SOCIAL POLICIES FOR OLD AGE

INTERNATIONAL LIBRARY OF SOCIOLOGY
AND SOCIAL RECONSTRUCTION

Founded by Karl Mannheim
Editor: W. J. H. Sprott

*A catalogue of books available in the INTERNATIONAL LIBRARY OF
SOCIOLOGY AND SOCIAL RECONSTRUCTION, and new books in
preparation for the Library will be found at the end of this volume*

SOCIAL POLICIES

FOR OLD AGE

Your Joking!

A Review of Social Provision
for old Age in Great Britain

by
B. E. SHENFIELD

LONDON
ROUTLEDGE AND KEGAN PAUL LTD.

First published in 1957
© by Routledge and Kegan Paul Ltd.
Broadway House
68–74 Carter Lane,
London, E.C.4
Printed in Great Britain
by Butler and Tanner Ltd.
Frome and London

CONTENTS

CONTENTS

INTRODUCTION

FEW problems in the fields of the social sciences have received a more rapidly rising degree of attention in recent years than those concerned with the ageing of the population. This book is intended to make a general review, in the light of the considerable literature of research and discussion now available, of the foundations of present-day social policies for old age; and to examine some of the perplexing open questions which those policies expose.

These questions are perplexing, partly because in large measure they raise difficult problems of choice for the community, but partly also because our knowledge of the basic facts upon which social policies ought to be founded has itself been radically altered by recent studies. Thus the statistical forecasts of only a decade ago of the future numbers of the aged have had to be substantially revised, and the alarm of a few years ago at the magnitude of the 'burden of the old' has been considerably relieved. But social policy is not always easily shaped to the latest development of factual knowledge. For such reasons a general study of fact and argument bearing upon these problems may perhaps be judged to be of value. And it is hoped that the student seeking a broad introduction to the subject may find it useful to have material from numerous scattered and specialized studies gathered together and brought under review.

Further, we have had some considerable experience of the operation of services for the old, and it is now possible to make some assessment of their measure of success. For example, the progress made in ameliorating environmental conditions in order to enable the great majority of old people to stay in their own homes has not been as great as is sometimes supposed. A study of home living conditions among the more elderly is, therefore, included here (Appendix III) because although the material was collected in 1948, the difficulties and needs which came to light in this survey appear to have altered little, notwithstanding the growth since then of services for the aged.

Some major questions, especially with regard to the financing of old age, remain unanswered for lack of data upon which to found conclusions. In certain cases we are still obliged to rely largely upon the untested anecdotal evidence of doctors and social workers. These questions point the way to avenues for future research.

Ageing is a natural process continuous throughout life, and in this sense we are growing old before we are born. When we speak of 'old age', however, we think only of the later years of the life span, in which certain familiar physical changes strike the eye.

It needs hardly to be said that the mere tally of years may be a poor measure of ageing, for though the ageing process cannot be arrested it can be delayed or accelerated, and the rate at which it takes place varies widely among different individuals and between different periods of life. Hence the choice of particular ages for the social recognition of old age (as in the case of eligibility for pensions, for example) reflects the wealth and social conscience of a community as much as, or perhaps more than, any recognition of changes in health or the onset of senescence.

In the following pages the conventional definition of old-age as those years following 65 for men and 60 for women is adopted, unless otherwise stated. But clearly one of the major difficulties in formulating social policies for old age is to make them flexible enough to take account of the wide variation in individual adjustment to ageing in a changing social environment.

A stocktaking of present policies must include a sober reckoning of the difficulties which the growth of old age dependency no doubt creates for the community. Yet it would be deplorably wrong to approach the expansion of life as if it were simply a burden to be shouldered. It is in fact a social change which presents the community with a new challenge to its capacity for intelligent and imaginative adaptation of social policy.

CHAPTER I

PRODUCERS AND DEPENDANTS

THE broad picture of the ageing of the population of Great
Britain is sufficiently well known to need little re-statement.
Tables I–VII in this chapter indicate briefly[1] some of the main
changes which have taken place, and the likely future trends in
population growth, which are relevant to a discussion of provision for old age.

From Table I, it may be seen that the numbers of old people
have grown at a rate much greater than the population as a
whole, and that this is not a recent development but a trend
which has been continuous during the first half of the century.
The rate at which this change occurred was especially rapid
between 1921 and 1941, but the numbers of the elderly are not
likely to increase so quickly during the next twenty-five years,
and the numbers who will be of pensionable age in 1979 may
not be so great as has sometimes been predicted.[2] The Beveridge
Report assumed that the population of pension age would rise
to 21% of the total by 1971, whereas later forecasts estimate
that pensioners will only form 18% by 1979.

These population trends have been conditioned by the course
of birth and death rates, both of which have markedly declined
in the past fifty years. The fall in the number of annual live
births has been uneven, the decline being temporarily checked
by higher post-war birth rates. But the mid-century level of
births, while it is above the average for the thirties, is below
birth rates before 1920, and it is from the larger generations
of the last century that the present old people have sprung.

[1] For a more detailed discussion see the Memorandum by the Government Actuary, Appendix II of the Report of the Committee on the Economic and Financial Problems of the Provision for Old Age ('Phillips' Report',
Cmd. 9333.)

[2] See, e.g., Table XI, Section II, p. 91, *Social Insurance and Allied
Services* (the Beveridge Report).

PRODUCERS AND DEPENDANTS

TABLE I

The total population and the numbers of the elderly (men aged 65 years and over, women aged 60 years and over) 1901–79: Great Britain (*thousands*)

Year	(1) Total population	(2) Percentage increase on total of preceding census or estimate	(3) Men aged 65 and over and women aged 60 and over	(4) Percentage increase on total of preceding census or estimate	(5) Col. 3 as a percentage of Col. 1
1901	37,000	—	2,284	—	6·2
1911	40,831	10·3	2,748	20·3	6·7
1921	42,769	4·7	3,349	21·8	7·8
1931	44,795	4·7	4,295	28·2	9·6
1941	46,565	3·9	5,571	29·7	12·0
1951	48,840	4·8	6,620	18·8	13·5
*1954	49,630	—	6,890		13·9
*1964	50,860	2·4	7,760	12·6	15·3
*1979	52,230	3·0	9,500	22·4	18·2

2 million

* Cmd. 9333, *op. cit.*, Appendix II.

died not at coal at S.

At the same time, reductions in mortality have taken place, especially in the younger age-groups, and the resultant increased expectation of life has enabled larger numbers of persons to survive to pension ages. So great has been the progress in reducing mortality among children and young persons, that the amount of further life conservation possible is very limited, and the area where the greatest improvements remain to be made is among the elderly. The decline in death rates at high ages, however, has so far been very small, especially in the case of men, and there has not been any significant lengthening of the average lifetime beyond retirement ages.

The reduction in mortality which has taken place does not alone account for the ageing of the population. A decline in death rates in younger age groups, which is where the most dramatic reductions have in fact been made, by keeping up the numbers of the young prevents the ageing of a population at least for a time. In countries where a reduction in death rates has not been accompanied by declining fertility, the population is not yet ageing, and the dependency burden is that created by large numbers of very young children for whom support must be provided.

It is the pattern of a coincidental decline in fertility and mortality which has produced striking changes in the age distribution of the population of Great Britain. In the first half of this century, while the child population has fallen by 10%, and the active[1] population has grown by 2%, the percentage of old people (men aged 65 years and over, and women aged 60 years and over) has more than doubled. From being 1 in 17 of the total population at the beginning of the century and 1 in 10 in 1931, the old had become 1 in 7 of the population by 1954, and the proportion is likely to be near 1 in 5 in the next twenty-five years. There is, however, nothing abnormal in this age-distribution of the population. It was to be expected that the proportion of old people would rise as the rate of population growth slowed down and mortality fell. In fact it can be shown[2] that the proportion at present over retirement age is not as high as would be expected in a stationary population with present levels of mortality.

THE PATTERN OF DEPENDENCY

Nevertheless, these trends in population growth have given rise to anxiety about what has been termed 'the burden of dependency' which must be borne by the working population. Before it can be judged whether there are any grounds for such fears, it is necessary to consider the total number of dependants and the ratio this bears to the working population. For it must be remembered that the old are only one group of dependants, and that there are children, housewives, the sick and the disabled and numbers of other non-earners, who for shorter or longer periods are dependent upon the current earnings of others. In examining the problems of dependency we have therefore to look at the claims of other than elderly dependants, notably children, and to consider pensions and welfare services for the old as one item only in a Budget which must provide the cost of many other public social services.

[1] The active population is taken to mean men aged 15–64 years and women aged 15–59 years.

[2] See 'The Economics of an Ageing Population', W. A. B. Hopkin, *Lloyds Bank Review*, January 1953.

PRODUCERS AND DEPENDANTS

It is important for another reason to recognize the needs of the old as a part of the total pattern of interdependence in family and community over each individual's lifetime. It may help to correct the unfortunate psychological effects which frequent public discussion of the 'burden of dependency' sometimes has upon the old, who cannot but be distressed to hear themselves repeatedly described as a 'burden' upon the rest of the community.

The age distribution of the population and the numbers who fall into the active and dependent age-groups can be seen in Table II, where to the experience of the last forty-three years is added an estimate of likely trends during the next twenty-five.

It appears that the proportion of the total population which old and young dependants constitute has actually fallen since 1911, and though this will rise again slowly, it is unlikely during the next twenty-five years to exceed more than very slightly the proportion in the first decade of the century.

However, the conventional division of the population into active and dependent age-groups with reference to minimum school-leaving and retiring ages gives only a very approximate estimate of the number of producers and dependants in the population at any given time. The active population is not synonymous with the working population; some persons over 65 years continue to work and some juveniles do not enter the labour market until they are over 15 years old.[1] Similarly the proportion of women between the ages of 15 and 59 years who are 'gainfully occupied' may fluctuate with changing economic and social conditions.[2] Nor are the present ages at which the majority of persons enter or leave employment immutable. Fifty years ago, children went into employment at much earlier ages than the present school-leaving age, and greater numbers of older workers, who were not then provided with pensions, continued in employment until their strength failed. In the future the extension of compulsory education, or a trend towards earlier retirement financed by better pension coverage, could significantly alter the ratio of producers to dependants.

[1] Only 574 per 1,000 at age 15 years and 774 per 1,000 at age 16 years are employed contributors to National Insurance (Report by the Government Actuary on the First Quinquennial Review of the National Insurance Act, 1946, Appendix 6, Table H).

[2] See C. E. V. Leser, 'The Supply of Women for Gainful Employment in Britain', *Population Studies*, Vol. IX, No. 2. November 1955.

TABLE II

The age distribution of the population of Great Britain 1911–79, and the ratio of old and young dependants to the total population (*thousands*)

Year	Total population	Under 15 years	15–39 years		40–64 years	40–59 years	Males 65 and over and females 60 and over	Ratio of the old (Col. 7) to the total population (Col. 1)	Ratio of the young (Col. 2) and the old (Col. 7) to the total population (Col. 1)
			Males	Females	Males	Females			
(1)	(2)		(3)	(4)	(5)	(6)	(7)	(8)	(9)
1911	40,832	12,588	8,196	8,834	4,300	4,125	2,748	6·7	37·5
1931	44,795	10,825	8,666	9,388	5,895	5,718	4,295	9·5	33·7
1951	48,840	10,986	8,350	8,724	7,292	6,860	6,628	13·5	35·0
1954	49,630	11,160	8,520	8,510	7,570	6,980	6,890	13·9	36·3
1964	50,860	10,730	8,620	8,500	8,150	7,060	7,760	15·3	36·3
1979	52,230	10,510	9,100	8,750	7,180	6,590	9,500	18·2	38·3

Based on estimates of the Government Actuary, Appendix II, Cmd. 9333.

Thus, although the age structure of the population determines broadly how many very young and very old persons there will be at any time who are certain to be dependants, within these limits changes in law or custom or economic conditions may operate to vary the numbers of producers and dependants. At the present time, for every hundred workers, there are about one hundred and thirteen dependants, twenty-five of them old people, forty-eight children, and forty adults.

THE WORKING POPULATION

The Ministry of Labour[1] has calculated the size of the working population over the next twenty-five years on the assumption that the same proportion of persons is employed in each age-group as at present, and on this estimate the ratio of producers and dependants will show little change. By 1979, there will be one hundred and fourteen dependants to every hundred workers, but a larger proportion of the dependants (33%) will be elderly and there will be 5% fewer children.

If, as estimated, the working population grows at a greater rate (5%) than the active population (2%) this will help to offset the growth in the numbers of the elderly, and may largely remove anxieties about a 'burden of dependency' being created by the changing age-structure of the population. But the assumption that the same proportion of persons in each age-group will work in the future as at present is by no means certain to prove a correct one.

The size of the active population has fallen since before the last war because although the numbers in the age-groups 15–64 years have scarcely changed, the decision to regard 60 years as the pension age for women has removed 1·3 million[2] of them from the active to the dependent category. On the other hand, the size of the total occupied population of all ages has increased by about 2 million. This illustrates aptly the elasticity of the concept of the producer-dependant ratio within the broad demographic framework. It is not possible to make completely accurate comparisons between the size and distribution of the labour force before the last war and after 1948, because manpower statistics have been presented in a different form since

[1] Cmd. 9333, *op. cit.*, p. 1, para. 87.
[2] 1940.

the operation of the National Insurance Act (July 1948).[1] Nevertheless, allowing for this, and for the man-power requirements of the Armed Forces, there has been a marked growth in the numbers engaged in civilian employment in Great Britain reaching a total in 1954 of 22·3 million persons.

This increase has been mainly due to a higher level of employment, the entrance of more women into the labour market and, more recently, some apparent halting of the trend towards earlier retirement. To what extent can we rely on these factors operating in the future?

The Phillips' Committee has pointed out that if a rate of 4% of unemployment (which is the rate assumed in ordering the finances of the National Insurance Fund) is in fact experienced, this would extinguish the increase anticipated over the next twenty-five years in the employed population. An increase in unemployment would also be likely to cause some groups of workers, such as married women or workers of pensionable age, to withdraw from the labour market altogether. Unemployment at the rate of 4% and in addition a reduction by 20% in the number of workers of pensionable age and of women between the ages of 35 and 59 years who are expected to be in employment, would reduce the numbers at work by about 1·8 million.

On the other hand, given a high level of employment, there is every reason to suppose that the present trend towards a larger proportion of women seeking paid employment will continue, even though the proportions who are married will show a substantial further increase. Whereas in 1931 approximately a third of women aged between 35 and 55 years who were in employment were married, twenty years later 56% of women occupied in these age-groups were married. The pattern with which we have now become familiar of earlier marriages and small families appears to facilitate the return of married women to paid employment. It is true that an increase in the working population created by the employment of married women, who now form 45% of all female employees, may not be all gain.

---

[1] The old manpower series (Ministry of Labour and National Service) did not include private indoor servants, non-manual workers earning more than £420 per year, persons of pension age still working, and two part-time workers were reckoned as one full-time worker. From July 1948 all persons over 15 years who are at work or available for it, are included, and each part-time worker is counted as one worker.

To the extent that it is only possible to add the labour of married women to the employed population by making available substitute services in part care of homes and children, other competing claims may be made upon national resources. There is as yet no evidence that any large number of women are prevented from entering employment because of their responsibilities in the care of elderly relatives, but if more daughters are married and 'gainfully occupied' they may be forced in future to rely more upon domiciliary or institutional welfare services to help them in the care of their parents.

It is by its effect among women over pensionable age that the change in the proportion of women married may directly influence the size of the working population. As the proportion of single women and widows falls over the next twenty-five years and there is a corresponding increase in the proportion married, this may affect the numbers of older women who remain in employment beyond pension age. About three-quarters of such women who are employed at present are single or widowed, and more than half the increase in older employees of both sexes between 1950 and 1953 was accounted for by women who were not married. If however a new generation emerges of older married women who have been occupied *immediately* before reaching retirement ages, more married women of pensionable age may continue in employment, and a reservoir of labour may be found among them which is as yet untapped.

In examining the ways in which the working population may contract or expand in the future, the Phillips' Committee took an optimistic view about the postponement of retirement. Pointing out that between 1950 and 1953 there was an increase in the employment of elderly men of 10·5%, and among elderly women an increase of 21·1%, the Committee states 'the prewar tendency to earlier retirement has been arrested and perhaps even reversed'.

Apart from the possible effect of marital status upon employment of older women, there are other reasons for thinking that it may be too early to conclude that the trend towards earlier retirement has been halted. In the last twenty years a considerable expansion has taken place, and is continuing, in the coverage of occupational pension schemes, and there is evidence to show that these tend to encourage retirement at minimum pension ages. Age limits beyond which employees are not retained are commoner in employment covered by occupational pension schemes,[1] and even where retirement is optional, the prospect of a pension added to savings influences the decision to cease work. Less than a million pensioners are drawing occupational pensions at present, but more than seven million are members of pension schemes and are building up future claims for benefits. This factor is therefore going to be of increasing importance in future.

There are also some workers over pension age who are continuing their employment and contributions in order to qualify for a retirement pension and who will retire as soon as they have secured a title to their pension. These workers are a transitional class created by the regulations governing National Insurance pensions, and until ten years have elapsed from the introduction of the National Insurance Scheme in July 1948, we do not know how this group is affecting temporarily the number of old people in employment.

Such increase as there has been in the number of older employees has coincided with a period of overfull employment. It is difficult to decide whether this increase is tied directly to a very high demand for labour and would be reduced correspondingly if the level of employment fell, or if it represents a more permanent change in working habits.

Workers over pension ages constitute about 4% of the total working population at present and are expected, if the same proportions in these age-groups continue to work, to account for 6% of the population in twenty-five years' time. The Phillips' Committee concluded that it would require 'a major change in retirement habits' to raise the proportion to 7% and thus add 1% to the total working population. On the other hand half the anticipated increase in the working population over the next twenty-five years is expected to come from the employment of workers over minimum pension ages. It appears then that the possible gain to the total labour force by further postponement of retirement is not likely to be great, but widespread retirement at earlier ages than at present would seriously affect the expected growth in the size of the working population.

[1] Reasons for Retiring and Staying at Work. Report of the Ministry of Pensions and National Insurance (1954). See also Appendix II, p. 212 below.

PRODUCERS AND DEPENDANTS

TABLE III

Age Analysis of Employees, 1950–4 * (*thousands*)

	Males				Females			
	1950	1954	Increase or Decrease		1950	1954	Increase or Decrease	
			Nos.	%			Nos.	%
All employees								
15 and over	13,700	13,840	+140	+1	6,950	7,350	+400	+5·7
15–54	11,443	11,414	−29	−0·2	6,286	6,521	+235	+3·7
54–59	994	1,041	+47	+5·7	389	485	+96	+24·9
60–64	777	844	+67	+8·6	169	224	+55	+32·5
65 and over	486	541	+55	+11·3	106	120	+14	+13·2
65 and over as percentage of all employees	3·6	4·0		0·4	3·9	5·0		1·1

* *Ministry of Labour Gazette*, June 1951, June 1955.

If the assumptions[1] on which the Ministry of Labour has estimated the size of the future working population prove well founded, the change in the ratio of workers to non-workers between 1952 and 1979 will not be great and will be well capable of absorption by an expanding economy. In addition, a high level of employment improves contribution income to the National Insurance Funds and keeps unemployment benefit claims low.[2]

If, for the reasons suggested above, these assumptions about working habits prove incorrect the ratio of producers to non-producers may be less favourable. On the assumption that by 1979 unemployment will rise to 4%, and that the numbers of pension ages and women aged 35–59 years at work will drop by one-fifth, the ratio of workers to non-workers will fall to 76 workers for every 100 non-workers. This would still represent

[1] The proportions that were occupied in each age-group in the population in 1952 are assumed to remain constant through the next 25 years.

[2] The rate of unemployment assumed for the purpose of ordering the National Insurance Funds was 8½%, reduced in 1951 to 4%, but in fact unemployment has averaged 1½% for the insured population. The savings on unemployment and other benefits, the incidence of which proved to be over-estimated, have helped to offset the cost of pensions.

TABLE IV

Number of Workers in Relation to Non-Workers

Based on the estimate of the working population of Great Britain, 1954–79 made by the Ministry of Labour for the Phillips' Committee [1]

Year	Ratio of workers per 100 non-workers
1952	90
1954	88·5
1964	90·5
1979	87·6

a rate of increase in dependency (15% over 25 years) which is likely to be slower than the increase in productivity, even if the latter is slower than in recent years and unemployment is higher than at present.

YOUNG AND OLD DEPENDANTS

So far all non-workers young and old have been grouped together as 'dependants'. It is necessary to examine the changing composition of this group more closely in comparing the cost of dependency at different periods of time. In the first place, though the proportion of all dependants to the total population may be no greater now than it has been in the past, the cost per dependant has grown and it is likely to increase further. For example, public expenditure on pensions and assistance for the elderly was only about £23 million in 1910, but by 1953 (excluding occupational pension schemes) it had risen to £404 million. This increase has to be related of course to changes in the value of money and the size of the National Income, as well as to the increased numbers of old people. Even so the increases in real terms have taken place. Between 1910 and 1954 the numbers of old people rose by two and a half times, but the proportion of the National Income transferred to the elderly in the same period quadrupled. The corresponding value in 1954 of the 1925 ten-shilling pension has been officially calculated[2] to be six shillings, so that if this calculation is accepted

[1] *Op. cit.*, p. 1, Cmd. 9333, Appendix III, Table I.
[2] Hansard, Vol. 535, 10, p. 89. 13th December 1954, E. Marples. This estimate is calculated on the basis of the Cost of Living Index 1914–47 and

the retirement pension of forty shillings is nearly two and a half times greater than the pensions of thirty years ago. As the standard of living of the community rises there is likely to be a demand for a corresponding improvement in pensions and other benefits, and the estimates of the future cost of social benefits will have to allow not only for increasing or decreasing numbers but for a steady improvement in real terms in social provision for the dependent age-groups in the population.

In addition to the likely changes in the cost per dependant, the composition of the group we call dependants has altered considerably in the first half of this century. In 1901 the elderly were less than one-fifth of all young and old dependants, but by 1951 they had become 37%, and by 1979 they will become 47%. This raises the question whether old and young dependants[1] can be treated interchangeably in calculating the costs of dependency.

It is difficult to compare the cost of children and old people even in the narrow sense of their claims upon public expenditure. The cost of services like education and family allowances may be set against expenditure on pensions and old people's Homes, but it would be very difficult to try to apportion, for example, housing costs in relation to the numbers of children and old people in the population.

An attempt has been made to estimate the relative costs of the groups who make up the dependent sections of the population by Professor Paish and Mr. Alan Peacock.[2] Their calculation deals only with the cost of some selected (though it is true the most expensive) social services, which can be most readily allocated between different age-groups. These are Edu-

the Interim Index of Retail Prices from 1947 onwards and probably under-estimates the loss of value of the pound. The Treasury's evaluation of the loss of purchasing power of the pound between 1925 and 1954 (R. H. Maudling, Hansard Parliamentary Debates, 7th December 1954) based on the Cost of Living Index, 1914–38 and the Consumer Goods Index 1938 onwards, estimates that the 10s. pension of 1925 was worth 4s. 10d. in 1954. Some improvement in real terms has taken place in the value of pension between 1925 and 1954, but the indices used above are not very satisfactory yardsticks by which a realistic measurement of this change can be made. (See 'The Purchasing Power of Pensions', The Times, 22nd October 1954.)

[1] Even young dependants have to be considered in different age-groups since the cost of children age 10–14 years is greater than that of the cost of children 0–5 years.

[2] 'Economics of Dependence', F. Paish and A. T. Peacock, Economica, Vol. XXI, No. 84, November 1954.

cation, Family Allowances, National Insurance, National Assistance and (very approximately) the National Health Service. Even so the comparison of expenditure on different age-groups is very striking. The expenditure per head on these five major social services is £34·9 for children up to fourteen, £18·4 for men and women of working age, and £69·6 for pensioners, so that twice as much is spent *per capita* on pensioners as on children and more than three and a half times as much *per capita* on the elderly as upon the active population. These costs are related to the conventional definitions of those falling inside and outside working-age and to this extent are not necessarily realistic, but the difference in expenditure is of such an order as to leave no doubt that the elderly make much heavier claims per head upon this kind of social service expenditure than other age-groups. More old people and fewer children, even though the sum of their respective members remains constant, will necessitate much heavier social service expenditure on the non-working sections of the population. Further, even if the relative costs of the young and the old could be equated, it cannot be assumed that a rise in the numbers of the elderly will be wholly offset by a fall in the number of children. If one group of dependants decreases in size there is not automatically a *pro rata* reduction in expenditure on them. A fall in the size of the school population, for example, is most likely to be made the occasion for smaller classes and more spacious accommodation and not for a reduction of total expenditure on education. In future, facilities for extended and higher education may further change our concept of dependency[1] for the younger age-groups and increase the cost of supporting and educating them.

In addition to the difference between the needs of young and elderly dependants, there is a wide variation in the degree of dependency within the older age-groups. Among those over pensionable age are persons still in employment, others well able to live independently during their retirement, and only a comparatively small number who need special accommodation and welfare services.

Table V shows the age and sex distribution of persons over

---

[1] 'Our business is to persuade as many boys and girls as we can to stay at school until they are eighteen.' Sir David Eccles, Minister of Education, introducing the Government's policy of secondary education at the Conference of the National Union of Teachers, 13th April 1955.

pensionable age in Great Britain, 1951 (one per cent sample Report of the Census, 1951).

TABLE V

Older Persons and the very Elderly (*hundreds*)

Age	Men		Women		Total men and women	% of all men 65 and over and women 60 and over
	Nos.	% of total 65 and over	Nos.	% of total 60 and over		
60–64	—		1,327,9	30·0	1,327,9	20·0
65–69	866,7	40·0	1,153,3	26·0	2,020,0	30·0
70–74	648,0	30·0	929,7	20·0	1,577,7	24·0
Sub-total under 75 years	1,514,7	70·0	3,410,9	76·0	4,925,6	74·0
75–79	416,6	19·0	594,8	13·0	1,011,4	16·0
80–84	177,0	8·0	305,3	7·0	482,3	7·0
85 and over	66,5	3·0	142,1	30	208,6	3·0
Sub-total 75 and over	660,1	30·0	1,042,2	23·0	1,702,3	26·0
Total	2,174,8	100·0	4,453,1	100·0	6,627,9	100·0

Women outnumber men heavily in the older age-groups. At ages 65 and over there are 144 women for every hundred men, and women are 62% of all persons over seventy-five. Lower mortality rates for women and the heavier male losses due to wars and migration have throughout the last century (1851–1951) produced an excess of females at all age-groups except in the child population. The masculinity ratio is now improving and the excess of females in the adult population will in future years decline, though it will be many years before the ratio of females to males is much affected in the high age-groups.

Of the 6·6 million persons of pensionable age enumerated in the 1951 Census, just a half were under 70 years old, about three-quarters under 75 years of age, and only 3% over 85 years old. This age distribution of the older sections of the population has changed very little in the last hundred years, and the recognitions in recent years of the need to provide better care for the frail elderly is not, as is sometimes supposed, a consequence of a greater proportion of old people living to very advanced years.

TABLE VI

Percentage age distribution of the estimated future elderly population of Great Britain (Report of the Government Actuary, Cmd. 9333)

Year	Age distribution					
	65–69	70–74	75–79	80–84	85 and over	Total 65 and over
1954	37	29	19	10	5	100
1964	37	28	19	11	5	100
1979	35	29	20	11	5	100

Nor, assuming that death rates will continue to decline year by year at the same rate[1] as that experienced in the first half of this century, is there any reason to suppose that the age distribution of the elderly will change significantly in the next twenty-five.

This is not to deny however that demands are likely to be increased for health, housing and other social services by the presence in the community of 3·3 million old people over the age of 70. The claims of the very elderly are likely on the average[2] to be heavier than those made by other old people upon health and welfare services, and it is improbable that more than an exceptional minority of those over 70 years will continue in employment, so that proposals which aim to prolong employment and thus reduce pension costs, are limited by the age and sex composition of the pensioner group. At the last census 20% of men and 5% of women over 70 years were occupied. Many more women up to the ages of 75 or 80 years, though not in paid employment, are active and helping to

[1] See pp. 19–20 below.
[2] This must not be exaggerated, since even among those over eighty a surprising number remain active and independent. An inquiry by the National Assistance Board into conditions among their clients who are over eighty and live alone has recently confirmed this. See National Assistance Board. Annual Report, 1954.

maintain a household, as inquiries[1] into living conditions of old people have confirmed, but it is scarcely likely that they will re-enter the labour market.[2]

Marital status, especially of women, is particularly important in considering the needs of those in the higher age-groups. At the last Census 9% of men and 16% of women of pensionable age were unmarried, and it may be noted here that the lack of family care sometimes complained of is not unseldom found among these people, and their plight mistakenly quoted to support the unfounded generalization that children are no longer willing to look after their elderly parents. A high proportion of older women have been married but have survived their partner. Among all women of pensionable age, 42% are widowed and after age 75 years the proportion rises sharply to reach 71% among those who are over 80 years old.

TABLE VII

Age and Marital Status of Women 60 Years and over (*hundreds*)
(one per cent sample Report of the Census, 1951)

Age	Total Women	Single		Married		Widowed		Widows as % of all persons 60 and over
		Nos.	% of total	Nos.	% of total	Nos.	% of total	
60–64	1,321,8	210,7	16	752,2	57	358,9	27	15
65–69	1,150,9	193,6	17	536,0	46	421,3	37	21
70–74	927,9	152,4	16	338,2	37	437,3	47	26
75–79	594,4	98,2	16	151,7	26	344,5	58	34
80 and over	447,0	76.5	17	55,6	12	314,9	71	46
Total * 60 and over	4,442,0	731,4	17	1,833,7	41	1,876,9	42	28

* Excluding 11,000 divorced women.

Over the next twenty-five years the proportion of women who are widowed, which has been abnormally increased by the casualties of the 1914–18 war, is expected to decline. But at

[1] See Appendix III. Also J. H. Sheldon, *Social Medicine of Old Age*.
[2] For further discussion of employment of older persons, see Chapter III.

present and for some time to come, elderly widows, who are 28% of all persons over pensionable age, form a large part of the demand for all kinds of financial support including pension funds, National Assistance and family resources.

A recent study[1] of the cost of the National Health Service has shown the close relationship between marital status and the need for hospital care in old age. The single, and to a lesser extent the widowed, are much more likely with advancing years to require hospital beds than married couples.

Similarly the type and amount of housing accommodation provided for old people will have to be planned to take account of the present high proportion of single and widowed women among women over pension age.

DEPENDENCY RELATED TO THE NATIONAL INCOME

Whether the increase in the numbers and proportions of the elderly creates an unmanageable economic burden for the community depends finally upon the prospective growth in the National Income. A progressive improvement in productivity could enable satisfactory provision to be made for larger numbers of old people without absorbing for their needs a greater *proportion* of the national product than at present. Indeed, even if the size of the working population does not increase as anticipated, and the ratio of dependants to producers rises, it does not necessarily follow that standards of living must be adversely affected. A stationary or even slightly smaller working population may, with the aid of technical progress, continue to expand the National Income. It is true that the expansion of the National Income which has taken place in recent years has been achieved at a time when the working population was growing and that this has been one of the factors making increased production possible. But if we allow for little further growth in the working population and some ageing of the labour force available, and assume a rate of increased productivity only half as great as that recently experienced, this would still produce a greater rate of increase in national wealth than the rate of increase in the numbers of the elderly. This way[2] of relating the

[1] 'The Cost of the National Health Service in England and Wales', B. Abel Smith and R. Titmuss. See Chapter VII, p. 182 below.
[2] See 'Providing for Pensions', *Planning*, Vol. XX, 364, 24th May 1954.

cost of maintaining all dependants to the resources of an expanding economy has applied a valuable corrective to the earlier[1] more gloomy predictions about the economic burdens of an ageing population. An increase in productivity of the order of $1\frac{1}{2}$ per annum, which it seems reasonable to assume may be maintained in future, would enable the economy to absorb the cost of pensions and other services for old people without these proving an insupportable burden. Hence it might appear that the problem of supporting the aged will be merely the fiscal and budgetary one of arranging the necessary transfers of income. But we can only accept this comforting conclusion if we can be sure that the community will be prepared to transfer enough income to the aged *despite other claims*, the satisfaction of which may appear to be a prior condition of the growth of productivity, for example, the demands of the producers themselves.

Assuming however that the direct economic consequences of changes in the ratio of producers to dependants will be slight, there are still considerable fiscal and budgetary problems involved in effecting large scale transfer payments to the elderly. Even if no further increases in benefits are granted (which is unlikely), the deficit in the National Insurance Funds will be £364m. in 1979. If the whole of this sum has to be found from the Exchequer, the liability will aggravate an already high level of taxation, and unless other commitments are reduced, could prevent any hope of reducing fiscal burdens. If a greater part of the increased cost is met by raising National Insurance contributions, these will still have to be paid by the working population. No device of insurance or taxation can evade the claims of the old upon income currently derived from the labour of others.

Moreover the method of financing pensions as well as the magnitude of the payments is associated with general economic considerations. For example, if pension arrangements impede the process of capital formation (as may well happen in the unfunded National Insurance Scheme or other occupational pension accounts which in future will show a mounting deficit), or if they restrict the mobility of labour (which may be one of the consequences of increasing occupational pension schemes), the method of transferring income to the elderly may have in-

[1] E.g., Chapter I, p. 2. *Old People* (Rowntree), Nuffield Foundation, 1947. And Chapter II, Royal Commission on Population, Cmd. 7695.

directly damaging consequence for the economy and restrict rather than increase productivity.

FUTURE MORTALITY RATES

To these economic uncertainties must be added another imponderable, mortality rates in the older age-groups. So far it has been assumed that we can predict confidently the numbers of pensionable age likely to be in the population over the next twenty-five years, but these calculations are based upon assumptions about future mortality which may be falsified by events. Maximum future mortality, giving the lowest likely estimate of numbers of the elderly, may be ascertained by assuming that death rates at the higher ages remain constant at present levels. The downward trend at all ages which has been going on for half a century is not likely to be suddenly reversed, but it is possible that little in the way of any further reduction may be experienced.

The decrease in mortality at higher ages has only been very small and the decline among those aged 65 and over did not set in until the beginning of the present century. Whereas deaths per thousand of the population in the age-group 0–14 fell from 21 in the years 1900–02 to 2·8 in 1950–2, deaths per thousand of those aged 65 and over fell from 82 to 72 per thousand in the same period. Moreover the death rate among those over 65 had already fallen to 75 by the years 1920–2 so that the rate of decline in the last thirty years has been very slight.[1] Life conservation among elderly women began to improve earlier than among older men, and the downward trend is still apparent among women aged 50–75 years, though not beyond this age. As improvements in life conservation among males have in the past followed those made at earlier dates for females[2] it has usually been assumed that male mortality would not fail to fall to present rates among females. But the Government Actuary reports[3] that there has been little or no change in the last decade in the death rates for men aged 55–64 years, and among men over these ages there is some

[1] Appendix II. Memorandum by the Government Actuary for the Phillips' Committee, Cmd. 9333, p. 97.

[2] Wallis Taylor, 'Changing Mortality 1841–1947 measured by the Life Table' in the *British Journal of Social Medicine*, Vol. 5, No. 3, July 1951.

[3] Cmd. 9333, *op. cit.*, p. 1, Appendix II, p. 100.

suggestion of an increase rather than a decline in mortality. He adds a warning that it would be 'unduly pessimistic' to conclude without further evidence that the downward trend in mortality has worked itself out, but what we know at present about the secular trend in mortality does not justify alarm about the possible 'medicated survival' of increasing numbers of very elderly persons.

On the other hand the possibility of a dramatic fall in death rates among the elderly in future cannot be ruled out. No one can be sure that there will not emerge at any time some advance in medical skill which might substantially extend the life-span. If this happens the numbers of old people and their proportion in the population in the next quarter of a century may have been seriously under-estimated. This is a matter of speculation, and we can only be certain that a very large increase in the numbers of the elderly in the next twenty-five years will take place, since without any further decline in mortality the size of the population at present middle-aged will cause the numbers over 65 to rise by one-third by 1979. If mortality rates remain constant at present levels, the increase in the numbers over 65 years will rise by 1·88 million between 1954 and 1979 instead of, as has been assumed by the Government Actuary for the purpose of calculating the cost of pensions, by 2·5 millions, and the deficit in the National Insurance Funds may not be so large as anticipated. Alternatively a sharp decline in death rates at high ages, an eventuality not yet apparent but which cannot be excluded, would make the increase in the numbers of the elderly over the next twenty-five years at least half a million more than we are expecting, and possibly very much greater.

It would be unnecessarily pessimistic to conclude because of the difficulties outlined above that the prospective growth in the numbers of the elderly is likely to depress living standards in the foreseeable future. Nor is the changing age-structure of the population necessarily an argument for raising retirement ages or limiting pensions. Nevertheless the very large number of persons involved and the correspondingly heavy mortgage upon future national income to meet their needs, calls for a sober appraisal of the financial problems involved, and some unequivocal decisions about social priorities.

CHAPTER II

EMPLOYMENT OF OLDER WORKERS— (1) AGEING AND INDUSTRY

ONE way of preserving the independence of older men and women, and at the same time of enabling them to contribute to the national wealth, is to facilitate their continued employment beyond what are now regarded as normal retirement ages.

A policy of encouraging older people to remain in employment wherever possible was advocated in the Beveridge Report on social insurance,[1] and retirement pension regulations were designed with this purpose in mind.[2] Since then alterations in the 'earnings rules' (i.e. earnings permitted without involving deductions in the pensions drawn) and additions to the pension increments earned by deferred retirement have been made with the express intention of providing an incentive for continued employment.

Successive Governments, Employers' Associations and Trades Unions have endorsed this policy, and a National Advisory Committee on the Employment of Older Men and Women was appointed in February 1952. The first report[3] of this Committee states emphatically, 'The need for encouraging the employment of older persons is a present as well as a long-term one.' With so much official support in a period of over-full employment it is perhaps surprising that the response to this policy has not been greater. It would seem that the traditional

[1] The Beveridge Report, *op. cit.*, p. 1.
[2] Although the Beveridge Report recommended (p. 96, para. 244 *et seq.*) and the National Insurance Act introduced, retirement as a condition for receiving pensions, a system of increments added to deferred pensions was devised expressly to encourage the postponement of retirement beyond minimum pension ages.
[3] Cmd. 8963, H.M.S.O., October 1954.

work and retirement patterns are only yielding slowly to this new approach to the use of the older worker.[1]

The volume of employment among older persons will be conditioned by two factors; on the one hand by the number of older workers both willing and able to continue employment, and upon the other by the job opportunities available to them. These opportunities themselves will depend upon the level of employment and the general state of trade. Prognosis in these matters is notoriously difficult and here it may only be noted that it is important to decide whether the older worker is inevitably a *marginal* worker who will be the first to be extruded from any occupation if and when the volume of employment contracts.

All demographic approaches to this problem have emphasized that the need to keep older persons in economic employment will be a continuing one. Thus the Royal Commission on Population[2] quoted with approval the appeal of the *Economic Survey*, 1947 (Cmd. 7046), 'This need to increase the working population is not temporary; it is a permanent feature of our national life', and adds, 'if this appeal is to be fully successful more flexibility in the conditions of employment than exists at present will have to be introduced to meet the special needs of older workers'. As the first report of the National Advisory Committee on the employment of Older Men and Women puts it, 'the change in the age-structure of the total population requires a similar change in the age-structure of the working population'. If this is true, how far is it desirable and practicable to encourage the employment of older workers?

Bearing in mind that the most hopeful chance of providing employment for older workers is to retain them after pension age in their former employment (if not in exactly the same job at any rate in the same industry and if possible in the same firm), we must examine which industries would in fact have their labour force substantially augmented if much larger numbers of older workers remained in employment after pensionable age. Are these industries which require additional labour, and could they use older labour for their needs? Of course we

---

[1] See p. 10, Table III, above. Also the proceedings of the Trades Union Congress Annual Conference, September 1955, section D, motion carried concerning retirement ages.

[2] Cmd. 7695.

want to know not only the industry but the kind of job and process on which an older worker can maintain his performance. There are some light jobs even in what are generally classed as heavy industries and some skilled work is often associated with work which is mainly an unskilled occupation. But it is important to know in which trades a more than average proportion of elderly workers is found, and why this has happened. Ought the elderly to be encouraged to remain in contracting industries where their skill is still useful while the young are encouraged to seek employment in expanding industries? Or do the contracting industries need a high degree of flexibility and initiative (unlikely to be characteristics of an ageing labour force) to adapt their resources to meet a changing market? In the case of redundancy due to fluctuations in the general level of trade there may be no hesitation in deciding that the elderly pensioner must go and the younger family man be retained. Where, however, a particular industry has shown a decline over a lengthy period in the numbers employed and the volume of trade, to retain the young, who are wanted for employment in expanding industries, and to discard the skilled elderly, may prove to be a short-sighted policy.

THE NUMBERS AND DISTRIBUTION OF OLDER PERSONS AT WORK

The actual numbers of older persons in employment were in some doubt until figures became available from the 1% Sample Report of the Census of Great Britain published in July 1952, and only an approximate calculation can be made of post-pension age employment from 1946 to 1951. It was stated in 1949 that two-thirds of the men and half the women reaching pensionable age did not draw their pensions but continued in employment.[1] It is difficult however to reconcile this with the estimate made in July 1948, of 200,000 women over 60 years and 500,000 men over 65 years[1] in employment, an estimate subsequently revised to a total of 583,000 (Ministry of National Insurance Report, 1944-9).[2] These figures of two-thirds of men and just under a half of women continuing in employment

[1] Hansard, House of Lords, 31st May 1949.
[2] See 'Employment of Older Persons', *Manchester Guardian*, 1st May 1951, B. E. Lewis (Shenfield).

need to be further corrected by looking at the period during which they deferred retirement. Though at July 1949, 60% of men reaching pensionable age did not draw their pension, in the following six months this had fallen to 52% and in twelve months to 45%. Women deferring retirement similarly dropped from 45% of those reaching 60 years in July 1949, to 36% in July 1950.[1] Of those men reaching pensionable age in 1946 (when the new retirement pensions were introduced) 28% were still at work in 1951 when they were reaching 70 years, and of women reaching 60 in 1946 and deferring their pension right 24% of them worked nearly five years later. The numbers continuing in employment for any lengthy period are therefore lower than might be suggested from the figures given in the reports of the Ministry of National Insurance for those who, on reaching pension age, defer retirement.

On the other hand the records of the Ministry of National Insurance of those continuing at work after pensionable age do not include men over 70 years and women over 65 who may draw their pension without fulfilling the conditions of retirement imposed up to these ages. Nor does it include any estimate of part-time or casual employment which yields no higher income than that permitted by the earnings rule.

An analysis of workers employed over pension ages in the Midland Region 1945–8 (see Appendix I) showed a decline in all industries except in miscellaneous services in the percentage of older workers employed in this period. In so far as this record can be taken as broadly representative it shows that in no industry except Banking and Insurance did the proportion of older workers rise above 5·5% even in 1945,[2] and by 1948 the proportion for all manufacturing industries was 3·3% and for all non-manufacturing industries 2·6%.

Some decline in the number of elderly employees was to be expected as older workers who had remained or re-entered industry retired, and were replaced by returning Service men. It soon became apparent however that post-war conditions of full employment were still creating a high demand for labour, and it might have been expected that the numbers of older workers

---

[1] 2nd Report, Ministry of National Insurance, Cmd. 8412, pp. 18–19.

[2] Individual firms of course may have had a much higher proportion of older workers. See *Old People*, Rowntree Report, *op. cit.*, Appendix 9, pp. 152–4.

would rise again to war-time proportions. By 1951 however the proportion of employees over pension age was 4% for men and 4·7% for women and in 1953, the proportion still stood at 4% for men and 4·7% for women.[1]

The one per cent sample Report of the 1951 Census enables us to get a clearer picture of the numbers and occupational distribution of older workers. From Table VIII it may be seen that the men aged 65–69 (i.e. the age-group among whom the continued employment is most likely and valuable), who remained in employment formed only a small percentage of the total male labour force, approximately 2·7%. The largest *numbers* of male workers aged 65–69 were in agriculture, metal manufacture and allied trades, in distributive trades and miscellaneous unskilled occupations. The highest proportions of these were to be found in agriculture, in personal services and in leather and fur trades. If all male workers over 65 are taken into account, agriculture, leather trades and miscellaneous occupations still had higher than average percentages of older workers, but textiles and clothing industries had equally high proportions as they retained more workers over 70 than most industries.

The ratio of elderly workers to the total labour force in any particular industry is of course conditioned by the age structure of that industry and especially by its experience of recruitment of younger workers, as well as by the numbers working beyond pension ages. A more significant calculation is the rate of retirement, or conversely the rate of retention of workers in the years immediately following conventional retirement ages.[2] Table VIII, column 4, shows this for male employees for ages 65–69,[3] the period during which continued employment is most likely to be a practicable and economic proposition. Leather trades and wood and cane work firms retain 66% of their 60–64 year old workers in the following five years, and distributive trades,

[1] *Ministry of Labour Gazette,* June 1954.
[2] See also, M. Abrams, 'The Grim Truth about Our Ageing Nation' in *The Director,* November 1953.
[3] These figures refer to different groups of men and not to the same cohort of men continuing or ceasing to be employed as they move into the higher age-groups. Any group of men aged 60–64 may be larger than the group aged 65–69 in the same industry in part because of differential birth or death rates or fluctuations in recruitment to the industry in particular years. This index nevertheless gives a broadly representative picture of the rate of retirement from major industries.

TABLE VIII

Employment and Retirement in Selected Occupations,
Males—aged 15 and over (*hundreds*)

(Census of Great Britain, 1951. One per cent Sample Report)

	(1) Total Nos. occupied aged 15 and over	(2) Nos. occupied aged 65–69	(3) Col. (2) as % of Col. (1)	(4) Nos. occupied aged 65–69 as % of those occupied aged 60–64	(5) Nos. retired aged 65–69
Agriculture, Horticulture, Forestry	1,104,7	44,3	4·0	56·3	33,4
Mining and Quarrying	684,0	19,5	2·9	49·1	26,6
Metal Manufacture, Engineering and Allied Trades	2,525,2	41,7	1·6	38·9	44,7
Textile Workers	226,0	7,4	3·3	41·6	7,3
Leather, Leather Goods and Fur	119,5	6,1	5·1	66·3	2,4
Makers of Textile Goods	134,8	4,1	3·0	47·7	3,1
Makers of Food, Drink and Tobacco	171,3	4,2	2·4	42·9	4,6
Workers in Wood, Cane and Cork	491,1	16,9	3·4	66·3	12,8
Papermakers and Printers	183,1	5,1	2·7	46·0	3,3
Building and Contracting	914,0	26,8	2·9	47·1	28,9
Transport and Communications	1,571,6	24,2	1·5	28·4	51,1
Distribution	1,225,2	42,6	3·5	57·5	26,7
Finance and Insurance	146,7	4,3	2·9	47·3	7,5
Professional and Technical	799,5	18,2	2·3	49·6	15,6
Personal Service	511,8	24,3	4·8	50·7	14,8
Miscellaneous Unskilled Occupations	1,259,9	48,2	3·8	46·2	34,7
All Occupations	15,662,2	422,4	2·7	46·0	403,2

agriculture and personal services retain between 50% and 60%. On the other hand, the retention index shows that in transport and communications, only 28% of the 60–64 year olds remain in employment in the five years following pension age.

Table VIII, column 5, shows the former occupations of retired men. Given that the best hope of extending employment beyond pension age is to retain older workers in their former jobs,[1] certain industries which now have a large number of workers retiring at 65 are the ones which would have to be encouraged to keep more people in employment after this age *if the number of employees of pension age is to be significantly increased.* For example, of 403,200 men aged 65–70 who are retired, the largest group, 51,000, were formerly occupied in transport and communications. Other occupations discarding very large numbers of workers at 65 years are, after transport, metal manufacture and allied trades (44,700), agriculture (33,400), building and contracting (28,900), distributive trades (26,700), mining (26,600) and clerical work (26,000) and miscellaneous unskilled occupations (34,700) (these being the industries and occupations of course with the largest labour force of all ages). Thus even if it were possible to arrange for large numbers of older workers to remain in those industries which appear at present to be able to use older men successfully, since they have already more of these than most industries, the total numbers involved would not greatly reduce the present numbers of pensioners. If for example *all* workers between the ages of 65 and 69 years, retired in 1951, but formerly employed in textiles, textile goods, leather and fur trades and wood cane work, had remained in employment in these trades, approximately 25,600 persons would be affected. Similarly in other trades such as the making of jewellery and precision instruments where craftsmanship and lifetime experience may be presumed to put a premium upon the older worker, only 5,400 workers are in retirement from these industries. If we turn to the industries which are annually shedding large numbers of older workers into the pensioner group, it is by no means certain that they could reverse this process, although they may need additional labour.[2]

Mining may be taken as an example of an industry which

[1] This is the conclusion of the 2nd Report of the National Advisory Committee on Employment of Older Men and Women, Cmd. 9628, p. 13.
[2] See B. E. Shenfield, 'Employment prospects for older workers in Great Britain'. *Old Age in the Modern World*, p. 305. (E. and F. Livingstone.)

needs, and is likely in the foreseeable future to continue to need, to augment its labour force. It is a skilled occupation and one in which working conditions are such that experience and familiarity with the industry are of considerable importance. It is also an industry which for some time has been noticeably short of young recruits. These are factors which are likely to be favourable to the employment of older men and it might be supposed that, with the urgent need for more miners, here would be an example of the desirability of using older labour. Of course mining is an arduous and sometimes dangerous occupation requiring considerable sustained physical exertion, but will not mechanization and improved techniques, better hours and conditions and health care eliminate part of the strain which used to fall on the underground worker? This argument is frequently advanced, viz. that older men and women who have worked shorter hours under better social and employment conditions, will be able to continue longer in our industries where in any case mechanization and other improved techniques are successively reducing the physical effort required to maintain high levels of productivity.

In the mining industry to date the reverse appears to be true. The shortage of manpower is a shortage of men to maintain work at the coal face.[1] Only a few older men can continue to maintain an output comparable to that of a younger man, and often before reaching 65 years they move away from the coal face.[2] There is some variation between different fields but, for example, in the West Midland Division of the National Coal Board, the age-structure of the mining labour force at October 1953 was as follows:

Under 16 years . . 707	41–50 years . . . 13,385
16–17 years . . . 2,261	51–55 ,, . . . 6,219
18–20 ,, . . . 7,702	56–60 ,, . . . 4,140
21–25 ,, . . . 4,356	61–64 ,, . . . 2,550
26–30 ,, . . . 6,435	65–69 ,, . . . 1,526
31–40 ,, . . . 11,970	70 years and over . . 587

From this it will be seen that the big drop in numbers occurs at ages 56–60 years when the labour force falls by a third. Of

[1] About 35% of the total labour force in the industry is engaged at the coal face.

[2] See also I. M. Richardson, 'Age and Work', *British Journal of Industrial Medicine*, 1953, 10, 269.

the total labour force 26·4% is over 50 years, 8·2% over 60 years, and 2% over 65 years. If all types of work, conveying, maintenance and surface work are included, the men continuing to work after pension age in this area are quite a high proportion (60%) of those in the industry in the five years immediately before retirement age, but the former are clearly a highly selected group and long before reaching the age of 60 years many miners have left the industry altogether.

It would be possible for some of these men to continue to work at the face if they took a smaller 'stint'. With this end in view the National Coal Board is prepared to encourage the working of variable stints, but such a suggestion is not acceptable among the men in most pits. This is a typical example of a trend which makes employment of the older worker more difficult now than formerly. The standardization of wages through collective bargaining and minimum wage legislation makes it difficult to pay the older worker (or indeed any other worker who is not as efficient as his fellows) a smaller wage commensurate with his reduced efficiency.

As far as work away from the coal face is concerned, new methods, far from making it easier to employ the elderly, may make it in fact harder. About 87% of coal is mechanically conveyed and 50% mechanically cleaned and many miscellaneous jobs[1] suitable for older men are now being eliminated by the use of machinery, though there is a wide variation in different fields dependent upon how far the coal is mainly got by hand or by machines.

Numbers of older men have already been displaced in this way and this is likely to be a continuing trend. The lighter jobs and simpler tasks still available have to be apportioned between the Disabled Persons Quota, ex-accident and compensation cases to whom the industry feel a special obligation, and young 'green' labour progressing via the less exacting tasks to work at the coal face. Older men cannot be used very widely to induct younger recruits to the industry since conditions and methods are rapidly changing and to some extent this outmodes the older man's knowledge and skill. The problem in some pits already is how to make some effective use of the labour of older men who *want* to remain in employment. Where a pit is

---

[1] E.g. hand-picking of nuts and cobbles or removal of dirt and shale which is now increasingly done by conveyor belts.

EMPLOYMENT—

becoming worked out and there is some redundancy, it is difficult to maintain production if younger men are offered work elsewhere and older men allowed to remain (on the ground that it is harder for older men to secure and settle in alternative employment). Such a policy may well advance the time when the pit has to be closed as an uneconomic undertaking. In areas where a number of uneconomic pits have to be closed and miners are encouraged to migrate to neighbouring fields where their labour can be utilized, it is not easy to find employment for older men. The demand is for younger men able to work at the coal face, and the pits which are anxious to secure such labour usually already have their own accumulation of disabled and older workers and few vacancies of this kind.[1]

It may also be questioned whether a very much higher number of older miners than those now offering their services will, in fact, in future desire continued employment. Miners now have a supplementary scheme[2] which, together with National Insurance pensions, will reduce the drop from earnings to pension payments on retirement and will make it possible for men to retire from this very strenuous occupation with less financial loss and hardship than formerly.

If it is objected that mining is one of the industries which must be excepted from a policy of encouraging post-pension age employment because of the strenuous nature of the work, we may turn to another apparently more suitable occupation which passes very large numbers of older workers annually into the pensioner group, the distributive trades. Both because the distributive trades contain many small businesses, marginal enterprises, and a high proportion of employers and the self-employed, and by reason of the nature of the work involved, it might be expected that many older persons could be occupied until they chose their own retirement date.

Commercial occupations do in fact have the largest number (96,200) and the fourth largest percentage (6·1%) of men over pension age still occupied. This is clearly influenced by the unusually high proportion (23·7%) of those engaged in this in-

[1] See Hazel Heughan, *Pit Closures at Shotts and the Migration of Miners*.
[2] About 80% of miners are covered by the Miners Supplementary Pension Scheme; though this figure varies in different parts of the country and is influenced by the existence or otherwise of pension schemes of longer standing.

30

dustry who are employers or working on their own account. Among *employees only* (Table IX, column 5) in distributive trades (as also in agriculture and professional services) the proportion of older workers is much lower. Employers and the self-employed tend to retire later.

Occupational pension coverage has increased in recent years in this industry and no doubt some fit men retire because of the operation of these schemes. More flexibility in pension and retirement arrangements might thus enable a greater number of shop assistants and managers to stay in the distributive trades to higher ages. Since, however, nearly a quarter of men occupied are employers or the self-employed no alteration of retirement rules can affect their rate of retirement.

There are far fewer men at all ages now employed as shop assistants than formerly, but the decline is greatest among young men. This lack of young male labour, notwithstanding the widespread substitution of female labour which has already taken place, may make opportunities increasingly available for the retention of older men in this section of the distributive trades. This type of work also may lend itself more readily than other occupations to the organization of part-time work or intermittent periods of work (as relief staff during sickness of permanent employees, or for seasonal demands, etc.).

In considering industries such as the retail trades which appear suitable for prolonged employment it must however be remembered that there is some selection by physical fitness automatically in the existing occupational distribution of the labour force. Some workers in lighter industries like distribution will have taken this work because their health could not sustain more physical strenuous occupations. They may reach retirement age as physically impaired, if not more so, than some workers in heavier industries. If the results of a recent inquiry[1] into reasons for retirement may be accepted, the proportion of men retiring from retail distributive trades at age 65 who gave as their reason ill health or strain, is higher (18·5%) than the proportion retiring for this reason in all industries. This would seem to suggest that it does not necessarily follow that we can look for more prolonged employment among men engaged in trades which are less physically exacting than most.

[1] 'Reasons for continuing or retiring from work', Ministry of Pensions and National Insurance. See also below, pp. 63–67.

TABLE IX

Males Occupied by Industries and Industrial Status (*hundreds*)

(Census of Great Britain, 1951. One per cent Sample Report and *Ministry of Labour Gazette*, June 1952)

	(1) Total Nos. occupied * aged 15 and over	(2) Nos. of employers and those working on own account	(3) Col. (2) as % of Col. (1)	(4) % occupied aged 65 and over, of total occupied*	(5) % employed aged 65 and over, of total employees
All	15,662,2	1,293,3	8·2	4·3	3·7
Agricultural, Forestry, Fishing	997,5	324,4	32·5	7·0	5·5
Mining and Quarrying	849,1	6	·07	3·8	3·3
Non-metalliferous Mining	257,3	2,7	1·0	3·4	3·5
Chemical and Allied Trades	334,0	1,0	0·3	2·5	2·3
Metal Manufacture	517,3	6	0·1	3·4	3·7
Engineering, Ship-building and Electrical goods	1,452,4	13,6	0·9	3·9	3·5
Vehicles	851,0	32,8	3·8	2·4	2·5
Metal goods	327,0	11,7	3·6	4·5	3·1
Precision Instrument Jewellery	103,9	11,3	10·8	5·4	4·6
Textiles	456,6	3,4	0·7	6·0	5·5
Leather Goods and Fur	47,4	2,9	6·1	7·1	6·2
Clothing	234,0	35,2	15·0	7·9	5·6
Food, Drink, Tobacco	480,3	18,6	3·8	3·8	3·6
Wood and Cork	253,6	23,3	9·1	4·6	3·6
Paper and Printing	336,8	6,5	1·9	5·2	4·6
Building and Contracting	1,358,8	125,7	9·2	3·9	3·3
Transport and Communications	1,529,0	39,9	2·6	2·8	2·1
Distributive Trades	1,562,7	371,2	23·7	6·1	4·0
Insurance Banking, Finance	295,0	10,0	3·3	4·7	3·3
Professional Services	644·2	89,5	13·8	6·1	3·6
Misc. Services	697,3	163,3	23·4	8·4	7·3

* Including unemployed.

AGEING AND INDUSTRY

In transport and communications, another occupational grouping in which a large labour force is employed up to normal retirement ages, there is a much greater percentage drop in the numbers of older workers in the years immediately following pension age than the average for all industries. Among railway workers, for example, men employed aged 65–69 years are only 15·6% of the number working who are aged 60–64 years. For all workers in these services the 'retention rate' is only 28%. Is it likely that these numbers could be increased or desirable that they should be? Among road transport workers over three-quarters of those occupied are drivers of vehicles. Any defects of vision more prevalent among the elderly, or slowness of reaction in a potentially dangerous situation, would make the older driver anything but an asset in public or private transport services. In passenger transport services, in the interests of the travelling public, medical examinations demanding high standards of physical fitness are regularly carried out, a process which eliminates numbers of older men whose slight impairment of function would pass undetected in other forms of employment. On the other hand, this group of workers are a medically selected group from the time they enter this type of employment, which to some extent may give them a better survival rate for employment at older ages.

Apart from this kind of elimination on medical grounds, and the further voluntary retirement not unrelated to the strain imposed by the nature of their work upon the 'platform' staff in transport services, there are other objections to continued employment after pension age in this kind of occupation. These arise from the organization of the work in some sectors of the industry. Among railway workers particularly, a steady promotion from lower to higher grades accompanied by improvements in qualifications, status and remuneration is a very rigidly defined process. This inevitably leads to a rigidly applied retirement and pension age, since promotion is directly and visibly blocked all down the line by the retention of a man of pension age in a senior position. Apart from the very lowest grades of unskilled labour, the railway workers are not normally prepared to see men retained after pension age in their existing positions. Theoretically, if retained, a man would have to start again at the bottom in the junior grades. The only departure from this practice is both unsatisfactory and expensive, namely for the

33

pensioner to be retained but for the next man whose promotion is delayed to be given the increased salary which would be attached to his promotion. This kind of arrangement is sometimes negotiated for railway supervisory and clerical staff, but it is not common and, where used, very unsatisfactory since the employer pays more than the usual rate for the same work. From every point of view this rigid attitude is unfortunate as the railway industry, being old compared with road transport, already has 47·3% of its labour force over 45 years of age.

With regard to policies directed towards continued employment for older workers it is interesting to note that in transport and communications where relatively few workers aged 65–69 are retained (28%), large numbers of these workers are employed by *public* authorities. The situation is similar in water, gas and electricity services (29·4%) and in Local Government services (27·2%). Can public authorities as employers set a better example in making the maximum use of the labour and skills of older workers in the services for which they are responsible?[1]

The experience of one public authority in this respect is of interest. A large transport undertaking, though finding it impossible to retain many railway workers for some of the reasons suggested above, has tried to use older workers in road transport as long as they wished to remain in employment. (The retention is subject of course to fitness ascertained by annual medical inspections.) The transference of men to maintenance work can only be a limited outlet for the older transport worker, since not more than about one-third of all staff is likely to be employed on maintenance and miscellaneous duties, but it was found possible to recruit about 4% of the labour force for this work from men over 65 years. Among operating staff no more than 1·6% of those employed were over pension age.

Transport is not a popular industry and in a period of full employment the disadvantages involved in duties which fall outside normal working hours are not sufficiently offset by current rates of pay to attract and retain the labour force needed to man existing services.

[1] See *The Aged and the Nation* (Amulree, Seldon and Lewis). Local Government Superannuation arrangements are being revised to encourage later retirement.

This is especially true in areas such as the industrial Midlands where light engineering jobs offer relatively good wages for a five-day week of normal hours. In such an area one city transport department reported in 1953 that in a staff of 9,000, 2,000 left voluntarily during the year though only 93 employees were compulsorily retired by reason of some disablement. Further these transport workers are covered by Local Government Superannuation schemes under which a man is entitled to a disability allowance if he is unfit to continue his service before retirement age. Such men may be fit for other employment and are not lost to the labour market, since most of them take other work demanding less rigorous standards of eyesight and general physical fitness, and they can, of course, do this without any loss of their disability allowances.

Despite the shortage of platform staff in most transport services, there is no sign that these undertakings are making up their labour shortages to any significant degree from elderly workers. As the experience of the transport undertaking quoted above has shown, a minority of men are retained, but in general other sources of labour, such as women, are being recruited by inducement of equal pay to offset awkward work schedules. In the immediate future it is more likely that changed techniques such as operating some routes with one conductor-driver or re-designing vehicles to accommodate more passengers, that is, new methods of seeking to economize in the size of the labour force required, will be employed, rather than more elderly workers.

Employment conditions in the three industries mentioned throw some light on the present difficulties which hinder a wider use of older workers in under-manned industries. In two of them, mining and transport, there does not seem to be any immediate prospect of using many more elderly employees, and for older workers from such industries alternative occupations would have to be found to keep them in employment. In the case of the distributive trades there does appear to be some possibility here of deferring retirement for more older workers. But already the numbers working in the five years following pension age are nearly 60% of the numbers occupied in the years immediately before and presumably these include already many of the men who are fit and willing to remain in full-time work. The most hopeful chance for extending employment would seem to be in reducing any wastage due to fixed retirement rules and extending part-time and temporary employment and, where appropriate, employment at less than minimum wages.[1]

EMPLOYMENT OF OLDER WOMEN

Thus far the possibility of extending employment for men beyond pension ages has been considered, but the number of women who fall into the pension age-groups far outnumber men, women forming 67% of all persons of pension age. Owing to the earlier age at which pensions are payable to women and their greater life expectancy, older women will make heavy claims upon pension funds. Already more than 60% of the current cost of National Insurance pensions goes to women in receipt of payment either on their own or their husband's insurance. These claims might be reduced if the employment of older women could be extended, though in their case even more than in the case of men there are obvious limitations to such a development. 29% of all persons of pension age and 45% of all women of pension age are women over the age of 70, from whom further employment can scarcely be expected.

Further, many older women are not in gainful employment immediately prior to reaching pension ages. At ages 55–59 about 27% of women are occupied. Re-entry into employment at late ages after a long absence from the labour market is not impossible but it presents more difficulties for these older women than for men and women who have worked up to retirement ages.

There is also the effect of marital status on the employment of all women, including those of pension age.

An increase in the numbers of women aged 35–54 in employment has occurred coincidentally with an increase in the numbers of women married in this age-group,[2] and we do not know yet how far this change in social habits will be extended in future among older women. Notwithstanding, therefore, the

---

[1] By permission from the Ministry of Labour Wages Council.

[2] Between 1931 and 1951 the percentage of women occupied aged 35–54 rose by 11% and the proportion who were married and occupied in this age-group rose by 25·5%.

TABLE X

Proportion of Women Occupied and Married aged 35–69

(Census of Great Britain, 1951. One per cent Sample Report)

	Age			
	35–54	55–59	60–64	65–69
No. of Women	7,268,100	1,480,300	1,327,900	1,153,300
% of all women occupied	34·2	27·7	14·3	8·9
% of all women married	78·8	66·2	56·6	46·4
% of all women occupied and married	19·1	10·3	3·7	1·6

prospect[1] of an increase in the numbers of women over 55 who are married, it is possible that more of them will wish to remain in or re-enter employment than at present.

Table XI shows women's principal occupational distribution and the numbers who were at work in 1951 in the five years following minimum pension age. The largest numbers of these older women are occupied in personal service, in commerce and finance and in professional and technical services and they form the highest proportions of the total female labour force in the same industries. The retention rate for women aged 60–64 for all industries is 46·5%. Among all occupied women over the age of 60 years the highest percentages are in agriculture, the distributive trades, professional services, clothing, textiles and miscellaneous services. As in the case of men in some of these industries the proportions of older women occupied is substantially raised by the presence of a higher than average incidence of employers and self-employed persons in the industry. For example, in distribution 5·4% of all women occupied are aged 60 and over, but only 2·6% of *employees* are over minimum pension age.

The distributive trades, like personal services, seem more

[1] See the Report of the Government Actuary on the First Quinquennial Review. National Insurance Act, 1946, Appendix 6, Table D, p. 52.

likely by their nature to be suitable for older women who want to remain in or re-enter the labour market, than industries such as engineering which demand women's labour for rapid repetitive work paced by machinery. Yet the proportion of older

TABLE XI

Females: Employment in Principal Occupations at ages
60–64 years (*hundreds*)

(Census of Great Britain, 1951. One per cent Sample Report)

	(1) Total Nos. aged 15 and over	(2) Numbers occupied aged 60–64	(3) Col. (2) as % of Col. (1)	(4) Numbers occupied aged 60–64 as % of those occupied aged 55–59
Agriculture and Horticulture	105,4	2,8	2·7	46·6
Metal Manufacture, Engineering and Allied Trades	225,1	3,4	1·5	36·9
Textile Workers	418,9	10,0	2·4	37·5
Leather, Leather Goods and Fur	71,0	1,3	1·8	31·0
Makers of Textile Goods	469,5	12,4	2·6	51·0
Food, Drink and Tobacco	99,2	1,7	1·7	39·6
Paper Makers and Printers	101,3	1,2	1·2	33·3
Transport and Communications	145,2	2,7	1·2	27·9
Commercial and Financial	849,5	24,1	2·8	51·2
Professional and Technical	587,1	19,0	3·2	52·1
Personal Service	1,580,1	87,9	5·6	51·6
Clerks, Typists	1,415,7	12,9	0·9	35·9
Miscellaneous unskilled occupations	371,2	5,4	1·5	38·6
All industries	6,916,3	191,1	2·8	46·6

women employed in distribution was lower in 1952 than in most industries (2·7%). It may be a practicable possibility, at any rate in larger stores which have a range of functions (supervision, sales, stockroom, clerical, canteen, etc.), to retain more older women by a change of job or part-time employment, and also to absorb some new older employees.[1] On the other hand part-time help in retail trade is often required to assist during very busy periods, and the pressure of rush-hour conditions, when speed in dealing with customers is essential, may make this work too great a strain for the older woman. If commission or a bonus is calculated on individual sales the older shop assistant who deals with fewer customers will be paid less, and this may rightly reflect her reduced capacity. Often, however, it may reflect the time and care taken by the older assistant in suiting the customer's precise requirements. Whether this is a greater asset to business than the more rapid and perfunctory service sometimes offered by younger saleswomen will depend on the kind of merchandise being handled.

The possibility of finding more part-time employment for older women may be in some ways easier than for older men, because the tradition of part-time work for women, especially married women, is already established. At the Census of 1951 80% of part-time women workers were married, and just over a fifth of occupied married women aged 55–69 were in part-time employment. Some of the kinds of work in which substantial numbers of older women are found such as personal services (including domestic work) lend themselves more readily to part-time arrangements than other occupations, but the part-time employment of married women is spreading into teaching and nursing and other services and this may be a continuing development which will help to utilize the services of older women. At present among women engaged in professional services, 75% are occupied as teachers and nurses. The transference of older women's labour, not hitherto thus employed, to undermanned occupations like nursing and teaching is hindered by the lack of professional qualifications, though it is possible to use some older women in these services to a limited extent upon auxiliary tasks of a more domestic nature.

Much more detailed studies will have to be made of trends in employment of women at all ages in relation to their occupations and marital status before any conclusions can be drawn about the employment potential of women of pension ages. To date the increased demand for women's labour has been met mainly by using the services part or whole time of younger (i.e.

[1] Since this was written the proportion of women employees in the distributive trades who are over pension ages has risen to 4·0% (1954).

under pension age) married women. In considering the problem of the ratio of workers to pensioners we have to remember this possible source of more woman power. Earlier marriages and small families mean that for many women the heaviest responsibilities in rearing children are now over by early middle age, and they are able to work regularly outside their own homes.[1] Such labour will be preferred by employers, and until a saturation point is reached in the employment of younger married women it is unlikely that employers will want to retain or engage many elderly women except possibly in so far as any further part-time work is a practicable arrangement.

EMPLOYERS' ATTITUDES TOWARDS USING OLDER WORKERS

This very brief examination of the immediate possibilities of the employment of more older workers in some industries is not meant to imply that it is not possible for individual firms, or particular trades or public authorities, to increase their numbers of workers who postpone retirement for one, two or more years beyond present pension ages. It does however suggest that no large-scale extension of employment of older workers can be looked for in the immediate future either as a means of reducing pension payments, or of significantly augmenting the labour forces of undermanned industries.

It is clearly desirable that wherever their labour is economic[2] workers should be encouraged to continue in employment as long as they are able and wish to do so. But it must be remembered when we consider the possibility of employing more older workers that at present just over half of men aged 65–69 are in employment, and no doubt these already include most men who are healthy and vigorous or have skills and experience which are in demand, or are in a trade or occupation the nature of which is conducive to a prolonged working life.

The chief source of additional workers would seem to be

[1] This is one way in which fewer children and more old people may check the rise in the total cost of dependency. More women are likely to be tied to the home by the care of young children than by the care of elderly relatives, and with fewer children more women are freed for 'gainful' employment.

[2] The possibility of providing useful occupations for the elderly through social agencies (e.g. the Finsbury Employment Scheme) is excluded from consideration here.

among those who have been compulsorily retired or discharged and not all of these may be employable. A less rigid application of retirement rules by employers, for example, might lead to fewer retirements but to more discharges. Even for those workers who are willing to defer retirement it is by no means always easy to find them acceptable employment.

If in the long run, however, employers are faced with a labour force containing a very much higher proportion than now of workers over 50 years,[1] and if full employment continues, they will be forced to make considerable adjustments in productive processes either to try and reduce their total demand for labour by further mechanization, or to find ways of successfully using older labour, despite the difficulties noted above. An example may be quoted of a firm who have already found themselves with just such a situation, and whose response to it illustrates the problem.

The firm in question are manufacturers of machinery employing approximately 2,557 men and 462 women. Among male employees about 41% are engaged in work termed skilled, about 22% in clerical work, and the remainder on unskilled or semi-skilled occupations. Among females, the greater numbers, nearly 80%, are clerical workers, including a few part-time staff. Immediately after the war this firm found itself short of juvenile labour, especially boys and girls from the local grammar schools. Although the lower birth rate of the 1930's had been to some extent offset by the coincidental growth of the town in which this firm was situated, this very development led to new claims upon the annual supply of school leavers in the area. This situation, together with the raising of the school-leaving age to 15 years, faced local industries with an immediate shortage of juveniles. Those juveniles they had were becoming 'frozen' in their first jobs because to transfer or promote them created shortages of staff in departments dependent upon this labour. With transfers or promotion withheld, the better educated and more ambitious youngsters who after three to six months wanted to move from the very elementary jobs, were found to be increasingly dissatisfied and likely to look for other employment.

In this situation the firm made a careful study of the existing

[1] Already (May 1952) 49% of male employees are in the age groups 40 and over, i.e. our labour force is already middle aged.

use of juvenile labour and a brief job-analysis of the work customarily undertaken by youngsters. They found it possible to replace juveniles by a smaller number of adults in such departments as the internal postal and messenger department, the specifications office, accounts department and various records offices. A number of fetch-and-carry jobs in other departments usually consigned to juveniles could also be transferred to adult workers. In this way the company decided that some 57 adults could replace 70 juveniles. Provided adults and juniors were not mixed together, and the scope of work in the departments in question was slightly changed in form and title to avoid, on psychological grounds, the idea of adults doing junior jobs, it was felt that with careful selection adult disabled and older workers, old servants of the company needing transfers to lighter jobs, or those past normal pension age could be utilized. In the case of men transferred from the factory to this type of lighter work the minimum office rate was a little higher than the standard labourer's rate in the works, and they enjoyed the benefit of staff sick pay benefits, so that the problem of demotion to a lower rate of pay did not arise. The comments of some of the departments consulted are interesting: 'Happy to dispense with all juveniles, could accept four disabled in replacement of juveniles for messenger and miscellaneous recording'; 'Clerical work could be done better by older clerks. Disabled or old men could do the work'; 'Juveniles represent 25% of Accounts staff. Most of the boys could be replaced by old or disabled men'; 'If necessity demands, could replace all juveniles by alternative labour. Not so convenient in view of fatigue proneness of elderly people'; 'Owing to time off allowed for attending school, a department with a number of juveniles is constantly disturbed by their absence. The Cost Office nominally has sixteen juveniles, but in terms of working weeks they do not have more than fourteen. If old and disabled men work a full week every week it would probably be cheaper and less trouble to employ them.'

An experiment was commenced of using more older men, including men already over 65 at the date of the employment and who in some cases had retired already from other occupations. The group contained at one stage an ex-railway man, two former employees of the Post Office services, a salesman and a labourer, as well as moulders, skilled workers and labourers from the Fitting Shop already in the employment of the company. This was in addition to the company's normal policy of retaining older workers at their own jobs wherever possible, especially in skilled work. No special concessions were found to be necessary for these older employees and the record of their punctuality, attendance and conscientious application to their work was most impressive. The jobs found most suitable for them were as one would expect, those requiring care and responsibility but not speed or quick decisions. These resolved themselves into two main groups, 'pot-boiling' jobs of a routine kind often done badly in the past by bored juniors, or jobs requiring special skill and knowledge only obtained by long service. The older messengers carrying internal post moved more slowly than the juniors they had replaced but they had no girl friends to lark with on the stairs. As the Personnel Manager expressed it, the situation was analogous to the race between the hare and the tortoise, and the post was delivered if anything more promptly. The sedentary clerical work, especially in handling records, was equally successful and about $5\frac{1}{2}$% of the male clerical staff were over 65 years of age at July 1948.

Despite the successful operation of this policy, by the end of 1952 the company had to re-examine the size of its labour force and the need arose to effect some reduction. Two ways of making this reduction were adopted, first by ceasing recruitment and allowing normal wastage to take place and secondly by altering the policy regarding retirement. Those workers recruited from outside above the normal ages for recruiting workers had to leave first and a retirement policy was formulated which laid down 65 as the normal retiring age for men (both works and staff) and 60 years for women. This was not meant to be inflexible and men could be invited to remain to 67 years and even beyond that age in very special circumstances. The views of advisory panels from the works and staff committees, together with medical reports were to be used to arrive at decisions to retain certain men over 65 years. The policy was to be implemented gradually with adequate notice for the existing staff over 65 years and an improvement in the company's pension benefits also helped to eliminate any hardship. Having initiated such a policy early in 1953, the company were by mid-1954 again embarrassed by a shortage of recruits and their

43

retirement policy was revised again to include raising the possible limits of 65–67 years to nearer 67–70 years with medical examinations and annual reviews.

These fluctuations were directly conditioned by assessments of labour requirements in relation to order books and trading prospects, and illustrate very well the role of the older worker as a marginal worker. This experiment has given the company in question an experience of transferring the older worker, at any age from 50 years and over, and the reorganization of clerical work carried out originally for the pension-age workers can be used for any men who begin to fail in their jobs on the factory floor in the last ten years before retirement. The company's conclusion is that an upper limit must be fixed for retention, but that within this, a considerable degree of flexibility is possible in response to changing labour requirements, and that simple job-analysis and reorganization of methods may yield satisfactory and economic employment for older workers.

There was here no question of philanthropy or occupational therapy. The shortage of juvenile labour was met by employing older workers. During the last war, and it can happen similarly in a post-war period of full employment, employers will retain or recruit older workers, for want of any other labour. But in circumstances where it is possible to choose between older and younger applicants, unless the post is clearly one requiring maturity, experience and qualifications not possessed by a younger man, there is little doubt that a candidate over 50 will be rejected in favour of a younger applicant. Employers who are well disposed towards their older employees and speak most highly of their services will yet nearly always have this prejudice in engaging new labour.

During inquiries[1] made by the writer amongst more than fifty firms of varying sizes and trades in the West Midlands the response of employers and their personnel managers was almost always the same. They commended their older employees for their punctuality and attendance records and their conscientious attitude to their work. Most of the employers stated that they had no prejudice against retaining older workers, who were willing and able to remain beyond normal pension age. The visitor was then taken to see 'Old Bill', who had been with the firm for fifty years, but further questioning established that

[1] Appendix II.

44

these old gentlemen were rather exceptional and the number employed beyond pension ages was very small indeed.

Further, whilst most employers expressed themselves as in no way averse to employing people in any occupation for the first time after they had reached pension age, many then went on to demonstrate that this would be quite impossible in *their* particular trade.[1]

Similarly a survey of old people and their employment in 1950[2] found that one quarter of employers thought there were no prospects for using older workers in their field and another quarter thought it would be possible only if the older workers were already on their staff. Only half the employers in this sample favoured the idea of employing older persons.

Among the Midland firms it appeared that certain jobs had been found by experience to be unsuitable since older workers could not maintain the output achieved by younger employees and themselves requested transfers to different work. Other jobs were tacitly assumed to be unsuitable though there had never been any inquiry or experiment to prove this. Work at great heights or involving very heavy materials or extremes of temperature were generally excluded as possible employment for older workers, although in fact some older workers could be found successfully undertaking just such work. When employers were asked to state what work they considered suitable and could offer to older men they tended to list a few light auxiliary jobs,[3] usually not part of the main production line, though this definition of suitability was sometimes contradicted in their own firms by the employment of some men on very heavy work, whose high ages went unnoticed. Until some job-analysis has been made or experiments conducted to determine more precisely the criteria of 'suitability' of different processes for older workers, employers will continue to use common sense and convention as the only guides in selecting jobs for elderly employees, and this policy tends to yield only a very narrow range of jobs in most industries. In the long run as the labour force ages, employers will have less choice, but in the short run each

[1] For a further discussion of employers' attitudes see Appendix II, pp. 323-5.

[2] G. Thomas and B. Osborne, 'Older People and their Employment', *The Social Survey*, 1950.

[3] See also 'New Jobs for Older Workers', Le Gros Clark and Dunne, Nuffield Foundation, 1955.

will seek wherever possible the younger man. These observations refer mainly to industrial employment and apply with perhaps less force to some employment in professional, managerial and executive posts. But to a great extent the older employee, and certainly the man over pensionable age, is at present a marginal worker, drawn into the market when there is no alternative supply of labour and very much less easy to employ if the level of employment falls. Fifteen years of full employment have not yet significantly modified the older worker's role in the labour force.

TRADE UNION ATTITUDES TO EMPLOYMENT OF OLDER WORKERS

Even where employers may wish to retain older workers it is difficult for them to do so in the face of any redundancy among the young. One large firm reported that they had been faced with just this situation. After the war they found it necessary to reduce their number of employees and though they would have preferred to retain their pensionable employees who had stayed or returned to help the firm through an exceptionally busy period, they had to accept the demands of the Union concerned to let the elderly go in order to retain younger men, some of whom had only a very short record of employment with the firm. This is not to say that Trade Unions are not sympathetic towards the needs of the older worker,[1] but that where any substantial number of younger men are involved in the prospect of unemployment, the Union is likely to demand that the pensioners must go first. An extreme form of this was experienced in the period of heavy unemployment in the 1930's when schemes were proposed for lowering retirement ages and getting men out of employment at 55 or even 50 years in order to leave jobs to younger men.

As Mr. Roberts[1] points out, from the days of the earliest craft unions an attempt was made to protect regular employment for their members by restricting the number of workers competing in the labour market, and one way of effecting this was to exclude children, older persons, and in some cases married women. It was thought that older men ought to be helped

[1] See A. Roberts, 'British Trade Union attitudes to the Employment of Older Men and Women', a paper presented to the Third Congress of the International Association of Gerontology, London, July 1954.

by pension schemes, and unions and Friendly Societies often provided payments of this kind as long as older workers did not create a reserve of cheap labour competing for scarce jobs. The 'right to work' can be extended to the 'right to work for all adults irrespective of age' only where it can be shown that the labour of older workers is needed in addition to the full employment of men with families, 'where there has to be a choice it is in favour of the age group with the greatest domestic responsibilities'.[1] Clearly the worker over pensionable age is regarded as a marginal employee by many trade unionists. On the other hand the unions have always been perturbed by age-barriers erected against middle-aged workers, and lend their full support to any efforts to reduce the prejudice which often operates against workers changing their jobs as early as at 40 or 45 years.

In the short run therefore wherever the labour of young and older men is directly competitive, the older worker is likely to be regarded by both employers and unions as a marginal worker. No amount of official statements to the contrary will *per se* alter this.

OLDER WORKERS AND FULL EMPLOYMENT

In a period of full employment, however, it might be supposed that older workers could be readily employed. The obstacles which prevent the wider use of older persons in some industries have been noted above, and even when there is an overall shortage of labour this has to be examined carefully to eliminate labour needs which older employees would be very unlikely to be able to fill. Recruitment to the Armed Forces, Police and Fire Services and similar occupations cannot be considered by the elderly, though the gaps left in industry by the withdrawal of fit younger men to such occupations may be filled by older men.

Even industrial needs in the so-called 'light' industries are by no means always suitable for older men. Many such advertised vacancies are for women experienced in quick deft repetitive work. Women themselves are often unable to maintain their speed of performance with increasing age in this type of

---

[1] Roberts, *op. cit.*, p. 46.

work, and find difficulty in learning new processes.[1] It is unlikely that older men could acquire at a late age the necessary dexterity to be able to maintain the pace set by machines. It would be more expensive to employ men's rather than women's labour and not easy to fit older men into the supervision arrangements planned for young women. Moreover older men anxious for employment may be willing to take work formerly done by youths, for example internal postal and messenger services, but would sometimes rather leave than accept what they term contemptuously 'wenches' work'.[2]

It is scarcely useful therefore at present to suggest that the numbers of married mothers in industry could be replaced by the greater employment of the elderly. We should, of course, beware of traditional prejudices and remember that in certain occupations the relative numbers of men and women have greatly changed in recent years, e.g. male nurses and female 'bus conductors, but this has usually been an interchange of the young and physically fit rather than of older workers for young.

THE CAPACITIES OF OLDER WORKERS EXAMINED

The view of the older worker as a marginal worker is often said to be based on an erroneous undervaluation of older workers in relation to specified jobs. A number of investigations, notably those conducted by the Nuffield Research Unit into Ageing at the Psychological Laboratories at Cambridge[3] have attempted to re-examine some of the common assumptions about the capacity of older workers. The most common of these assumptions are that the older worker is slower, unable to continue in some kinds of heavy manual work, more prone to accidents; that he lacks the necessary flexibility to adjust himself to changes in production and finds difficulty in learning new skills. To the older business manager or public servant is attributed a generally conservative outlook and a reluctance to accept major changes in policy and practice. Some of these assumptions are not supported by the evidence available.

An examination of accident rates in industry does not show

[1] R. M. Belbin, 'Difficulties of Older People in Industry', *Journal of Occupational Psychology*, Vol. 27, October 1953.

[2] B. E. Lewis (Shenfield), 'Employment of Older Workers', paper read to the British Association, Brighton, 1950.

[3] A. T. Welford, *Skills and Age*, O.U.P., 1950.

a greater frequency rate among older workers. On the contrary statistics relating to awards of Industrial Injury Benefit quoted by the National Advisory Committee on the employment of older men and women, show that the award of benefit is twice as high among men under 30 as among men over 60. It is true that recovery may be slower and the 'severity' rate of accidents judged by the number of days lost is higher among the over 60's but even so it is only slightly higher than the average for all ages. The Chief Factory Inspector has reported similar findings. His report (1951)[1] quotes a steel works employing 6,000 persons where 17·5% of the workers are over 60 years and 5·5% (300) are over 65 years, and where the frequency rate of accidents was higher among those under 60 years than over. Other firms similarly have a frequency rate of accidents among older workers which is not in any way abnormal. This is confirmed in the Annual Report of the Chief Inspector of Factories (1954) which notes that[2] for the third year in succession accident rates for male and female workers over 60 years were lower than for workers in the prime of life. Divisional inspectors state that they feel that most of the accidents happening to the older worker could have happened to anyone and that, in general, older persons are not more prone to accidents than other workers. The old seem especially susceptible to falls and the results of these are more serious than among younger workers. Of all industrial accidents, 14% are caused by falls, but among elderly workers accidents due to falls are more than 20% of the total.

Any attempts to make comparisons of accident and sickness rates between younger and older workers are open to two serious objections. First, workers who are retained after retirement ages are very often transferred to lighter work well removed from accident hazards, and are therefore not subject to the same risks as younger workers. An extensive policy of keeping older workers in their former jobs with the same degree of risk attendant might lead to higher accident rates among elderly employees. Secondly, those workers who continue after minimum pension age may be a highly selected group, encouraged to continue just because they can safely maintain work performance and good attendance. The performance of

---

[1] Annual Report of the Chief Inspector of Factories, 1951. Cmd. 8772.
[2] Cmd. 9605.

this minority does not necessarily represent the potential capacity of all older employees.

A more significant comparison would be to match the accident rates of younger men and men in the last ten years before usual retirement age. In this latter group will be found men whose general performance is deteriorating and who expect to retire promptly at the customary age, as well as those who are both willing and able to continue in employment beyond pensionable age. Such a comparison has been made in a detailed study[1] of 17,800 workers in 109 plants in the United States, which analyses work injuries among different age groups. In this inquiry accidents are divided into disabling injuries, i.e. causing disablement for at least one shift, and non-disabling injuries. On this analysis the total of disablement for workers between 55 and 60 years is about the same as for the ages 45 to 49 years and only a little higher than for ages 24 to 34 years. The average number of days of disability rises with age from 40 but is never as high as in the 20 to 24 year old workers. Non-disabling injuries were found to decrease with age and a record of visits to industrial medical clinics for treatment of minor ailments showed that such visits were more frequent among those below the 45–49 age groups, than among those above. It is the experience of some employers that older workers do not readily report minor accidents for fear that this may draw attention to some supposed failing on their part, and this may influence the age analysis of the incidence of reported non-disabling injuries.

The possibility cannot be excluded that if very much larger numbers of old people were retained in industry in their former jobs, absenteeism due to industrial injury might rise, but among older workers at present employed there is no evidence to show that there is any serious excess of accident frequency or absenteeism due to industrial injury, over the rates experienced for younger employees.

LIGHT EMPLOYMENT FOR OLDER WORKERS

Transference of older workers to light or lighter work (not necessarily the same thing) is often advocated as the best way

[1] M. D. Kossoris, 'Absenteeism and Injury Experience of Old Workers' (*Monthly Labor Review*, 1948, Vol. 67).

of using the changing but still useful capacities of older workers. This rests on the assumption that heavy manual work demanding considerable physical exertion is generally unsuitable for older employees. Inquiries into current practice in heavy industries do not wholly support this view.

It is certainly true that an older worker is not likely to be able to engage successfully in heavy work if he tries to enter this kind of occupation at a late age, but numbers of older men habituated to heavy work are able to continue surprisingly often beyond retirement age. Long practice perfects their performance and enables them to economize on the muscular effort required by their work. Continuous heavy physical exertion is likely to create strain greater than can be tolerated by most older workers, but intermittently strenuous work in which the worker can control the pace of the operation can be found being done successfully by some older men over a wide range of industries.

Some industrial processes make such heavy physical demands upon those employed in them that some men begin to move away from these jobs long before they approach retirement age. Those who remain in these heavy industries after middle age are already a selected group since numbers of men will have left the industry at younger ages to seek lighter employment.[1]

A study of older workers in two foundries and a coal mine[2] showed that the number of transfers to lighter work began at about age 40 and from then on rose sharply with age. As might be expected, the percentage engaged in light work at ages 60–69 years was 12% higher than at 50–59 years for foundry workers, and nearly three times higher among miners. It appeared from this study that an injury or illness frequently precipitates a desire to move to lighter work even after full recovery, 12% of the men interviewed had moved to lighter work after an injury. Dr. Richardson describes industrial injuries as 'triggers' which may release a new consciousness of strain of which the worker was not fully aware before.

Despite this general trend of workers being moved to lighter jobs as they grow older, a substantial minority continued to perform heavy work up to and beyond retirement age. Nearly a

[1] See p. 29 above.
[2] I. M. Richardson, 'Age and Work', *British Journal of Industrial Medicine*, 1953, 10, 269.

fifth of the foundry workers and just over a quarter of the miners aged 60–69 years were in work classed as heavy, and it was similarly found in an analysis of the age-structure of iron and steel companies[1] covering 110,000 employees, that some firms had as many as 10% of workers over 65 years, and some of their departments, including blast furnaces and coke ovens, had over 13% of their operatives over pensionable age.

This retention of older workers in heavy industries may be because many of these occupations lack young entrants and employers are aware of the need to conserve the services of older skilled men, but there is some evidence to show that in making an occupation unsuitable for older workers, work paced by a machine may be more important than slower physical exertion controlled by the individual operative. Welford[2] found that the age-distributions for men on heavy and lighter work were very similar, and that it is when 'time stress' is associated with heavy work, thus demanding continuous effort from the operative, that heavy work discriminates against older people. In this inquiry there appeared a striking tendency for people to move away from heavy operations if they were rigidly paced. There was no evidence of moves from heavy work not involving time-stress. It may not, therefore, be practicable to think in terms of moving many old people from heavy to lighter jobs as is often suggested. Rather, older workers may successfully manage heavy work which is performed at a pace controlled by the worker himself, or at any rate where frequent pauses are permitted. Light work in which more emphasis is placed on speed than accuracy or where the operation is paced by the machine may be the least suitable employment for older workers. The lighter jobs which are found successfully for workers near or over retirement age are often miscellaneous tasks which are auxiliary to, but not directly a part of, a productive process.[3] It is true that there may be some semi-skilled jobs which involve speed but neither precision nor complex mental processes and which are carried out by familiar operations, where the older worker can maintain his performance

---

[1] C. Fleming, 'The Employment of the Elderly', *British Journal of Physical Medicine.* See also 'The Employment of Elderly Workers', the Industrial Welfare Society, 1950.

[2] Welford, *op. cit.*, p. 48.

[3] See Appendix II, p. 199.

successfully,[1] but in general it is found difficult to move old workers formerly accustomed to slower heavy work on to light work requiring continuous performance at high speeds.

The problems of pace and time stress which emerge so clearly from the studies at the Nuffield Research Unit are of the very greatest importance in considering suitable employment for older workers. Many other characteristics of older workers which can be readily observed in industry are directly related to the difficulty they experience in maintaining pace. It is well known that older workers are often found working apparently happily in small groups. It is significant that in small groups the speed of work can be adapted to suit individuals and the work is often of a kind which demands care and accuracy rather than a large output. Most important, the work is not part of a production line where other operatives may be held up or work accumulates if the older worker is more slow and deliberate in his movements. There is usually less strain and pressure in the small group and, left to organize his own task and develop his own rhythm of work, the older worker can often maintain a satisfactory performance. Sometimes the older worker's performance may deteriorate in some respects, but show a compensatory improvement in others, so that the overall output remains constant. In this respect older workers are not necessarily good people to train newcomers since their methods, adapted to their own changing capacities, may not be a suitable training for younger workers learning the operation for the first time. Of course these compensatory changes of performance can only operate where the work itself permits a variety of methods in carrying it out.

Again the tendency for older workers to be found on operations paid by a time rate more often than on piece rates is not due to the system of payments as such but because characteristics unfavourable to the elderly, such as the paramount importance of speed, are often associated with piece rates, while the need for a high degree of quality and accuracy is linked with time rates.

The Cambridge inquiry[2] into the acquisition and retention of skill in later years also studied learning difficulties among older

[1] See 'Age of Semi-skilled Workers in Relation to Abilities', G. W. Brown and E. E. Ghiselli, *Personnel Psychology*, 1949.
[2] Welford, *op. cit.*, p. 48.

persons and although it clearly refuted the contention that old dogs cannot learn new tricks, it demonstrated that older persons certainly learn in a different kind of way and appear to experience difficulties which do not trouble younger people so much. Wherever the older person can bring to a task methods and skills formerly acquired, there seems no impairment of ability even in learning a new procedure. But where the data are fresh and cannot be interpreted by 'preformed' methods, difficulties arise for older persons. They may be distinctly slower in apprehending what is required and experience difficulty and strain in carrying out a technique which is new to them and in which they cannot usefully draw upon their previous experience.

Thus changing techniques and conditions in industry on which hopes have been pinned for making it easier than formerly to retain older workers in employment, may have the very opposite effect in so far as they involve greater speed of operation fixed by the movements of machinery. Far from making work lighter and easier and therefore more suitable for the elderly, new and speedier methods may in future create more difficulty for older workers than some heavier and slower operations do now.

CHAPTER III

EMPLOYMENT OF OLDER WORKERS—
(2) REASONS FOR RETIRING OR
CONTINUING AT WORK

TURNING from employment opportunities available to older workers, how many more are likely to want to remain in employment should suitable work be offered to them? The rate of retirement after 65 for males and after 60 for females undoubtedly increased between 1931 and 1951 (Table XII) and the earlier census was taken in a period of heavy unemployment, when neither opportunities for employing the elderly were likely to be available nor would public policy or opinion encourage it. The great difference between these two periods is that a higher level of pension payments (even allowing for increased prices) underwritten by the National Assistance Board, wider industrial pension average, and other forms of social aid have made it possible for some older workers to retire, where formerly they could not have afforded to do so.

In this situation, assuming more flexible retirement policies and employment opportunities available to them, how many men and women reaching retirement age, who are fit, are likely to *choose* to prolong their working lifetime?

Retirement decisions first involve financial considerations: what means of maintenance will be available in lieu of earnings? The attraction of rest and leisure on retirement may be offset by the prospect of a marked reduction of income. If, as seems probable, the decision to retire is largely affected by the availability of pension and superannuation payments, the growth of pension provision in recent years will tend to reduce the financial pressure to continue employment.[1] Furthermore,

[1] Provided that the value of these pensions is not seriously reduced by rising prices without any compensatory increase in pension levels.

TABLE XII

Analysis of Retirement: Great Britain, 1931–51 (hundreds)

Ages	1931 Males				1951 Males			
	60-64	65-69	65 and over	70 and over	60-64	65-69	65 and over	70 and over
Number retired	92,1	199,2	647,6	448,4	105,3	403,2	1,320,0	916,8
Number occupied	761,6	422,7	682,8	260,1	918,2	422,4	695,3	272,9
Sum of retired and occupied	853,7	621,9	1,330,4	708,5	1,023,5	825,6	2,015,3	1,189,7
Retired as percentage of retired and occupied	10·8	32·0	48·7	63·3	10·3	48·8	65·5	77·1

Ages	1931 Females					1951 Females				
	55-59	60-64	65-69	60 and over	70 and over	55-59	60-64	65-69	60 and over	70 and over
Number retired	15,9	25,7	37,7	131,7	68,3	17,9	67,1	70,9	254,0	116,0
Number occupied	226,7	160,0	94,2	315,1	61,0	410,2	191,1	103,6	357,1	62,4
Sum of retired and occupied	242,6	185,7	131,8	446,8	129,3	428,1	258,2	174,5	611,1	178,4
Retired as percentage of retired and occupied	6·6	13·8	28·6	29·5	52·8	4·2	26·0	40·6	41·6	65·0

where pensions are conditional upon retirement at a fixed age, the older worker has a direct encouragement to retire and claim his pension. This does not mean that those with, say, a claim to a National Insurance pension and superannuation will necessarily find themselves financially able to retire. For many who have reached retirement after the war, provision which seemed sufficient by pre-war prices has proved very inadequate indeed. But, in general, financial pressures to continue in employment have been reduced, though by no means eliminated, for the bulk of industrial workers.

Where a choice can be exercised (for ill-health or retirement rules may leave some employees no retirement choice at all), it is not easy to determine precisely the reasons which induce older workers to defer retirement, but there are four major reasons, or some combination of them, which can commonly be observed. The first is a financial one, the desire to continue to receive full wages or salary and later a pension increased in amount by reason of this deferment. The other three reasons are 'non-economic' or social. They are first, interest and pride in work, secondly, status, and thirdly the social relationships associated with a particular occupation for the individual worker. To which perhaps also should be added, habit!

Of the incentives to remain in employment perhaps the most easily observed is the satisfaction derived by older workers from the continued pursuit of a craft or skill. Men of advanced years, up to 75 years old and beyond, can be found undertaking work requiring a lifetime's skill and experience. There is usually no problem involved in the employment of such people. A Birmingham engineering firm advertised (July 1954) 'Skilled toolmakers required. No one under 60 years of age.' The management commented, 'We feel there is still room for older men. They may be a bit slower but they are the real craftsmen.' Some highly skilled craftsmen want to go on working and industry is usually ready to maintain them as long as there is any demand for the products of their skill. Their slower movements or more frequent need for rest is more than offset by their specialized knowledge. These older craftsmen derive an unconcealed satisfaction from their work. They are aware that they are indispensable and their attitude to ageing is confident. They have usually never had to work at the same pace as machine operators or handle such heavy materials as heavy manual workers, and in this way they have conserved their energy and are usually less physically exhausted than the average unskilled or semi-skilled worker of the same age. There are few industrial enterprises where management cannot take their visitors with benevolent pride to see an older craftsman, and ask him the question, to which both know the answer: 'Let me see, how many years have you been with us?' This kind of situation keeps everyone happy but it is restricted to a very small part of modern industry. It is reflected in the higher proportions of elderly workers found in certain industries (see Table VIII) which employ a higher than average number of craftsmen and highly skilled workers.

Professional men, to the extent that they are self-employed and choose their own retirement date, may also prefer, apart from any financial considerations, to continue to exercise their skill because of the satisfaction they derive from it.

Apart, also, from the satisfaction derived from carrying on a craft or profession which may outweigh considerations of leisure, there is the second factor which may be combined with it, that is the fear of loss of status. The old often occupy positions of prestige and authority and find it difficult to surrender senior executive positions to younger men. To give up such positions involves an overt recognition of advancing years and lessening powers, and forces the older man to contemplate his future role and status and the narrowing opportunities remaining to him. Relationships in the home may also be affected, and some men feel a loss of domestic prestige in their own household following retirement.

These kinds of considerations may be powerful in delaying retirement for some people but they cannot be said to apply to those industrial workers who practise no special skill or craft and whose working life is not mainly conditioned by hopes of promotion to positions of authority. The strongest non-financial motive for them appears to be the need for occupation and especially occupation which brings opportunities for social contacts. Membership of a working group involves an important set of interpersonal relationships. Position in an occupational group gives opportunity for the display of personality and the development of relationships which have significance for the individual.

It may be a matter for regret that substantial numbers of

older people remaining in employment do so because they lack ways of using their leisure in hobbies and other interests.[1] Adult education, and the development of the old people's clubs and interest groups may in time alter this. But at the moment there are undoubtedly some older workers who would be lonely and bored if unable to continue to work in the place and at the tasks with which they have a long-established familiarity. Their limited educational background gives them little appreciation of cultural diversions, especially[2] those which they would have to pursue alone, and they are ill-equipped for the public work and voluntary service which occupy the time and energies of some of their contemporaries. Regular employment gives them purposive activity and economic independence.

It is also often claimed that continued employment is good for the health and general well-being of older persons and may help to defer the onset of senility. There is, however, no clear evidence on this point. Sheldon[3] suggests that the continued ability to find something useful to do in the way of domestic tasks is 'of immense value to the physical health of old women'. 'It undoubtedly', he says, 'plays a part in the fact that very old women are able to outlive men while carrying a great burden of physical defect.' He admits that it is possible that the female body is by genetic constitution more durable than the male. Bearing in mind the superior survival rates of females at younger ages, we cannot dismiss the possibility that it is this which accounts for the apparently greater will to live among older women compared with older men.

In general the weight of medical opinion is that sudden disuse of mental and bodily functions, previously regularly exercised, such as may happen through retirement, is likely to cause atrophy and degeneration which are harmful to the health of older persons. It does *not*, however, follow that continued paid employment of the elderly is necessarily the only or the

[1] See also 'Reasons given for Retiring or Continuing at Work', Ministry of Pensions and National Insurance, *op. cit.*, para 32, p. 9.

[2] It should not be assumed that lack of interest in later years is directly linked to social and occupational class in all cases. The more a man has been absorbed in his work to the exclusion of other interest the less he may be prepared for retirement, and this can apply with equal force to the business or professional man, irrespective of educational background or financial resources.

[3] *The Social Medicine of Old Age, op. cit.*, p. 16.

best way to avoid this, or that the pursuit of hobbies does not equally nourish vitality in old age.

While it is clear that some older people prefer to remain at work, and apparently take no harm from this, if indeed they do not derive positive benefit, it is less certain whether these people are a transitional class. Will future generations, accustomed to shorter hours of work and wider opportunities for the use of leisure, want a continued employment as a means of occupation and interest in their later years? If in our present organization of industry many workers do not derive much satisfaction from their work and it is largely divorced from other aspects of their social life, it seems unlikely that many, given adequate pension provision, will want to continue in employment beyond conventional retirement ages. Attitudes to retirement arise directly out of attitudes to work, and the larger numbers of older men remaining in employment in America (three-fifths of those aged 65–69 are in paid employment, and one-fifth of those over 75 years are working) may be the reflection of attitudes to work formed in a very different cultural pattern.

Two investigations,[1] carried out in 1945 and in 1950, have tried to disentangle the mixed motives of older workers in reaching decisions about retirement. In 1945 conditions were still favourable to the employment of a large number of older persons. They were able to supply labour which could not be obtained from any other source, compulsory retirement rules were not enforced, and many continued beyond normal pension ages at the request of their employers. In this situation in the 1945 inquiry, one in five of the older workers interviewed said they were in employment and worked solely because they preferred it, and a further one in four said they worked because they had to (i.e. for economic reasons), but that they also preferred it. Increasing age modified this figure. The over 70's referred more frequently than those between 60 and 70 years to the companionship of other workers and interest in their job. About one-third of those over 70 who went to work had no direct need to do so other than their own feelings of liking to continue. In giving their reasons for their attitude to continued

[1] 'Employment of Older Persons', G. Thomas and B. Osborne, *The Social Survey*, and 'Older People and their Employment', G. Thomas and B. Osborne, *The Social Survey*.

employment, 87% of older workers said they liked the job and 29% of the men and 24% of the women said they would be bored and lonely at home, and the proportion who gave this reason went up with increasing age. 66% of old people said they would go on working as long as they could and only 10% expressed a definite intention to retire and these were among those aged 65–69 years. (These figures refer to 1945 before the introduction, in October 1945, of the new pensions at a higher rate conditional upon retirement.) These results seemed to indicate that, while the majority of older people were working because they felt they had to, there was a proportion, probably more than a third, who preferred to work anyway. This was likely to be reduced, however, if allowance was made for the numbers who said they would retire when qualified for pension or when the labour shortage was less acute.

By the time that the second inquiry was made (1950)[1] some men had retired when the war-time need for their services had disappeared and some older men had been displaced by returning ex-servicemen. Some firms enforced again retirement rules which had lapsed during the period of acute labour shortage. (About a third of the men in this inquiry (1950) said their firms imposed a retiring age.) The number of older workers in employment was found to have fallen in 1950 as compared with 1945, from 64% of men aged 65–69 to 46% and from 34% of men aged 70–74 to 29% The main decline was roughly at the ages 65–69 years. The effect of pension provision on retirement is illustrated when those remaining in employment aged 60–75 years are divided into pensioners (i.e. persons receiving any kind of pension) and non-pensioners. In the summer of 1945 44% of pensioners and 81% of non-pensioners were working full or part time. In the spring of 1950 30% of pensioners and 85% of non-pensioners were in employment.

Only 11% of those still working said they had remained in order to get a bigger pension, though 31% of those below pension age said they would stay for this purpose. This may mean that the increased tendency to retire because of pension rights may be to some extent offset as the idea of the deferred increased pension becomes known and acceptable. The larger increase now earned by deferment and the fact that a widow can have her pension increased by her husband's continued

[1] *Older People and their Employment, op. cit.*

employment, meets some of the criticism raised about the original regulations for National Insurance pensions. Before these changes were made men complained that if they paid their contributions, deferred their pension, and attempted to work up to 70 years, they might die before they or their dependants could 'get anything out of it'.

Of the men in full- or part-time employment aged 65–74 years who were questioned in 1950, about the same proportion said that they worked mainly because they liked it, but nearly twice as many said that they had to work and preferred to remain in employment. It seems likely that a proportion of those saying they worked because they had to in 1945 took the first opportunity of retirement on pension and the proportion of those working because of direct financial need was correspondingly reduced.

Many of those interviewed (over 60%) were aged 55–64 years and had not yet reached retirement ages, so that they were expressing ideas and opinions about a future possibility. Where there is a marked difference between the views of those now retired and those who will retire over the next ten years, it is impossible to say how far this represents genuinely changing attitudes, or how far the views of the 55-year-olds will be modified by their own experience of ageing in the next decade.

Even the statements of those already retired have to be interpreted with caution. It is usually a combination of circumstances which produces a 'voluntary' decision on the part of the employee to retire. In interviewing old people who have retired, or in examining industrial records, it appears that one meets much rationalization about reasons for retirement. Apart from clear cases of ill-health most firms consulted feel there is no reliance to be placed on the explanations given by the employee for retirement, and in any case these are usually very vague. The man who says to the works manager or foreman 'I think I've had about enough' may have reached this decision for reasons of general health, or the strain of the particular job he is doing, or some difficult domestic circumstances, or because of the acquisition of other means of income to eke out his pension or a number of other reasons.[1] Sometimes the man himself would find it difficult to assess his own motives, and when inter-

[1] See I. M. Richardson, 'Influence of the Home on Decisions about Retirement', *Old Age in the Modern World*, 1954.

viewed such men seem unable or unwilling to elaborate the vague type of reasons quoted above. Some men tend to rationalize their decisions and seize readily upon explanations suggested to them by inquirers. It is interesting to note that Thomas and Osborne found in their survey inconsistencies in the answers given. For example less than half the men who *said* they would like to return to employment if offered the opportunity had, in fact, tried to find any employment. Similarly in 1951 when retirement pensioners were given the opportunity to 'de-retire' and seek employment with the opportunity of taking advantage of the scheme of increments for deferred retirement, only a negligible minority responded. The authors of *Older People and their Employment* comment on these apparent contradictions in their survey. 'It is evidence not so much of muddled thinking, but of real difficulty in sorting out the motives for working, different aspects of which are thrown into relief by different questions.'

A further study of the pattern of retirement was made by the Ministry of Pensions and National Insurance in 1953.[1] This inquiry covered a group of some 26,000 persons who, during the period studied, established a claim to a National Insurance retirement pension at that time, or subject to subsequent retirement. Included among these older men and women interviewed were 2,581 persons who though still working were automatically entitled to a pension on reaching age 70 (65 for women). The results of this investigation present, as the title of the Report carefully indicates, the '*reasons given*' by individuals for their decision to cease or continue work and, except in the case of compulsory retirement, no attempt was made to check their statements. In rather less than half the cases of men and women who had retired[2] the answers given by individuals were checked with their former employers and in general their answers closely corresponded with each other. It may safely be accepted therefore that where the major reason given for retirement is related to the decision of an employer to terminate service, those reasons are likely to be accurate. But when the reasons given for retirement or continuance (either to employers or to the Ministry's questionnaire) rest upon the individual's assessment

---

[1] *Op. cit.*, p. 9.
[2] No information was sought from employers of persons still at work after pension ages.

of his own financial need or ill-health, there is no objective definition of these conditions or verification that they are being experienced. There is no reason to suppose that men and women answering the questions put to them in this inquiry did not give truthful answers in describing what they felt were the reasons actuating their decisions. Their answers, however, must be interpreted with some caution.

Some of the questions asked, despite the care which no doubt was exercised by the Ministry's interviewers, were inevitably 'loaded' questions. As anyone who has discussed retirement decisions with older men will readily confirm, the question[1] 'What made you decide to give up regular full-time employment?' frequently evokes a defensive response if the decision has been a voluntary one and not enforced by an employer. Among men of pension age in industrial employment a 'voluntary' decision to retire is usually explained in terms which seek to avoid confession of a consciousness of failing powers and the desire for rest and leisure, unless these can be ascribed to definable disabilities. It is not unlikely, therefore, that the reasons for retirement which are described in this investigation as 'heaviness or strain of work' and 'wish for rest and leisure' may be understated. Only 6·7% of those retiring at 65 said they did so because they wanted more leisure. When asked later in the interview whether the prospect of more leisure influenced their decision, 15·9% said it had influenced them 'a lot'. Similarly, while the men aged 65 who gave ill-health and strain as a reason for their retirement had more incapacity than men giving other reasons, 30% had no record of incapacity in three years and eight months preceding their interview, and 60% had not been incapacitated for work in the previous eight months. This is not to suggest that there are not substantial numbers of older men and women whose retirement is clearly dictated by failing health which in effect compulsorily retires them. General feelings of tiredness and failing powers may, however, be more important as compared with recorded sickness and specific disabilities in influencing retirement, than might appear from this Report.

For some groups of older workers, of course, the reasons for retirement at minimum pension ages are beyond doubt. A

[1] *Op. cit.*, p. 9, see Appendix 2, p. 62, Question 3, Part IV, Interview with Informant.

quarter of men and 14·9% of women were suffering from chronic sickness and 28·4% of men and 7% of women were retired or discharged by their employers. For others the decision to retire is a choice compounded of a number of considerations which have to be weighed against each other, and the decision when it is reached has to be expressed in a form which is not too damaging to self-respect. The attempt in this report to establish for each individual one main reason for retirement tends to over-simplify the motives of those questioned, and leads to some discrepancies in the answers given. This applies even more forcibly to the reasons elicited for postponement of retirement. Nearly half the men remaining at work gave other reasons in addition to their 'main' reason for continued employment, and, as is admitted in the report (p. 79, Table II and footnote) assumptions and adjustments were made subsequent to the interviews about what was to be recorded as the informant's main reason for staying at work in a substantial number of cases (14%). No great reliance can be placed upon this evidence of motives for continued employment, and it is not surprising that there are apparent contradictions between answers given to different parts of the questionnaire. For example, among men choosing to stay at work at 65, 54% said financial need was the most important reason, and this was also stated to be their reason by 43% of those working at age 70. Yet when the same men were asked what would be most likely to make them leave work, only 6·2% of the 65-year-olds and 4% of the 70-year-olds said 'sufficient means'.

The inconsistencies in these answers show the difficulties which some men and women have in explaining the factors which have influenced their retirement and the relative weight of each in reaching their final decision. 'Felt fit enough to go on working' is a common explanation offered by those whose health is good and who have no inclination to retire, but who have not been very introspective about their motives. This was the reason given by 15·2% of men and 9·4% of women in this inquiry who continued to work, but, as is noted in the Report, this is not a reason but a pre-requisite for continued employment. The fit older man or woman, unless subject to compulsory retirement rules, has often a choice available to work or to retire, but fitness does not dictate, as ill-health does, what the choice will be.

Though one may have some reservations about the interpretation of all the answers given in this subjective inquiry into retirement decisions, the major features in the profile of early retirement are clear. A quarter of men and one in seven women who took pensions on reaching minimum pensions ages were classed as chronically sick. Another 24·8% of men and 30·2% of women fall out of the labour force as soon as they are entitled to a pension because of ill-health. None of the first group, and unless working conditions can be very substantially modified very few of the second group, could or would continue in employment.

The biggest single reason for early retirement among men is one however which might be largely eliminated—28·4% of men retiring at 65 were compulsorily retired or discharged by their employers. 80% of these men were retired because of the operation by their employers of an age-limit for retirement, and three-quarters of them said they would have been willing to go on working with their old employers. 60% of these men, as compared with 30% of all men reaching pension age, were covered by employers' pension schemes.

The findings of this report confirm that where employers' pension schemes operate, they are associated with a high rate of retirement at minimum pensions ages, and a high rate of retirement by employers and discharges. Unless the operation of pension schemes can be dissociated from inflexible retirement rules the present trend towards wider pension coverage of workers in all types of industry and public service may encourage more retirement at minimum pension age, especially as those compulsorily retired will have less financial pressure to seek other employment.

Among men aged 70 receiving their pensions and staying at work, of whom 43% said they did so because of financial need, only one in ten was covered by an employer's pension scheme. In future an extension of pension coverage may have some effect on the numbers working at high ages who at present are only entitled to National Insurance pensions. On the other hand, in this group the proportion who said they preferred to work and felt fit to do so was 45·7% of the whole and it seems likely that a good proportion of men working after age 70 is a select minority of more than average fitness and vitality as compared with their contemporaries who have retired. Such men may prefer to continue in employment even if they become eligible for employers' pensions as well as National Insurance.

In view of the doubts which have been raised about the value of the increment to deferred pensions as an incentive to continued employment, it is interesting to note that only seven in a thousand men in this inquiry said that their reason for staying at work was to earn an increased pension, though a quarter of those staying at work said the knowledge that a higher rate of pension would be available had influenced their decision to go on working.

The older women interviewed in this survey included only those insured in their own right and a quarter of these had retired for more than five years, so that their answers cannot be taken as applying generally to older women. Chronic sickness and ill-health figure largely among reasons for retirement, in this group of women as for men. Fewer women are compulsorily retired, and more retired for family reasons. Of those women who were continuing at work, widows and single women, as would be expected, gave financial need as their reasons more often than married women and rather fewer women than men said they continued because they felt fit and preferred to be employed.

If the results of this inquiry may be taken to be broadly representative, at any rate as far as the reasons given for early retirement are concerned, possibly about a quarter of men aged 65–69 and 9% of women aged 60–64 who are now retiring might be willing to continue in their work if employers were prepared to retain them. This would add approximately 107,000 persons (100,000 men and 7,000 women) over pension age to the labour force, if employment could be found for them. Equally important, it would help to make the 'choice' which faces older workers as they approach minimum retirement age more of a reality, allowing those who are fit and willing to continue at work, while not seeking to compel those who are feeling strain to postpone the rest and leisure to which they have looked forward.

Apart from the kind of information about attitudes towards prolonging working life which is revealed in these surveys, where at least 60% of the sample interviewed are manual workers, some groups of professional workers and public servants have expressed their collective views on this matter.

Among these groups the problem of delayed promotion is a very real one and fewer of them seem perturbed by the thought of enforced leisure at 60 or 65 years. Indeed the view is often expressed among them that to lengthen working life is a retrograde step which represents a fall in the standard of living for the elderly. The National Federation of Professional Workers, which has a membership of some 550,000 drawn mainly from the clerical, technical and advisory staff in the public service, after a careful study of the recommendations of the Ministry of Labour's committee,[1] rejects its conclusions with regard to flexible retirement arrangements on the general grounds that their members would thereby be deprived of something to which they are entitled. As would be expected from such a group of workers much concern is expressed about delaying promotion. Two proposals are made for the solution of this difficulty, either 'demotion without disgrace' to advisory or lower grade posts[2] or compensatory promotion[3] where expected promotion is delayed by the retention of a senior officer beyond pension age.

Even these arrangements are suggested with great reluctance and the Annual Conference (1954) of the Federation went on to pass additional resolutions which made it clear that members held the view 'that citizens have a right to expect to retire between the ages of 60 and 65 but not later than 65 years of age and the Federation would oppose any general move either by employers or the State to extend the age of retirement beyond its present 'limits', and again, 'in the absence of satisfactory demonstration of the absolute necessity of such a step this Conference places on record its determination to oppose any suggested deferment of the National Insurance Acts pension age. In its views such deferment would be a further serious inroad into the benefits provided under social service legislation.'

It can be argued that the average working lifetime would not be much lengthened by raising the pension age by two or

---

[1] *Op. cit.*, p. 21.　　　　　　　　　　　　[2] See p. 34 above.

[3] 'Under compensatory promotion the senior officer is retained in his existing post on his existing pay, but a promotion is made to that grade in question as though the officer had retired. The promoted officer receives an increase in pay equal to the difference between his existing pay and the minimum of the grade to which he is promoted. The promoted officer remains on his existing work. Consequential compensatory promotions are made right down the hierarchy', Annual Report of the National Federation of Professional Workers (1954).

three years when account is taken of the later age of entry into industry; still less would it be lengthened proportionately in view of the improved expectation of life now enjoyed. It may also be pointed out that even if promotion is delayed, the position when reached by the next man is in turn held to a greater age, which makes up for the delay. Unfortunately this is little consolation to a man who finds himself waiting for a promotion at that period of his life when family needs, especially in educating children, may be at their maximum.

Among some groups of workers (for example, civil servants), where early retirement on an adequate pension has been one of their recognized advantages, proposals to raise retirement ages are unlikely to meet with wide approval. Among officers holding less responsible posts and engaged in much routine work, major interests are often developed outside their work. Far from being dreaded, retirement is regarded by them with pleasurable anticipation as a period when hobbies and other interests may be pursued uninterrupted by the necessity of daily attendance at the office. It is to be expected that a determined resistance will be developed among some public servants against any compulsory raising of pension ages, though some progress has been made department by department. The age limit for recruitment in some occupations has been raised, and some posts have been offered specifically for those over 45 years. Retiring ages are more flexible and maximum periods of service on which pensions are calculated have been extended. Local Government Superannuation schemes have also been amended to raise the maximum age for pensionable employment to 70 years and to add appropriate increments to the deferred pension when finally received. Greater progress has been prevented by the coincidental policy of reducing in size, if not eliminating entirely, some public service departments. Established civil servants who have not yet reached retirement age have had to be transferred for this kind of reason and have, if only temporarily, made it unnecessary to try to retain other officers past pension age.

Among these salaried workers conditions might seem likely to lend themselves to prolonged employment. Their work does not involve heavy physical strain or performance at high speeds, and those qualities of conscientiousness, reliability, and experience so often noted as important assets possessed by older staff, could be displayed to advantage in public service. Unfortunately even if problems of promotion could be satisfactorily solved, it is among this group that the strongest views are held about the right to retirement and pension at a fixed age. Such people can be encouraged to go on working and arrangements made which facilitate employment beyond normal pension ages for those who are willing to continue. But to compel them to work longer by raising pension ages could only be justified if it could be clearly demonstrated that the withdrawal of their labour at existing pension ages created an irreplaceable deficiency of skills which the community needed, and that they were adding to a burden of dependency which was seriously depressing the standard of living. Thus in a field which seems suitable and is often recommended for prolonged employment (especially as the State and local authorities as employers could initiate this), the attitudes of employees discourages the hope of any rapid progress.

UNEMPLOYMENT AMONG OLDER WORKERS

There are of course a number of older workers who we know wish to continue in employment because they are registered at Labour Exchanges and Appointment Bureaux as 'capable, available and ready for employment'. Some of these people will have been compulsorily retired from their former employment. A Ministry of Labour survey in 1949 showed that in manufacturing industries 28% of male 'white-collar employees' and 26% of female clerical and staff employees retired at fixed ages, while 19% of male works employees and 15% of female works employees had a fixed retirement date. Among a representative sample of banks, insurance companies, Building and Friendly Societies, accountancy firms, dock, canal, gas and electricity undertakings, and shipping companies covering 127,000 clerical workers, and 68,400 other workers, 79% of male and 76% of female clerical and administrative employees were covered by compulsory retirement provisions and even larger numbers of other workers in this group of occupations were subject to fixed retirement, 95% of the men and 89% of the women. Among Co-operative Societies and large retailers, it was found that half of the firms, employing about one-third of the male shop assistants and clerical workers, and 50% of the male and female manual workers in this group of employees, had schemes for compulsory retirement. Since the date of these inquiries there has been considerable publicity and persuasion by the Ministry of Labour to modify some of these inflexible retirement policies, though on the other hand the growth in the same period of industrial pension schemes, which are often associated with fixed retirement ages, may have offset this. There is no need for retirement benefit schemes to impede the recruitment of older workers or their retention beyond normal pension age, and under many schemes it has been common practice to grant the employee the full actuarial equivalent of the pension withheld in the form of an increased pension on eventual retirement. In so far as the existence of a pension[1] scheme does prove a bar to employment of older men, the Life Office Associations made it clear (statement to the Press, July 1953) that they are willing to amend and revise schemes which may possibly have this effect if the employer wishes it. Unfortunately it is well known that employers sometimes use the terms of their pension scheme as a polite excuse for the rejection of older applicants for the vacancies they offer.

Although the position is very different now from the 1930's, with active encouragement to both workers and employers to make retirement decisions more flexible, it is common experience that the older workers, even when 'older' is interpreted to mean over 45 years, may suffer protracted spells of unemployment even in a period of relatively high and stable employment. In December 1952, while males unemployed aged under 20 years were 1·2% of employees in that age-group, and males unemployed aged 40–49 years were 1·4%, among male employees aged 55–64 years, the proportion was more than twice as great (2·9%). The corresponding figures for women unemployed were, under 20 years 1·5%, 40–49 years 1·8%, 55–59 years 2·7%.[2] The percentage suffering over 52 weeks unemployment is very much higher among men aged 55–64 than in other age-groups, and is twice as great as among men aged 50–54 and four times as great as among men aged 40–49. Among women the percentage unemployed aged 55–59 is three times as great as among women aged 40–49 years. The greatest difficulty in

[1] See G. W. Pingstone 'Insured Retirement Benefit Schemes', a paper presented to the Industrial Welfare Society, December 1953.
[2] *Op. cit.*, p. 21.

securing employment at later ages is found among those seeking managerial, clerical and unskilled employment.[1] The National Advisory Committee on Employment of Older Men and Women has emphasized that employment difficulties begin for older workers changing their jobs well before retirement age, and indeed it may be suggested that securing suitable employment for the over 50's is a more urgent and rewarding task than that of finding work for men entitled to a pension. On the other hand there is more mobility of labour in the last ten years before retirement than is sometimes supposed.[2]

The number of those over pensionable age and registered as unemployed and seeking employment is very small, though this is not a very good guide to the potential addition to the labour force which may exist among those at present retired.

TABLE XIII

Midland Region

(Numbers registered as wholly unemployed)

Age	June 1953	% of total unemployed all ages	December	% of total unemployed all ages	Age	June 1953	% of total unemployed all ages	December	% of total unemployed all ages
40–49	2,061	20·2	1,508	19·2	40–49	1,342	20·2	1,080	20·6
50–54	1,144	11·2	869	11·0	50–54	953	14·2	682	13·4
55–64	2,182	22·4	1,986	25·2	54–59	808	12·1	644	12·0
65+	259	2·5	221	2·8	60+	77	1·2	70	1·4
Total					Total				
40+	5,646	56·3	4,584	58·2	40+	3,180	48·7	2,476	47·4
Total All ages	10,154	100	7,947	100	Total All ages	6,591	100	5,108	100

[1] See also Thomas and Osborne, *op. cit.*, p. 60, for comparison of the greater incidence of long-term unemployment among unskilled older workers than among the skilled.

[2] See Appendix II, p. 339.

Apart from these small numbers registered as seeking work there may be others who, confronted with this discouraging situation, have retired prematurely or are carrying on part-time employment within the limits of the earnings rules (£2) permitted by retirement pension regulations. Against this must be placed the suspicion that among those registered as unemployed there may be persons who have little hope or indeed desire for continued employment, but to whom continued registration may be the means of getting their National Insurance contributions credited and their pension and other rights preserved.

Table XIII shows the record of unemployment among various age-groups in the Midland Region in 1953, and Table XIV shows that the record of placing older workers in employment during this period in the same region was as follows:

TABLE XIV

	Males			Females		
	15–40 yrs.	41–50 yrs.	51 yrs. and over	15–40 yrs.	41–50 yrs.	51 yrs. and over
4 week period ending 3rd June 1953	12,264	800	462	4,973	404	185
4 week period ending 16th Dec. 1953	13,776	846	652	5,805	527	324
4 week period ending 10th March 1954	16,007	1,087	743	6,072	587	363

This increase in the number of placings is, in the view of many people concerned in this work, to some extent due to an improved response to requests for consideration of older workers, and to more attention being given to careful placing,[1] but this evidence is too slight on which to base any conclusion.[2]

The jobs found for men aged over 51 years were mainly in building and contracting (193), manufacture and repair of

[1] Cf. the work of the Unemployment Insurance Commission of the Canadian National Employment Service. W. G. Scott, 'Placement of Older Workers', a paper presented to the Third Congress of the International Association of Gerontology, London, July 1954.

[2] The Ministry of Labour reports a sustained improvement in the placing of men and women over 40 between 1953 and 1955. Cmd. 9628, Appendix A.

vehicles and aircraft (92), metal goods and industries (85), engineering, shipbuilding and electrical goods (78), National and Local Government and Defence (65). For women most placings were made in metal goods (51), non-metalliferous mining products—pottery, glass, etc. (47), and miscellaneous services (116). These placings reflect the labour demands of local industries rather than work especially suitable for older persons, but employers who have once experienced using older workers are more ready to repeat or extend this policy, and in many cases the older workers impress employers by the enthusiasm with which they seize the opportunity afforded to them.

Here it is important to distinguish between the unemployed elderly and the retired, between those who have accepted retirement and those who are frustrated by unwanted leisure. Barron[1] found in a study of 1,000 males and 200 females in America that while 36·9% of this sample who had no employment considered themselves retired, only 4·9% of those with no occupation considered themselves unemployed, that is, still in the labour market and denied employment. It was this small group of the unemployed aged who were in every way more ill-adjusted and socially isolated than the retired who had accepted their status. From this kind of inquiry and the evidence which we have of those over pensionable age who attempt to obtain employment (through Appointment Bureaux, Labour Exchanges and other Agencies), it appears that there may not be a very large number of older persons not in employment who are actively seeking work, though we are apt to hear a good deal about the persistent attempts of the frustrated minority whose efforts fail.

MAKING CONTINUED EMPLOYMENT ATTRACTIVE TO OLDER WORKERS

If our intention is to try and persuade substantial numbers of older persons to remain as producers we shall have to look beyond the limited numbers registered as unemployed, some of whom anyway are physically handicapped. To arrive at any estimate of the numbers available for continued employment

[1] M. L. Barron, 'A Survey of a cross-section of the Urban Aged in the United States', *Old Age in the Modern World*, 1954.

we shall have to look to the numbers of fit, active older men who are at present retiring at age 65 or earlier.

If we want more of our fit older persons to work rather than retire, not only must retirement rules be made more flexible but some greater inducement than at present exists must be offered to them. During the last war many responded to requests to continue in their work for patriotic and other non-financial motives, but failing an appeal which could evoke a similar response, economic considerations will be the most important ones. Continued earnings and a larger deferred pension will be weighed against the attractions of rest and retirement. Not all pensions are conditional upon an absolute retirement from paid employment. Some occupational pension schemes award a pension, and often a lump-sum payment also, which leaves the recipient free, without any deductions (except liability for taxation on the pension payments when made), to retire completely or to seek other employment. National Insurance retirement pensions, however, are given only on condition of retirement from regular employment, though the regulations have been amended to raise the amount which may be earned by pensioners without deduction, and to increase the size of the increment for deferment. These changes were made with the express intention of encouraging those entitled to pensions to defer their claims; or if a pension was drawn, to add to it by part-time earnings.

It is too early yet to estimate the ultimate effect of this type of provision. In the first three or four years of the new insurance scheme the increment for deferment did not appear to have very much influence on the decision to retire, and many of those remaining in employment were the old 10s. pensioners who kept their pension at the old rate in addition to earnings, and who were not entitled to increments under the new scheme. As the larger increments, which may now also be added to a widow's pension, become better known they may prove a more attractive inducement in future. At present it seems that the monetary incentive will have to be greater than the present increment scheme to have any marked effect on the numbers who now prefer retirement. It might seem that the very considerable drop in income which a man taking his retirement pension often faces, would make it worthwhile for him to continue if he is fit and is offered continued employment. But a man earning £9 per week may reason that he 'loses' 65s. per week pension for himself and his wife which he might otherwise draw, and that he pays 6s. 9d. insurance contribution and has expenses of wear and tear on clothing and shoe leather, travelling fares, meals taken away from home, trades union and other subscriptions, and P.A.Y.E. deductions arising out of his employment. In these circumstances he may prefer to take his pension, earn £2 without deduction for part-time work, and obtain an income of about £5 for perhaps two days' work.

If pension payments together with permitted earnings, personal savings, or supplements from the Assistance Board are just sufficient to live on it is very likely that numbers of people will take the pension to which they feel entitled as soon as they reach minimum retirement age. Short of returning to the pre-war situation when a pension scheme limited both in amount and coverage kept older people at work from sheer economic necessity, the financial inducement to continue working must be made more attractive than it is at present if the numbers working over pension age are to be increased.

This raises the question whether for those eligible under the National Insurance scheme a basic pension could be granted at a fixed age irrespective of retirement, as was the practice under the former Contributory Pensions Act (1925). Those who chose to continue working and could find suitable employment, either by remaining in their old jobs or finding other work, would then be entitled to keep, subject to tax liability, whatever they were able to earn, and there would be no incentive for them to retire to claim the pensions to which they felt entitled.

Such a proposal would raise some difficulties at once. Trade unionists would protest against the possibly depressive effect on wage-rates of pensioners as competitors in the labour market, and the national pensions bill would be increased by payments to persons who might be considered as being in no need of them. It has been estimated[1] that the extra cost involved would be £55 million in 1955-6, falling to £20 million in 1979-80. Allowing for those incapacitated by ill-health and assuming that employer's retirement rules were made more flexible the largest addition to the labour force which might be stimulated by removing barriers to employment is about

[1] Cmd. 9333.

76

316,000 older workers. (Over a million men and women over pension age are already at work despite retirement conditions.) Would the contribution to the national output and revenue from taxed earnings of these 316,000 older workers outweigh the additional cost of pension payments?

The answer is almost certainly yes. Under a system of pensions paid at a basic rate to all eligible contributors reaching pension age no increments would be paid since no pensions would be deferred. The savings on increments, which are postponed payments that would have to be made in the future, will, over a period of time, almost balance the extra cost of paying pensions without the prerequisite of retirement. It may still be argued that to pay pensions and wages simultaneously is wrong in principle and this objection is considered again in discussing pension provision below (Chapter IV). Here we are only concerned to decide what influence paying pensions without a retirement condition would have on employment beyond pension ages. Would about another 300,000 older workers become available in the labour market? It must be admitted at once that there is no reliable evidence on this point. Indeed it may be held that the provision of pensions irrespective of retirement might make some older workers now in full-time employment seek a part-time occupation instead. This might be an excellent development from the point of view of the individual older worker since it would cause retirement to be a more gradual process. From the point of view of increasing the contribution of older workers to the national output however, an equivalent expansion of part-time working would have to take place if, at the same time, the full-time employment of older workers was reduced because pensions were paid without a retirement condition being enforced.

FITNESS OF OLDER WORKERS FOR CONTINUED EMPLOYMENT

In considering the numbers who might be induced by financial incentives to postpone retirement, we have to eliminate first those whose state of health would make it difficult and unprofitable for them to attempt to stay in employment. The National Advisory Committee on Employment of Older Men and Women[1] quotes the estimate of the Ministry of Pensions

[1] Op. cit., p. 21.

and National Insurance to the effect that over 100,000 of the 450,000 unoccupied men in the 65–69 age-group are chronically sick, and the Ministry's subsequent inquiry has confirmed this figure. The inquiry also suggests that in addition to 25% of men and 14% of women who are chronically sick when reaching pension age, a further 24·8% of men and 30% of women give ill-health as the chief reason for their retirement.

A useful contribution (though by its nature a limited one), is made to our knowledge of the part played by physical disablement in precipitating retirement, by a recent study of older workers in the building industry.[1] Le Gros Clark has studied a group of 320 older workers (100 craftsmen, 100 painters and 120 labourers) engaged on maintenance work for a Local Authority. In tracing the age of, and reasons for, retirement among these workers it was found that between 65 and 69 years nearly half of them left the industry. Of these 'leavers' about 24% died or became permanently unfit, and 23% were marginal cases, about whom it was considered doubtful whether they could have remained much longer in the building industry, though a few might have been retained a little longer by careful rehabilitation. 33% were discharged simply on account of age, being judged by the employing authority to be no longer fully effective. This would seem to imply some discernible deterioration in general capacity. The remaining 20% left voluntarily and had no record of sickness other than very slight complaints. Men over 70 years (and of the men working at 65, nearly one-third were still working at 70 years) seem to have been a selected group of fit older men, 44% of them leaving the industry finally in fairly good health. The fact that such fit old men exist may, as the author remarks, 'mislead us in our search for what is happening to the ordinary run of workers'. He concludes that it may be too optimistic to hope to salvage a large number of men for a prolonged life in this industry.

There is evidence to show that there is a considerable wastage immediately following minimum retirement age owing to ill-health, this being composed of employees who find their work a strain and who retire at the first opportunity which is available to them. Barron,[2] for example, found that while there was

---

[1] *Later Working Life in the Building Industry*, by F. Le Gros Clark, for the Nuffield Foundation. [2] *Op. cit.*, p. 74.

little difference in the extent of physical health problems between those working aged 60–65 years and those who were not employed in this age-group, those aged 60–65 years who considered themselves definitely *retired* (i.e. having no intention of seeking re-employment) had far more health difficulties than any other group, and it is likely that they had retired for this reason.

Thomas and Osborne[1] found that while there was little difference in the numbers reporting feelings of strain owing to their work in the age-groups 60–64 years, as compared with those aged 55–60 years, the incidence rose sharply in the years 65–69. 44% of those people working in this age-group reported strain though only 25% of those over 70 years suffered in this way, which probably means that those 70-year-olds in employment are a selected group of those enjoying particularly good health. For the majority between the ages of 70 and 75 years, as medical surveys[2] of elderly city dwellers have shown, there is a significant decline in fitness and in unrestricted mobility.

EMPLOYMENT POTENTIAL AMONG OLDER WORKERS

If the conclusions of the Ministry of National Insurance's inquiry into reasons for early retirement can be applied generally, at the very most 46% of those men aged 65–69 now retiring might be fit for employment, and this would give an additional 186,000 workers, assuming that they were willing to accept continued employment. Similarly 48% of women aged 60–64 formerly employed[3] and who are retiring at present for other than health reasons might be induced to postpone retirement. Taken together, the maximum numbers which could be added to the labour force would be approximately 316,550, an addition of less than 2% to the numbers engaged at present in civilian employment.

Thus if present pension ages were raised from 65 to 70 years for men and from 60 to 65 years for women, the addition of effective workers to the total labour force would be useful but not nearly so large as is often supposed, and many of those thus

[1] *Op. cit.*, p. 60.
[2] See, for example, *Health of the Elderly at Home*, W. Hobson and J. Pemberton, 1955.
[3] Approximately 28% of all women in this age-group were employed in 1951.

79

denied a pension would have to be given unemployment or sickness benefits. The reduction of expenditure on social insurance payments would be correspondingly small. Without a compulsory rise in the pension age, some of these fit older men and women will prefer and choose retirement, and in any case there would be the problem of matching their accustomed employment to the demands of the labour market. As has been suggested earlier,[1] the possibilities of older workers remaining in their previous employment is severely limited in some industries, though these may be the very industries which suffer from an inadequate labour force.

These arguments apply to existing conditions and circumstances commonly found in industry and commerce. Of course it may be found to be true that some of those who are considered unfit for further employment both by themselves and their employers might very well be occupied if conditions of work could be adjusted to their needs while still allowing their efforts to be economically worth while. Some simple re-adjustments like better lighting to offset any diminution of visual acuity, or arrangements for work to be undertaken by the operative seated, could make a surprising reduction in the strain felt by an older worker. There is room for a considerable amount of experiment in this direction. Welford and others[2] have demonstrated that older persons can learn new methods, but that they may learn in a different way, and that because they do not learn easily by the training normally offered to younger men and women we need not conclude that they are too old to learn at all. Firms who say they cannot teach older persons a new job may in fact be using the wrong methods of training, and here again the findings of the laboratory need to be elaborated and applied in industry.

Some older persons express a desire for part-time employment, and if this were available possibly some of those who now find full-time working too great a strain could continue in employment for shorter hours. In 1951 nearly 18% of women occupied over the age of 60 were in part-time employment, but only 3% of occupied men over 65 were engaged in this way. The part-time employment of women may be an arrangement related more directly to their domestic circumstances than to their age, and furthermore the type of work often done by older

---

[1] See Chapter II.   [2] *Op. cit.*, p. 48.

women, such as in domestic and personal services, lends itself more readily to part-time arrangements. The organization of part-time work for men creates some difficulties, but they are not insuperable. It is not popular with employers because it is thought to be difficult to organize,[1] and, since it is not yet common among men workers, older men do not always welcome part-time working. Concessions, for example, in the insurance contributions due from both employee and employer[2] for the regular part-time worker or raising the permitted earnings limit (£2) might help to stimulate more part-time employment for older men. If part-time working could be extended for older workers this would help to avoid an abrupt change from full-time employment to retirement. In this way the exit from employment, like the entrance into it, could be graduated by shorter hours and less strenuous working conditions.

CONCLUSIONS

The case for encouraging more workers over pensionable age to continue in employment is commonly based upon three main arguments. First it has been widely held that owing to the changing age-structure of the population and the mounting cost of pensions the labour of the elderly is needed to mitigate what would otherwise be an intolerable 'burden of dependency'. As has been suggested earlier (Chapter I) it is likely that this argument has been much exaggerated and there is no evidence on this point which would justify measures such as raising minimum pension ages to prolong compulsorily working lifetime. Nor should the same objective be achieved indirectly, but equally effectively, by allowing the purchasing power of pensions to fall in such a way that older workers are forced to remain in employment.

But allowing that it is an obvious advantage to the whole community to have more producers and fewer pensioners, will the amount added by the efforts of the additional number of

[1] The difficulties quoted by employers are sometimes derived from their experience of employing married women on a part-time basis where hours and attendance are often affected by family responsibilities. These are not likely to apply to older part-time workers who have good records of punctuality and regular attendance.

[2] At present a full contribution is demanded except for married women who have opted to pay no contributions.

older workers who might be induced to continue in employment make any substantial difference to the total national product? If we exclude the very elderly and older women unlikely to enter the labour market after many years away from it, and those so physically enfeebled that, if included in the labour force they would draw sickness and unemployment benefits, we are left with a possible addition on the most optimistic calculation of willingness and suitability of a further 300,000–320,000 men and women, and the actual number for whom employment could be found is probably very much less. Conditions of over-full employment and rising prices provide strong incentives to both employers and older employees to postpone retirement wherever this is practicable and already over a million older workers who are willing and able have responded by remaining in employment. Unless some rather unlikely changes are made in production methods (the trend of change is in favour of an increased pace of work and is therefore against the older worker's interests), or unless the physical fitness of older persons is markedly improved in the next few years, it is improbable that more than a very limited further addition can be made to the total working population by policies designed to encourage the employment of men and women over pension age.

This is not to despise the useful if limited contribution to national output which may be made by increasing the employment of older workers. Indeed if attention is directed to the arbitrary exclusion from employment of men and women over 50 years, a considerable economic waste may be prevented. But attempts to extend continued employment for workers *of pension age* is not likely to relieve the present cost of pensions for the remaining 4 million beneficiaries[1] by more than a very limited amount. If a recession in economic activity and a reduction in the level of employment make the so-called 'burden of dependency' look serious, in this situation the older worker, being largely a marginal worker, is not likely to find employment anyway.

From the point of view of the national economy therefore no exaggerated hopes should be entertained of reducing the pensions bill or extending the labour force. From the point of view

[1] Nearly three-quarters of pension expenditure is paid out to men over 70 and women over 65 among whom prolonged employment is less likely.

of individual older citizens, however, there may be other equally important considerations which make continued employment valuable.

It is frequently asserted that it is good for the general health and well-being of old people to continue wherever possible in remunerative employment. There is a good deal of anecdotal evidence in support of this view, and many members of the medical profession favour it. It is possible to detect, both by objective measurement and by the judgments of those questioned, apparently better health, and a greater degree of satisfaction with their status, among the occupied over pension age than among the retired. But no cross-section survey can give us any conclusive evidence on this point. We do not know whether older men who are fit and active are so because they are at work, or are able to be at work because they are fit and active. The high death rate in the first year following retirement is often quoted to prove that retirement may speed premature deterioration, but it is just as probable that poor health predisposes people to early retirement, and that their disabilities pre-date their withdrawal from work. In fact, it is just as likely that mental and physical morbidity leads to prompt retirement as that retirement leads to physical and mental deterioration. We do not know how far older workers are a highly selected group nor what factors make for this selection. Men and women up to 70 years of age can be found engaged as successfully as their younger fellow-workers in many walks of life, but we do not know how far they are exceptional. We need to study a cohort of men and women aged 60 or 65 years, and, in terms of morbidity and mortality related to occupational status, and other variables, trace them through the next five or ten years. Until we have some evidence from longitudinal studies of this kind, the hypothesis that continued employment is good for older persons cannot merit more than a verdict of not proven.

Allied to this belief that continued employment is beneficial for some old people, there is a further argument that it is a matter of social justice to remove unfair discrimination based only upon chronological age, which deprives active older citizens of the right to work. This third argument discloses a real problem. The compulsory retirement of still effective older workers and the repeated rejection of older candidates applying for posts destroy self-respect and confidence and rob many older people of economic independence. Arbitrary age-barriers erected against the entry of older men into employment without reference to individual qualifications are indefensible and these are often applied against men ten or more years before retirement ages. Indeed to remove discrimination against the older worker is far more urgent for men aged 50–65 years than for men over pension age.

For those who desire continued employment the removal of fixed retirement rules would be very helpful but not enough in itself to solve their employment problems. Many are prevented by the nature of their occupation from continuing in their customary work and if they are to remain in employment suitable alternative jobs must be made available for them. Whether industry and the public services can find annually a substantial number,[1] of alternative jobs, and will consider it worthwhile to do so, depends upon the maintenance or intensification of the present high demand for labour.

In modern industrial and urban societies it is not likely that very large numbers of older persons will want to remain in full-time employment to high ages, or that they could be economically employed unless productive processes are much modified; though more might successfully undertake part-time employment. We should not therefore go to great lengths to press older people into prolonged employment. We ought rather to think in terms of removing unreasonable barriers to their employment and encouraging them, if they so desire, to continue to exercise their skills to their own satisfaction and the community's benefit.

[1] See *Ageing in Industry*, F. Le Gros Clark and A. C. Dunne, 1955. The authors estimate that about 40,000 alternative jobs would be needed annually to absorb men who are capable of further work but who must transfer from their previous occupation or retire.

CHAPTER IV

PENSIONS

THE employment of persons of pension ages has been discussed at some length in the previous chapter because policies designed to secure this have often been advanced as though they were a complete solution to the problems of financing old age. Such policies sound attractive because they appear to maximize the satisfaction and well-being of older men and women while preserving their economic independence. Greater flexibility in employers' retirement rules and the encouragement of part-time working can indeed make a small but useful contribution towards financing old age. If however it is accepted that prolonged full-time employment is practicable and desirable for only a minority of those over pension age, and for only a part of their remaining life-time, the necessity remains of supporting the majority whose basic problem will be a financial one.

Anxiety over the cost and adequacy of pensions has tended to be focused upon the National Insurance scheme and this perhaps more than anything else has drawn attention to the charge on the community's resources which a large and growing number of pensioners is likely to make. But it must be remembered that the state of the National Insurance funds by no means reveals the full measure of the claims of the elderly. Occupational pension schemes, for example, represent a much larger future commitment of the national product than the total cost of retirement pensions.[1] Nor is the National Insurance scheme the only pension fund faced with the prospect of a deficit; the Teachers' Pension Account, for example, will have an actuarial deficiency of £324 million by March 1956.[2] Factors such as earlier retirement, improvement in mortality,

---

[1] See *New Pensions for Old*, B. Abel-Smith and P. Townsend.

[2] This is a calculation of future liabilities; payments out are not expected to exceed contributions until about 1970. For a comparison of public service pension schemes see 'The Report of the Working Group on Teachers' Pensions', *The Schoolmaster*, 29th July 1955.

the admission of late age entrants to full pension rights, and the inflation of prices have upset both the expectations of pensioners and the calculations of actuaries.

Pension provision in Great Britain takes a number of different forms, among which there are three major kinds of schemes of outstanding importance. The first is the National Insurance scheme, which includes retirement pensions as one of its principal benefits; secondly, there are both contributory and non-contributory pensions attached to certain forms of public service such as civil service pensions and local government superannuation arrangements; thirdly, there are private insurance schemes, including especially industrial pensions negotiated by business firms for their employees. These schemes often overlap each other in coverage since virtually the whole population will become eligible[1] for National Insurance retirement pensions, many will also have a claim to a pension arising directly out of their employment, and some people in receipt of both kinds of pension may choose to subscribe privately for some further provision for income in old age.

About three out of four retirement pensioners have other means in addition to their National Insurance pensions and these include superannuation benefits from other sources. Even among the 25% of pensioners whose resources are so limited that they are entitled to supplementary assistance grants, the Assistance Board found (1954) 55,000 superannuation payments, about half of which were taken in account in assessing needs.

National Insurance retirement pensions were never intended to provide anything but a minimum subsistence income,[2] upon which individuals would endeavour to build for themselves a more generous competence for their old age, and there is evidence to show that this is still an acceptable proposition to large numbers of people in all sections of the population. Despite the spectacle of disappointed expectations among those

---

[1] At present some groups of old people have never contributed or been included in National Insurance by reason of their age at the inception of the scheme, and other late-age entrants will not be qualified before 1958, when they will have contributed for a minimum of ten years.

[2] 'In establishing a national minimum it (the State) should leave room and encouragement for voluntary action by each individual to provide more than the minimum for himself and his family'. The Beveridge Report, para. 9.

who have reached pension age during the post-war period of rising prices, there has been a marked expansion in the growth of occupational pension schemes,[1] and apparently no lack of confidence in this method of providing more than the basic retirement pension can yield towards income security in old age.

It is not surprising, therefore, that there is a multiplicity of pension schemes both private and public, and that pensioners often draw their retirement incomes from more than one source. It is however disquieting to find that existing pension coverage leaves about a quarter of retirement pensioners so impoverished that they are eligible for National Assistance and that their numbers are growing annually.[2] Between 1945 and 1955 three increases have been made in the rate at which retirement pensions are paid in order to take account of rising prices, and five increases have been made in the scale rate[3] of the Assistance Board during the same period, but the conclusion of the Phillips Report,[4] which is supported by the evidence of other inquiries[5] was that the elderly 'often live on or near the borderline of poverty'. This indicates a most unsatisfactory way of dealing with the financial needs of the elderly. Notwithstanding the difficulties which inflation inevitably creates for pension financing an attempt must be made to evolve a more positive policy which does not leave the effects of demographic and inflationary trends to bear more heavily upon pensioners than upon others.

The avowed intention of the National Insurance scheme was that benefits, among which were included retirement pensions, should be adequate without recourse to assistance for the bulk of those making claims, and that they should be drawn as a right without investigation of means. The Beveridge Report allowed that, 'for a limited number of cases of need not covered

[1] See *Growth of Pension Rights and their Impact on the National Economy*, F. W. Bacon, B. Benjamin and M. D. W. Elphinstone, for the Institute of Actuaries and the Faculty of Actuaries.

[2] The rate of increase has recently slowed down (6·7%, 1954).

[3] The scale rate of the Assistance Board is a sum which is assumed to be sufficient for minimum subsistence for the applicant and his family excluding payment of rent. In so far as an applicant's income falls below this rate, it may be made up to the scale rate by an assistance grant, and to this is added an allowance for rent.

[4] Cmd. 9333, para. 109.

[5] See e.g., *Over Seventy*, National Old People's Welfare Committee, and *Poverty and the Welfare State*, Rowntree and Lavers.

by social insurance, National Assistance, subject to a uniform means test, will be available'. But it was never envisaged that by 1954 more than two and a half million persons would be provided for in whole or in part by National Assistance grants, of which one million and a quarter were being paid in supplementation of insurance benefits.

To keep pensions at a subsistence level as measured officially by the scale rate of the Assistance Board would require not only the addition of any sum by which at any time the pension falls short[1] of the scale rate currently used by the Board, but also a major addition of rent allowance[2] since the Board's calculation of a minimum subsistence income excludes rent and provides for this need separately. The cost which would be involved in gearing all retirement pensions to this definition of subsistence is formidable, but to fail to keep pensions at a level which is just sufficient to live on, even if no other means are available, is to retreat from the basic principles of social insurance as defined by Beveridge. It would mean the acceptance, as a permanent feature of our social services, of the use (at present increasing) of a personal needs test for the elderly. Income maintenance of the old would thus become an eleemosynary service rather than an insurance right. For those old people who are in such demonstrable need that they are already being helped by the Assistance Board, a subsistence pension will not in any case improve their circumstances, but only substitute a single pension payment for the pension plus assistance grant they now receive.

One way out of this difficulty would be to raise assistance rates to a more generous level and pay these only on proof of need. Raising the scale rate would cost more for the Board's present clients, and would extend the scope of the Board's help to persons at present ineligible to receive assistance, but this would still be a great deal more economical than raising all retirement pensions. This apparently logical remedy for reducing the cost of financing old age has, however, some serious disadvantages. It penalizes thrift, it is difficult to avoid dissatisfaction as between one client and another when varying

[1] The scale rate of the Assistance Board has sometimes been less and sometimes greater than the level of retirement pensions, see p. 101 below.
[2] The average rent allowance is 12/'d. (1954) and in most cases the full amount of the rent actually paid is allowed by the Board (Report of the National Assistance Board 1954, Cmd. 9530).

88

grants are made on the basis of confidential inquiries which cannot be disclosed, and it is reported to be very unpopular. It is difficult to estimate the importance of this unpopularity as there is very little firm evidence upon it. Individual old people can certainly be found who are too proud to accept assistance and prefer to suffer some hardship by voluntarily depriving themselves of help which they feel is detrimental to their self-respect; we do not know how widespread this feeling is. Reluctance to have help from the Board disappears in some cases after an initial courteous visit from the Board's officers, *CONJECTURE* and some of the more elderly clients are very confused about the difference between pensions and supplementary assistance, especially when, as in 1954, assistance grants were raised in February and then adjusted again in April to take account of higher pensions.

A study in Lancashire (Social Security and Unemployment in Lancashire, P.E.P. Planning, No. 349, 1952), on the other hand, demonstrated the reluctance of families to go to the Assistance Board during unemployment. *REFUTATION* Whether the strong dislike which undoubtedly existed for the old Poor Law and the household means test is dying out under a system of national assistance which is administered in a very different spirit,[1] it is impossible yet to say. It is still repugnant to some people, but we do not know how many, nor whether the response of temporarily unemployed workers to receiving assistance can be compared with that of old people drawing regular and continuous payments. If a policy of paying more generous grants on proof of need were to be adopted, reliance on the National Assistance Board as a national relief agency might increasingly replace the notion of a contributory insurance scheme as the normal provision for income in old age. The propensity to save and the willingness to submit to the compulsory deduction of substantial insurance contributions might be adversely affected. *IN OTHER WORDS INSTITUTE GENEROUS NAB NO ONE WILL CLAIM.*

Thus six years after the introduction of the much heralded social security legislation the country is already committed to annual pension expenditure of about £470 million (excluding national assistance payments to the old and occupational and

[1] In this connection Charles Booth's dictum, 'To select the poor is to pauperize, to select the deserving is to patronize, to do either is to humiliate,' may not be applicable to modern assistance payments.

PENSIONS

public service pensions), which is likely to double itself in the next twenty-five years, without either securing subsistence pensions for all or relieving poverty among the needy elderly. How has this impasse arisen so soon after the inauguration of a comprehensive social security system, designed, as its author said, 'to abolish the Giant Want, in some ways the easiest to attack'?

Several questions have to be answered before any reform of present pension financing can be attempted. Is the income maintenance programme for the old to be geared to individual need determined by some test of means, or are pensions to be paid as an inalienable right, irrespective of means but dependent upon individual contribution records in some kind of insurance scheme? If both systems are to be used what should their relationship be? Is the individual contribution record to be retained? (If it were to be discontinued it would be difficult to preserve any semblance of insurance, and the payments could be wholly financed out of taxation, either by an earmarked social security tax or from general revenue.) What role should be played by occupational pension schemes subsidized by tax relief in financing old age? In short, what test or combination of tests should be applied, such as contribution records, occupational status, limited means or residence as criteria for deciding who are the 'deserving' and the 'undeserving' elderly? As Professor Titmuss has pointed out,[1] 'Already it is possible to see two nations in old age; greater inequalities in living standards after work than in work.' If this is the result it was certainly not the intention of post-war social policy in Great Britain nor a consequence which can be regarded as desirable.

ASSISTANCE OR INSURANCE? THE DEVELOPMENT OF OLD AGE PENSIONS 1908–48

During the post-war period there has been a considerable shift of opinion about the relative merits of insurance and assistance, both as a means of meeting effectively the needs of the elderly, and as a method of keeping the cost of pensions within manageable proportions.

[1] R. Titmuss, 'Pension Systems and Population Change.' *The Political Quarterly*, April–June 1955, Vol. XXIII, No. 2.

PENSIONS

These are the perennial problems of pension financing, and the arguments being put forward now are in many ways similar to those advanced in debating pension legislation in 1908 and 1925. There was then the same concern about discouraging self-help, the same alarm about increasing numbers and rising costs, and the same complaints about the inadequacy of the level of pensions in relation to the cost of living. We have had experience in Great Britain of using both an assistance[1] and an insurance scheme to provide old age pensions, and the results are instructive in considering our present difficulties.

When the first Old Age Pensions Act was introduced in 1908 after twenty years of discussion and delay, the Liberal Government of the day finally decided upon a non-contributory scheme. The limitations which were inserted in the scheme, such as the 'industry test', the disqualification of paupers, and the age and residence requirements, were defended both on the grounds that greater generosity in meeting the needs of the elderly could not be afforded, and because the scheme was only meant for the 'deserving' poor. It was allowed that at some later date it might be possible to make the scheme more liberal. The Trade Unions welcomed the legislation and their spokesman declared that the act was 'one of the greatest measures of reform that our day or any day has witnessed'.[2]

Opposition came chiefly from the Friendly Societies, who saw in it a threat to their interest in old age insurance. But in both Houses there were also speakers who distrusted the creation of this kind of social benefit, and who claimed that the provision of 5s. a week to the elderly poor would 'demoralize the working classes, abolish thrift, and undermine the recognized responsibilities of families to maintain their old and feeble relatives'.

The non-contributory pensions scheme was amended three times during the sixteen years which passed before contributory pension provision was introduced. Residence and industry qualifications were made less stringent, some resources both of income and capital came to be disregarded in assessing means,

[1] The Poor Law and subsequently Public Assistance administered by local authorities always assisted the elderly among other necessitous applicants after determination of need. Here we are considering only pensions schemes which make payments subject to investigation of means in contrast to contractual insurance benefits.

[2] Hansard, Parliamentary Debates, July 1908.

and both the maximum pension payment and the income limit were increased. In 1919 the income limit was raised by about 25% and the amount of pension was doubled. The elaborate provision for investigation of means was not so important as had been assumed, since 90% of pensioners received the maximum pension.

10/- week

The improvement made in these pensions in 1919 were in many quarters still regarded as unsatisfactory, and at the election of 1924 both the Liberal and Unionist parties stated their objection to the 'thrift disqualification' inherent in assistance pensions, and pledged themselves to its revision. The Chancellor of the Exchequer of the first Labour Government in 1924 met these criticisms of existing legislation by making more generous allowances for savings and other resources which could be disregarded in calculating the weekly rate of pension. It was estimated that this relaxation of the means test would permit all existing pensioners to draw the maximum payments, and some elderly people previously excluded now became eligible for pensions.

From this point non-contributory pensions were developed no further and in 1925 a contributory pension scheme was introduced.[1] Notwithstanding that it was presented to a public already familiar with unemployment and health insurance as an improvement on the old non-contributory pensions, it met with considerable opposition. Under the new contributory scheme the pension age was lowered to 65 years and the unpopular means test was avoided. Both were reforms which had been long demanded. But the motive behind these proposals, as the Government spokesman admitted, was to relieve future governments of embarrassment in paying gratuitous pensions to increasing numbers of elderly persons. Although a great deal was said about the virtues of thrift which pensions schemes should not repress, the main consideration was to remove part of the cost of pensions provision from the Exchequer to a fund built up by a weekly tax on workers and employers. The opportunity was also seized to keep the cost of pensions for those who were over 70 and insured, as a charge on the con-

---

[1] Non-contributory pensioners had their payments raised from 10s. to 26s. when this became the standard rate of pension under the National Insurance scheme. They have remained at this level since and are supplemented by National Assistance.

tributory funds, although pension liability for those over 70 had been accepted by the Exchequer since 1908.

The insurance scheme was opposed by Labour members, who declared that the wages of those they represented did not permit of any further weekly deductions. They pointed out that many workers already paid into insurance funds through trade unions and Friendly Societies and could not afford any more commitments of this kind. They demanded a pension without contribution for all workers unable any longer to support themselves by employment. The fear was expressed that the employers' contribution would be reflected both in prices and wages to the workers' disadvantage, and the contributory scheme was condemned as a tax on industry in contrast to a non-contributory scheme which would be a tax on wealth.

The other major objection was that a pension of 10s. a week was inadequate to meet the bare cost of subsistence, and was less than Poor Law Authorities were paying at the time to recipients of outdoor relief. The Government did not contest this, but made it clear that they regarded the pension as only a contribution towards income security in old age, and as a minimum to which people would be encouraged to add by personal thrift. Here again the overriding consideration was finance. A large 'back service' charge had to be met from the Exchequer in respect of initial entrants with no contribution record, and for other concessions, and the Government was unwilling to contemplate any greater financial commitments.[1] This problem always arises when a contributory pension scheme is initiated. Whenever it is introduced there are some people who are already over pension age, and others so near to it that they will make few contributions before retiring. An emerging deficiency was inevitable under the 1925 Act, and the subsequent actuarial deficiences of the National Insurance Scheme have arisen for similar reasons.

By 1939 about 20,678,000 persons were insured for old age pensions (a joint weekly contribution was made by them for Health, and Old Age, Widows and Orphans pensions) and about 2,103,700 pensioners drew a weekly payment at a cost of approximately £50,945,000 annually.[2] Because of the 'late

[1] For a detailed account of the early years of pension legislation see *Old Age Pensions*, Wilson and McKay.

[2] Statistical Abstract for the United Kingdom, 1939.

age' entrants, the State's contribution up to 1934 was about 25%[1] of the annual expenditure on widows, orphans, and old age pensions (65–70). In addition the sums necessary to meet fully the cost of non-contributory pensions, which were running at the rate of about £15,634,000, had to be met from the Exchequer. Thus the precedent of the Exchequer accepting very substantial liabilities in connection with contributory pensions was established before 1946.

The inadequacy of the 10s. pension, both contributory and non-contributory, was an oft-repeated complaint in the nineteen-thirties. Though clearly not all old people needed financial assistance there was *some* acute poverty among the elderly who had no other resources. Some 10% had to seek help from Public Assistance authorities, others had to be helped by their families, and some shrank from exposing their needs to inquiry and endured the resulting hardship. Rowntree demonstrated in his survey of York in 1936 that the poverty of old age was more acute than poverty due to any other cause, and the figure of 10% of the elderly applying for Public Assistance probably did not reflect fully the extent of poverty which in fact existed among old people.

The demand of the Labour Party and the Trade Unions for a subsistence pension was made more urgent after 1930 by the depression. In their plans[2] for better pensions they included the stipulation that pensions should be paid only to those who had retired from regular employment. It was argued that this would help to move older men out of jobs, leaving more work for younger men with family responsibilities. During these years the reduction of pension age to 60 or even 55 years was widely discussed as a way of reducing competition for jobs.[3] These ideas were in keeping with earlier trade union attitudes towards restricting the supply of labour by eliminating the competition of the cheaper labour of the elderly. In 1939 demands were pressed upon the Government of the day to improve pensions for the elderly and an inquiry was followed by legislation in 1940. In supporting the Labour Party's de-

[1] This does not include the cost of pensions drawn by right of insurance for those over seventy, a charge which was transferred in 1925. Expenditure on 'over seventy' insurance pensions was accounting for over half of the annual expenditure on old age insurance pensions in 1938.

[2] Labour's Pension Plan for Old Age, Widows and Children, 1937.

[3] The Exit from Industry, P.E.P., 1935.

mands for a higher pension, trade unionists well understood and accepted the need for higher contributions towards the cost, as they have done on subsequent occasions when improvements in benefits have been made.[1] In the Old Age, Widows and Orphans Pensions Act of 1940, contributions were raised by 2d. per week for men and 3d. per week for women (the employer to 1d. of this in each case). The extra contributions were to finance the first part of the new legislation which reduced the pension age for women from 65 to 60 years. Some savings were made in this way on sickness and unemployment, payments which might otherwise have been paid to women between the ages of 60 and 65 years, but the new benefit was estimated to be worth a good deal more than the benefits foregone. The first part of the Act was generally welcomed, but Part II was heavily criticized because it did not embody an increase in basic pension rates.

Instead, the Act entitled pensioners to be paid a supplement determined by a household means test. Those pensioners whose income fell below a scale rate for subsistence as defined by the Assistance Board, could have the deficiency made up by a supplementary pension. In addition to the scale rate for other needs, an allowance for rent was calculated as part of a pensioners' needs.

This was criticized on the grounds that a means test of any kind was an unworthy way of dealing with the problems of poverty among the elderly, and a household means test was particularly disliked. The use of a means test was not a new departure, as income tests had always been applied in the case of non-contributory old age pensions and the Unemployment Assistance Board had administered a household means test which had left bitter memories. Despite protests, a household means test was included in the 1940 Act, but to meet criticisms it was removed in 1941, when the Determination of Needs Act substituted a personal means test. This took no account of the earnings of children, except to assume a small contribution to household expenses, and allowed certain kinds of income and savings to be held without disqualifying an applicant from a

[1] See, for example, discussion on pensions at the Trades Union Congress, Brighton, 1954. To this it may be objected that readiness at present to pay increased contributions is due to confidence that the incidence can be passed on in new wage demands.

supplementary pension. Notwithstanding this more generous interpretation of need, supplementary grants after an inquiry into means constituted a serious departure from the idea of contributory pensions. The Acts of 1940 and 1941 were regarded both by their sponsors and by the Opposition which reluctantly accepted them as an interim measure as a war-time expedient to be replaced when the whole structure of pension payments was reviewed and co-ordinated[1] after the conclusion of hostilities.

This was the state of progress in statutory pension provision when Beveridge produced his Report in 1942. Old people were drawing income from contributory pensions as an insurance 'right' and from non-contributory pensions subject to age and income limits. Both kinds of pensioners could have their payments supplemented by the Assistance Board, but those who had no title to pension still had to seek relief from Public Assistance authorities. In 1942 over 12% (about 29,324 persons) of Public Assistance cases involved men over 65 years and women over 60 years, and about 69,350 old people were being relieved in institutions, of whom about 39,559 were not receiving old age pensions.[2]

The war-time experience of helping the elderly by assistance subject to a means test sharpened all the old objections to methods which help people on the basis of how poor they are, and Beveridge was undoubtedly in harmony with popular sentiment in including old age pensions in a national scheme of contributory insurance. On the other hand, his reservations on the ground of cost, which led him to devise a twenty-year transitional pension plan, were at variance with the demand for immediate subsistence pensions, and were accordingly discarded when legislation was drafted. The roles of assistance and insurance in providing social security were subsequently defined very differently by the National Insurance and National Assistance Act, but events have led us to do something very like Beveridge's original proposals by another route, and the rela-

[1] In June 1941 the Inter-Departmental Committee on Social Insurance and Allied Services was appointed 'to undertake with special reference to the inter-relation of the schemes, a survey of the existing national schemes of social insurance and allied services, including workmen's compensation and to make recommendations'.
[2] The Beveridge Report, *op. cit.*, Section 3, Appendix B.

tionship of assistance and insurance in meeting the needs of the elderly has still to be decided.

THE BEVERIDGE PLAN FOR OLD AGE

The problem of financing old age was specifically recognized and discussed at some length in the Beveridge Report, although one of the Report's most important recommendations in this respect was ignored when new legislation was drafted. It is open to question whether old age pensions should ever have been included in a comprehensive insurance scheme of flat-rate benefits, since the nature of the foreseeable long-term needs of the elderly are very different from need arising out of unemployment or sickness. Having made the decision to include this contingency some of our present difficulties might have been avoided, or at least managed more easily, had the original proposals, i.e. transitional assistance pensions rising over twenty years, of the Beveridge Report been followed.

Beveridge recognized the heavy claims likely to be made on social insurance funds in meeting the needs of old people, and he drew attention not only to their increasing numbers but also to the lack of uniformity of the economic consequence of old age. He quoted pre-war poverty surveys and the number drawing supplementary pensions in 1941 to demonstrate that old age may be accompanied by very great poverty or by no poverty at all. Bearing in mind, therefore, that many people would have made some provision for their old age by savings and superannuation schemes, and that the new retirement pensions were to be part of an insurance scheme and dependent upon contribution records, Beveridge did not recommend that a full subsistence benefit should be paid to all old age pensioners from the beginning of a national insurance scheme. Instead he proposed a twenty-year transitional period in which pensions would gradually be raised to the full amount. Those pensioners who were unable to manage on the initial pension would be entitled to assistance, and Beveridge defended this use of a 'means' pension on the grounds that the pension was meant to be a contributory one and could not be paid in full immediately to those who had not made any substantial number of contributions. 'There is all the difference in the world between a permanent system of pensions subject to a means test and a

PENSIONS

transitional system of supplementation of rising contributory pensions.'[1]

On the basis of these recommendations the Government Actuary estimated for the Beveridge Report the cost of retirement and assistance pensions for the first twenty years of the scheme. But the 'golden staircase' plan was later abandoned and pensions were introduced at the full rate (26s.) from the very beginning of the new scheme of National Insurance. In the event, before 1955 payments to the elderly through the National Insurance scheme had already exceeded £350m., and mean-tested pensions and grants were more than twice as great as had been anticipated.

TABLE XV

Retirement and Assistance Pensions. The Beveridge Proposal 1952 [2]

(Estimated cost, 1945–65. Actual cost, 1954)
(£m.)

Year	Estimated Cost			Actual Cost
	1945	1955	1965	1954
Retirement Pensions	126	190	300	351
Assistance Pensions	39	33	25	75*
Total	165	223	325	426

* Includes non-contributory pensions, supplements to non-contributory pensions, supplements to retirement pensions and assistance grants to those over pension age and not in receipt of pensions or benefits.

NATIONAL INSURANCE RETIREMENT PENSIONS

The hesitations of the Coalition Government (1940–45) which had considered the Beveridge Report were swept away with the victory of the Labour Party in 1945. One of its first actions was to pass the National Insurance Act in February 1946, which brought virtually the whole population within a comprehensive social insurance scheme. No new members of the scheme could qualify for pensions before they had contri-

[1] The Beveridge Report, *op. cit.*, p. 99.   [2] Beveridge, *op. cit.*, p. 199.

buted at least ten years, and the main change was to include the existing pensioners who had contributed under the Act of 1925 and to raise their 10s. pension to 26s. Non-contributory pensions were raised in a similar way to the new rate. The other important difference was that for the first five years after pension age (65 years for men, and 60 years for women) pensions were paid only on condition that the recipients had retired from their regular employment. The new Act permitted continued work to what was described as 'an inconsiderable extent', and this was interpreted to mean not earning[1] more than £1 per week (raised in 1951 to a limit of £2 per week). Those who had reached pension age but were ineligible for benefit by reason of employment, were entitled to a deferred pension increased by increments calculated on continued contributions up to five years after pension age. This device was expressly intended to encourage older people, who felt able to do so, to prolong their working life. The old contributory pension scheme had no such retirement condition, and a number of 10s. pensioners continued to draw this pension and work,[2] being entitled to the new rate of 26s. only when they retired or reached the age of seventy years if men, and sixty-five years if women. The number of such pensioners has decreased steadily and in 1953 was about 35,000 persons.[3]

In all this the Act embodied the main recommendations of the Beveridge Report, with the very important exception, already mentioned, that it did not include the scheme of transitional pensions rising to the full standard rate over twenty years. Beveridge's proposals were intended to deal with the difficulties of providing for those already over or very near pension age, but his scheme was not adopted, and in fact by a special arrangement the new rates of pension became operative for all pensioners from October 1946, though the general scheme of comprehensive insurance benefits did not commence until July 1948.

[1] See the decisions of the Umpire N.1. Pension pamphlet 1/1947 on the definition of retirement, some of which have discouraged part-time employment (e.g. Cases 14/47, 58/47, 68/47 and others).

[2] Only those pensioners who were already receiving payments as contributors under the 1925 Act at July 1948 were able to continue to receive them and work. There was some dissatisfaction among contributory pensioners reaching 65 years after July 1948 who felt that their right to pension *and* employment should not have been abrogated in this way.

[3] Annual Report of Ministry of Pensions and National Insurance, 1953.

PENSIONS

Not all the increase in the actual cost of pensions over the estimates of the Beveridge Report is due to the introduction of full pensions for those who had no opportunity to contribute at the new rates. Retirement pensions have been increased since 1946 by more than 50% and assistance scales by more than 80% in the same period (1946–55). It is no doubt true that rising prices would have forced a similar increase in the transitional pensions proposed by Beveridge had his method of payment been employed, but the great difference is that there would not have been the present numbers drawing a full benefit irrespective of other means.

PENSIONS AND RISING PRICES

In the enthusiastic debates on the National Insurance Act,[1] in which the principle of making benefits generally adequate, without recourse to assistance, was clearly accepted, no definite pledge[2] was given that benefits would be tied to a cost of living index. The then Minister of National Insurance (Mr. James Griffiths) thought it sufficient to affirm that benefits would be broadly related to the cost of living, and would be subject to a quinquennial review in which their adequacy could be reconsidered. At that time memories of unemployment and dislike of the old Poor Law approach to poverty were uppermost in the public mind and conditioned much current thinking about social insurance. It was not so readily appreciated then, as it is now, after more than a decade of rising prices[3] that inflation can be an even greater threat than depression to a subsistence standard of living.

The demand for an increase in pensions which began very shortly after the new rates became operative was met by referring those in need to the National Assistance Board. The scale rate, with reference to which the Board calculated its payments consisted of 40s. per week for a couple and a rent allowance, as compared with the retirement pension for a man

[1] Hansard, Parliamentary Debates, Vol. 432, No. 150, pp. 1380–1472.
[2] No Government at any time since the introduction of the National Insurance Act has ever pledged itself formally to benefits tied directly to the Cost of Living Index.
[3] See also 'Old Age Security in Britain', adjusting pensions to rising prices 1946–52, Helen F. Hohman, in *The Social Service Review*, Vol. XXVII, 2nd June 1953.

and his wife of 42*s*. A year after the new pensions were introduced about 18% of pensioner households were receiving a supplementary grant from the Board, and a further third of these had to have extra weekly payments in consideration of special circumstances. In addition a number of single lump sum payments were being made to meet exceptional temporary needs. Between 1946 and 1954 the number of grants made to retirement pensioners by the National Assistance Board has risen from 460,000 to 1,001,000 and in 1954 27% of pensioner households were in receipt of national assistance. (Since one grant may cover the needs of a married couple the number of pensioners dependent upon supplementation from the Board is now about 1,500,000.) Table XVI shows how both assistance scales and retirement pensions have been increased to take account of rises in the cost of living.

TABLE XVI

Assistance Scales and Retirement Pensions, 1948–55

	National Assistance		National Insurance Retirement Pensions	
	Single	Couple	Single	Couple
1948	24/–	40/–	26/–	42/–
1950	26/–	43/6	26/–	42/–
1951	30/–	50/–	30/–*	50/–
1952	35/–	59/–	32/6	54/–
1955	37/6	63/–	40/–	65/–

* Applicable only to retirement pensions over 70 (65 women) or those who had reached pension age before October, 1951.

Pensions and assistance rates have thus been adjusted to meet rising prices but unfortunately there is no general agreement about the way in which the admitted rise in living costs can be accurately measured. Any decision to tie pensions to a cost of living index would have to be preceded by the adoption of an acceptable index or the construction of a new one which reliably reflected the effect of changing prices on the living standards of pensioners. The weight normally given in a cost of living index to rent, e.g., may distort the index for those whose rent is in any case paid by the National Assistance Board, whereas the cost of fuel in the pensioners' budget may need to be differently weighted as compared with a younger household.

PENSIONS

Pension debates both inside and outside Parliament have frequently been pre-occupied with these calculations to the exclusion of any long-term considerations of the principles upon which pension financing can equitably be based. As living costs have risen the size of the pensioner vote, together with the concern widely felt by the public about financial hardships for the elderly, has forced improvement first in assistance and then in pension rates. The increases given have been regularly condemned as inadequate by the Opposition and defended by the Government on the grounds that no more can be afforded having regard to the mounting liabilities which are being undertaken. But in fact everyone knows that further liabilities will have to be undertaken if the purchasing power of pensions is seriously reduced by rising prices. At the end of 1954, for example, it was decided to raise the level of both assistance and pensions. One and three quarter million order books were laboriously altered to give effect to the new assistance rates by February 1955. Then two-thirds of all allowances (i.e. grants to those in receipt of insurance benefit) were revised again in April and May when the new pensions rates became operative. After these book-keeping transactions were concluded an uneasy peace descended for a brief period until complaints were resumed again about the inadequacy of pensions in view of rising prices. In December 1955 it was announced that assistance rates would be increased by 2s. 6d. and 4s. for single householders and couples respectively. After this official recognition of increased living costs there will undoubtedly be a renewed effort to raise retirement pensions in 1956.

PENSIONS AND THEIR PURPOSE

Schemes using assistance and those using insurance are not mutually exclusive, but in any long-term plans (if both are to be retained) one or other must be dominant according to the view which is accepted of the purpose of pension schemes. If instead of meeting a limited number of exceptional needs, assistance continues to be used to underpin insurance payments for increasing numbers of beneficiaries, and the payments are regulated to match rising prices, it may come to be relied upon as more adequate than the insurance benefits. A disparity between more generous assistance payments and admittedly inadequate insurance benefits would reduce the value of the insurance scheme to contributors.[1] If insurance benefits are only a basis for other benefits payable by the National Assistance Board there may be a reluctance to continue to pay large insurance contributions. The less deterrent and more generous National Assistance is, the more likely is it that this will happen.

The mechanism for securing an adequate income for the elderly must depend upon some basic assumption about the respective roles of the individual and the community in financing old age. Ought workers to have a right to maintenance in old age out of the community's resources in recognition of a lifetime of effort and service?

'The State must take this matter (of old age pensions) into its own hands, not as almsgiving but as the right that men have to be taken care of when, from no fault of their own, they become unfit for work. Why should regular soldiers and officials have old age pensions, and not soldiers of labour.'[2] This is one kind of answer that can be given. The 'veterans of industry' argument is often advanced and has much to commend it, but one query arises at once. Is the pension to be granted only when men become 'unfit for work'? Is it to be withheld while a man can still work, and what is the test of fitness to be? Is reaching a stated age of, say, 65 years, which medically speaking has been pulled out of the hat, a satisfactory way of deciding fitness or otherwise for employment? Are pensions to be regarded as a way of discharging a community responsibility to those unable to maintain themselves in the same way that support is organized for other disabled persons, or are they a reward for a lifetime of effort, a kind of deferred pay to which everyone should be entitled after a named period of work attendance and contributions? If the latter, then pensions schemes should create a right to retirement for all workers on a pension which is adequate to meet their basic needs, while they enjoy their well-earned rest. Those who choose voluntarily to continue to work should gain, either by receiving pension and wages, or by a larger deferred pension ultimately drawn, in recognition of the surrender of leisure which might otherwise have been enjoyed. The notion of creating a 'right' to a pension at a certain age is emphasized by the device of insurance as a

[1] See also Hansard Parliamentary Debates, Vol. 500, cols. 49–50.
[2] Bismarck.

method of financing old age. Whether a scheme dependent on a regressive poll tax on workers together with employers' contributions and subsidized by the Exchequer, ought properly to be described as insurance at all is open to question, but there is no doubt that the idea of contractual insurance rights is firmly implanted in the public mind in relation to national insurance benefits.

If, on the other hand, we are primarily concerned to relieve need among the elderly, and to do it as generously as the community can afford, we ought to provide something more than a bare subsistence for the smaller number of old people involved. To do this means using some method of determining needs and then granting assistance.

As noted above, the Beveridge proposals pronounced firmly for subsistence pensions as a right to be paid irrespective of the pensioner's other resources, when he or she retired from work. 'It follows that the plan must include provision of pensions up to subsistence level given as a right to people who are past work, regardless of other resources that they then possess, but in respect of service and contribution during working life.'[1] Thus Beveridge added a new condition to the qualification for pension. Not only must the pensioner have reached a certain pension age, but he must also be 'past work'. Beveridge treats this condition as though it were similar to other unexpected misfortunes like sickness or industrial injury or unemployment. But old age as a disabling condition preventing continued earning is very different from the other contingencies provided for in social insurance. In the first place, it is in no way unexpected. It is a foreseeable and certain need for which a long preparation may be made and to this extent the individual may be expected in normal circumstances to help substantially to make provision for himself. Secondly, whether a man retires or not is, for some men though by no means for all, a personal choice, which is not true of sudden sickness or accident, or widowhood or unemployment, which may strike any family unexpectedly. The decision as to whether a man is 'past work' may of course be settled for him by poor health, or by his employment being terminated at minimum pension age by a compulsory retire-

[1] The Beveridge Report, pp. 93–5. Beveridge made it clear that the pension he proposed, on condition that the recipients had retired from work, was to be a 'full subsidence income'.

ment rule, or a discharge decided by his employers. Some fit older men reaching pension age do however exercise their choice to take or postpone retirement, and in these circumstances applying a condition of retirement as well as an age limit creates some difficulties. It may encourage some older workers who have a choice to take their pension and retire since they feel that to continue means working hard for only a part of their nominal wages. The nearer pensions are to a reasonable subsistence level the more likely is this to happen, and the improved rate of increments to deferred pensions does not seem to have removed this dissatisfaction.

Retirement regulations hinder arrangements for part-time employment which some older men might be glad to undertake, and the loss of pension together with the need for full insurance contributions does not encourage the development of part-time employment for older workers.

There is a further consideration. The retirement condition imposes upon the bulk of workers dependent on National Insurance pensions a restriction on the use of their later years (i.e. if they receive a pension they cannot continue in any regular employment), which is not applied to retiring civil servants or business executives under their pension arrangements. This is a major difference between National Insurance and other industrial or public service pensions and creates an unjustifiable distinction between professional and manual workers. Occupational status involving different retirement rules should not be the determining factor in awarding or withholding pensions claims.

INDUSTRIAL PENSIONS

The purpose of pension schemes and the assumption on which they are based may be further examined by comparing National Insurance pensions with other kinds of pension provision. Industrial and occupational pension schemes have grown rapidly in number in recent years, covering both manual and non-manual workers. Individual firms, either by private funds or by arrangement with insurance companies,[1] have

[1] Group Life Pension Schemes began to be developed from about 1925 onwards. By 1953 it is estimated that staff life assurance and pension schemes covered about 1,654,000 lives, of which 319,500 represented new schemes begun in 1953 (*The Economist*, 16th October 1954, pp. 246–9).

provided mainly contributory pensions which are usually based on years of service and the rate of salary attained. Schemes for manual workers, whose earnings do not greatly vary over a lifetime, have sometimes consisted of a fixed payment after a named period of service. For salaried staff pensions have more often been calculated on retiring salary, or on average renumeration during the last ten years of working life, as well as on years of service. Non-contributory schemes and ex gratia payments at the discretion of employers have also been used, the latter being especially common in the smaller family firm. The number of these schemes continues to grow and many are now extended to cover all workers on a contributory basis. Larger industrial concerns may have two or three different schemes and those which have been initiated in recent years are likely to have been chosen with a view to minimizing the tax liability of the contributors. Schemes under the 1918 Act may suit works employees where contributions merely attract relief as life assurance premiums and no tax is deducted from any repaid contributions. Under the 1921 Act contributions are eligible for tax relief on an expense basis, which is advantageous for staff employees who are subject to income tax at the full rate.[1] 'Top Hat' Endowment Assurance Schemes[2] are used for higher executives and working directors, where tax liability is crucial, since part of the pension may be commuted in a tax free lump sum, and the handsome pension is in effect deferred pay. The latter have been criticized on the grounds that they involve a considerable loss of revenue to the Exchequer. They are themselves the product of a penal rate of taxation and are one of the few ways left of offering an incentive to maximum effort for the higher-paid business executive. Nevertheless the generosity of their terms, aided by tax relief, are in marked contrast to the very limited benefits for the elderly under the National Insurance scheme.

It may be asked why so many firms have decided to initiate pension schemes for their employees and if this is a development which should be encouraged? Individual firms may have a

[1] The Committee on The Taxation Treatment of Provisions for Retirement (Cmd. 9063) (The Millard Tucker Report) has recently reported on the diverse arrangements at present existing and has made recommendations with the object of securing more uniform treatment.
[2] Non-contributory schemes approved under section 388 of the Income Tax Act, 1952.

different approach to this matter but two considerations seem to be of general importance to employers. The first is that the offer of a pension after a stated number of years of service is an attractive condition of employment. It will be weighed along with present salary and future opportunities for advancement by prospective employees. A generous pension scheme may help a firm to recruit the best staff, and indeed if other firms are offering pensionable employment it may be necessary for their competitors to do so in order to secure a share of the new entrants in industry. In this way industrial pension schemes are very like superannuation and pension schemes for teachers or civil servants. They are an advantage associated with that kind of employment which has an influence in attracting candidates into the service. This has been of great importance to employers in a prolonged period of full employment. Arising out of these pension arrangements there is a further advantage to the employer that the employee with pension rights is likely to stay with the firm where he has acquired them, and will not lightly surrender the contributions made on his behalf and pay tax on his returned contributions which might happen (dependent upon the type of scheme to which he belongs) if he changed his employment. Against this, it may be said that while the individual employer may have less labour turnover, if pension rights impede the free mobility of manpower, maximum national efficiency may be seriously hindered.

Secondly a pension scheme with a normal retiring age enables an employer to retire an older worker when he is no longer fully efficient without great hardship to him. It is generally recognized that when a man has worked for many years in a business he should be paid over a longer period than his actual service with the firm,[1] and employers who have no pension scheme often find themselves forced to make ex gratia payments or retain older workers beyond their usefulness, because they feel unable to terminate employment for the man with no other resources. Add to this that the whole cost to the employers of a funded scheme approved by the Inland Revenue Authorities is allowed as a trading expense, and it is easy to see why industrial pension schemes have become increasingly popular.

Occupational pension schemes are often assumed to be

[1] *Op. cit.*, p. 106.

unquestionably desirable because they promote savings which might otherwise not be made,[1] and the saving thus made can be invested to enhance the country's productive capacity. The weight of this argument, which might equally be applied to national insurance contributions,[2] is difficult to assess since it is impossible to estimate how much of the savings made through occupational pension schemes replaces the savings which might otherwise have been accumulated in a different form. It seems probable that pension contributions whether deducted through the national insurance scheme or occupational pension schemes, result in some net addition to the volume of saving, but insufficient information is available to gauge the extent of this.[3]

The development of occupational pension schemes has other economic consequences apart from their effect upon the level of personal savings, such as the effect on prices of this addition to the cost of labour, the emergence of pension funds as a major source of capital not designated in advance for special purposes, and the effect of pension rights upon the mobility of labour. These important economic implications are not discussed here, but we may look at industrial pensions from the point of view of their effectiveness in helping directly to finance old age.

Pensions negotiated as a condition of employment in a particular firm or public service are a way of enabling people to provide more than the basic minimum which a state pension scheme can provide, and the inadequacy of National Insurance pensions has stimulated this development. Schemes are spreading from limited coverage for salaried staffs to workers in all levels in industry. The nationalized industries and public services, as for example the National Coal Board and the British Transport Commission, offer supplementary pension schemes to their employees and this example in the public sectors of industry is likely to be followed by similar demands in other public services.

So far only about one quarter of employees, other than those in public services, belong to industrial pension schemes, but the increase in pension provision witnessed in the post-war period is likely to continue. The more highly paid worker who suffers a correspondingly great drop in income on retirement is

[1] Cmd. 9333, para. 124.
[2] Paish and Peacock, *Manchester Guardian*, 8th February 1955.
[3] See *New Pensions for the Old*, B. Abel Smith and P. Townsend.

able and apparently willing to pay more than the flat rate of National Insurance contributions towards an old age pension. For such workers a funded scheme arranged through the life insurance offices gives security to this convenient way of saving for old age, and future benefits are not jeopardized by a fall in business activity in individual firms. Of course these schemes are not truly insurances any more than is the National Insurance scheme, because they are subsidized in effect by exemption from tax liability, with a consequent loss of revenue to the Exchequer.[1] They provide one kind of solution to the problem of easing the transference from full salary or wages to retirement pension. Without the prospect of an adequate pension, the last years of a man's working life are haunted by anxiety, unless he has been able to accumulate substantial savings.

With these admitted advantages, ought unions to be pressing for the extension of industrial pension schemes, as some of their American counterparts have done, to provide greatly increased income security in old age? Would this be the kind of development Beveridge foreshadowed and approved when he pleaded for voluntary action to provide something better than bare subsistence? At present pension schemes are mainly provided at the discretion of employers, but as they enjoy substantial tax concessions, it can be agreed that all employees should be enabled to set aside some part of current earnings in a pension scheme, and receive equal tax treatment in relation to it. Though trade unions have not found pension schemes attractive for their members as a means of tax avoidance, they have to some extent accepted them as a form of deferred pay, when no immediate wage increases could be negotiated. As long as pension rights are non-transferable and dependent upon the employer's goodwill, however, they may continue to be regarded with some suspicion in trade union quarters.

If occupational pensions are to be encouraged to develop more widely, some way must be found of minimizing or eliminating their major disadvantage which is their tendency to restrict the free movement of labour. To the employer this appears as an advantage, though it may not do so to his employees. The supplementary pension scheme for miners, for example, was unpopular with some of the men in that industry

---

[1] The Phillips Committee estimated that tax concessions to occupational pension schemes cost the Exchequer £100m. of revenue annually.

just because it made pension claims dependent upon being tied to the industry for a number of years. Where pension schemes are attached to employment which is fairly stable, and where people are expected to remain for long periods of service, or where pension rights can be fairly easily transferred as in different branches of a public service, this objection may not be of great importance. If, however, industrial pension schemes or superannuation arrangements are going to be used increasingly to provide for the average industrial worker, transferability of pension rights is essential if industrial mobility is to be preserved. Until a year or two ago the Inland Revenue Authorities exempted from tax liability an employer's pension contributions which were returned to a man leaving his service, only if the decision to grant this concession was entirely at the discretion of the employer. Now arrangements can be approved where an employee can receive the employer's contributions as of right without tax liability, on withdrawal from service after a specified number of years. This is one way of securing transferability without loss of rights, but whether many employers will be prepared to offer such arrangement remains to be seen.

It is perhaps less appropriate now than formerly to think of the employer's contributions to pension as a reward to old employees for long and faithful service, which can be withheld if a man changes his job. The more recent 'Top Hat' insurance schemes for example, although non-contributory, are a way of frankly treating pensions as deferred pay. If pensions can be regarded as a deferred claim then it should be possible to transfer these claims, including the value of both the employee's and the employer's contributions, or to retain them and base the ultimate pension on a composite figure made up of several claims accumulated at different places of employment. These two methods are used widely for employees in public services and in certain occupations.[1] Several schemes have been proposed which it is claimed would at a reasonable administrative cost secure transferability of pension claims.[2] There would have

[1] The F.S.S.U. Schemes have the most flexible arrangements. Superannuation rights can be transferred within a group of employers and policies can be handed over to employees who move to other kinds of employment.

[2] For a fuller discussion of transferability of pensions see, A. S. Owen, 'Transferability of Pensions', Industrial Welfare Society, Broadsheet 11, 1954.

to be some minimum period of service, say five or seven years, before transferable rights were recognized, and pensions would cost the employer a little more because there would be no windfalls added to the funds by withdrawals. From the employer's point of view, however, one of the main attractions of pension schemes would have been lost if transferability were unhampered, since pension rights would no longer be so effective in tying men to their employment. If approval of pensions schemes for tax concessions were made dependent upon the employee's having a right to the payments made on his behalf when leaving employment,[1] industrial pension schemes might become a good deal less popular with employers and this might prevent further expansion of these kinds of arrangements.

NATIONAL SUPERANNUATION FUNDS

Even so, partial coverage by industrial pensions does not solve the problem of adequate income after retirement for those covered by neither these nor public service superannuation schemes. A different approach to the problem is to explore the possibility of creating a national superannuation fund with a contribution from employee and employer. This could be a fixed percentage, with an upper and lower limit to the rate of pension. A man would draw a pension broadly related to what he had paid in and what had been paid in on his behalf.[2]

One of the major difficulties of the National Insurance scheme is that to have a flat rate of contribution and benefit means that the contributions, being a highly regressive tax, cannot be made high in relation to the wages of the earners in the lowest income groups, and the benefits are correspondingly inadequate to finance retirement at anything more comfortable than at best a bare subsistence level. Those not already covered by pension schemes other than National Insurance might welcome the opportunity to pay more and receive a higher pension, and the flat rate of benefit dependent upon a number of years of service could be replaced by one which reflects occupational success. This has always been a feature of public services and other pension schemes where payments are

[1] See F. W. Paish and A. T. Peacock, 'The Economics of Pension Funds', *Lloyds Bank Review*, October 1954.
[2] See also *Planning*, Vol. XX, No. 364, 1954.

calculated to take into account the peak salary earned. Unlike former social insurance schemes which only provided for those in the lower income groups, National Insurance demands contributions at all levels of income, and the question arises whether, rather than forcing those who want more than the insurance pension to belong to other pension schemes, it would be better to extend the insurance scheme in a way which would be made to cover most people's needs. The proliferation of pension schemes involves heavy administrative costs and tends to immobilize labour. While it is not suggested that any steps should be taken to eliminate the variety of alternative pension schemes now available, a national scheme with different rates of contribution and benefit might be an advantage. Such a national pensions fund would avoid the problems of transferability of pension rights and would not limit labour mobility. Those who already felt satisfied with the pension for which they were contributing would not need to pay for more than the basic pension. In this way a national pensions fund would not seek to replace existing pension arrangements, but would extend pension facilities to those in firms and services where no scheme at present exists. Since existing schemes are made more advantageous because they are permitted substantial tax exemption, it seems only fair that this privilege should be more widely extended and not restricted to a limited number of business firms, merely by employers' decisions.[1]

Another advantage of a superannuation scheme of this sort would be that contributions would be automatically increased as a percentage of higher wages. If wages and prices rise the additional funds created by larger contributions can help to maintain the purchasing power of pensions. The kind of industrial pension scheme for manual workers which offers a fixed pension after a number of years of service (on the assumption that the wages of such workers will, at a fairly early stage, reach their top rate), has become inappropriate in a period of rising prices. In paying National Insurance pensions the same difficulty has been encountered. The National Insurance scheme has no built-in regulator of the relationship between benefits and prices, except the provision for a quinquennial review.

[1] *Op. cit.*, p. 106. This argument has been extended to include the proposal that the self-employed should be allowed to benefit from the taxation advantages that are enjoyed by employees in recognized pension schemes.

Benefits can only be altered by amending legislation with an inevitable time-lag between a rise in the cost of living and an increase in pensions.

A national superannuation scheme with contributions forming an agreed percentage of wages would avoid some of these difficulties, but it would not be possible to base pensions on earnings in the last five or ten years of employment, as is often the practice in industrial pension schemes for executive and administrative staffs. If this were permitted, a difficulty would arise when there was any general increase in wages and salaries owing to rising prices. In these circumstances contributors who were near to retirement would pay increased contributions for only a short period, and their past contributions would not have been calculated to pay for a pension based on unforeseen increases in remuneration. Since it is impossible to demand retrospective contributions, it would be necessary to avoid serious deficiencies in the funds by basing pensions on average earnings and contributions over a lifetime. Even so, some deficiencies might have to be accepted, as has happened in the notional accounts of public service pensions.

DIFFERENTIAL CONTRIBUTIONS AND BENEFITS

A national superannuation scheme with contributions forming a fixed percentage of wages and with maximum and minimum levels set for benefits would in some ways be very similar to the American system of Old Age and Survivors Insurance. In this scheme the heterogeneity of economic conditions and living standards in the United States is recognized, and an attempt made to relate contributions and benefits to former earnings. Though more narrowly exclusive when it was initiated in 1935, by subsequent amendments coverage was extended by 1950 to include about 45 million workers.[1] The benefit payable is calculated as a percentage of average monthly earnings in 'covered' employment at the rate of 55% of average monthly earnings of $100, 39% of average monthly earnings of $200 and 31% of average monthly earnings of $350, which is the maximum sum subject to this tax. The minimum benefit

[1] The latest amendments in August 1954 have extended coverage further to include some employees and persons not previously eligible, as well as increasing benefits.

for single persons is $30 per month and for those already retired the maximum is $98·50, though the 1951 amendments raises the upper limit for those retiring after this date to $108·50. Wives over pension age can draw a benefit equal to half that of their husbands (subject to a maximum) and widows, parents and children also draw benefits under this scheme. Payments to dependants are related to the primary benefit calculated on the insured person's average earnings in covered employment.

Retirement is assumed unless earnings exceed $100 a month up to the age of 72 years, after which benefits and earnings may be retained. This is similar to our National Insurance retirement pensions which may be drawn without disqualification by reason of employment when five years after pension age have elapsed.

Contributions, like benefits, are linked to former earnings, and the percentage contribution is shared equally between employer and employee. These contributions in the form of a combined tax were supposed to begin in 1937 at 2% of earned income rising by 1949 to 6% up to the maximum amount subject to tax, and shared equally between employee and employer. In fact the tax was frozen at 2% for nearly twelve years and has only now risen to 2% from employees and 2% from employers and 3% from self-employed persons. One of the reasons for this was that the trustees of the Federal Old Age and Survivors Insurance Fund were not encouraged to build up a large reserve fund. The trustees were required by law to report immediately to Congress if they estimated at any time that during the next five years the fund would exceed three times the highest annual expenditure anticipated in that period, or if the fund seemed likely to become unduly small. The O.A.S.I. fund, which now stands at $18·6 billion[1] consists entirely of employers' and employees' and self-employed persons' contributions without any subsidy from public funds.

The numbers drawing benefits have steadily increased and are now more than 5½ million persons. This includes not only old people and their dependants but widows and their dependent children of younger ages; for example about one-quarter of these beneficiaries are dependent parents and children. At the same time the number of old people drawing old age assistance has declined to about 2½ million, and only about 10% of

[1] American billion = 1000 mn.

pensioners in America also receive relief as compared with nearly one-quarter of pensioners in Britain receiving additional grants from the National Assistance Board. This is a very approximate comparison since the conditions under which assistance may be drawn are somewhat different in America and there is considerable variation in the determination of need between different States. At the end of 1952 while one-fifth of all old persons in America were receiving old age assistance, in Louisiana five-eighths of the aged were being assisted and in the district of Columbia, one-twentieth. In twenty-five States the average payment per month was more than $50, but in some States it was as low as $27.[1] States have different policies regarding the assets of those applying for assistance and about the responsibility and contribution which relatives are expected to undertake towards the maintenance of the elderly. The personal means test and the policy of disregarding certain kinds of assets used by the National Assistance Board here are, on the whole, a more generous way of calculating need. To the extent that it is less stringent than American old age assistance inevitably a larger proportion of pensioners are eligible for help. However it remains true that in America the number of assistance payments to the elderly is declining and that of insurance benefits is increasing, while the opposite trend has been discernable in Great Britain, though the rate of increase has now slowed down.

The average monthly pension at present being paid under the O.A.S.I. scheme is about $50 for single retired persons and the average of assistance payments is $49. The comparable figures for Great Britain in 1954 were retirement pension payments at a flat rate of 32s. 6d., and an average assistance pay- *per week* ment to retirement pensioners of 14s. 3d.[2] The American scheme has never professed to provide a subsistence benefit. It has been assumed that the O.A.S.I. benefit, to which may be added by earnings any sum up to $100 per month, together with savings and perhaps industrial pensions, can provide an adequate income for most old people, leaving only a minority needing special extra assistance. Thus though old age benefits have not been geared to the notion of a subsistence minimum, the

---

[1] *Social Work Year Book*, 1954, The American Association of Social Workers.

[2] The average supplement for a non-contributory pensioner is 18s. 6d.

American system does not seem to have created the need for a large-scale recourse to public assistance now that this scheme is maturing. Moreover, the gradual transference of old people from assistance to insurance benefits, which has taken place in America, as contributory rights have been built up[1] and coverage extended, has permitted the accumulation of a substantial O.A.S.I. fund. This provides a contrast to British practice where, in 1946, we endowed most of the elderly with a claim to National Insurance retirement pensions irrespective of inadequate contributions records. The solvency of the O.A.S.I. fund, on which we may look with some envy when we reflect that our own National Insurance funds are likely in the near future to run into heavy deficits, has been partly achieved by limited benefits and the use of assistance until contribution records have been built up. Also it must of course be noted it is not a fully comprehensive scheme.

The American scheme has not been immune from the difficulties experienced in the British social insurance system, where rising prices have destroyed the value of benefits.[2] The increase of benefits, sanctioned by Congress in 1954, was a recognition of higher living costs. But inflationary pressure has been partly offset by the device of the percentage tax, which makes higher wages automatically yield higher contributions. A percentage tax on wages does not altogether avoid the difficulties of adjusting benefits to rising prices. For younger contributors it is true that when increases in wages are granted to meet rising costs, larger contributions towards their ultimate pension will be set aside by this method, which helps to adjust the pension level to the increased cost of living. However, for all employees and especially for older workers near retirement, increased contributions may have been paid for only a limited period and the calculation of average earnings will be depressed by the lower earnings of former years. Recent amendments in the American O.A.S.I. scheme permit some years of lower earnings to be disregarded in calculating an average, but it is not possible to base benefits on earnings over the last five or

[1] No payments were done during the first years of contribution to this scheme, thus enabling the fund to be built up.

[2] For a discussion of some of these difficulties, see 'Social Security in a Period of Full Employment', Eveline M. Burns, Proceedings of the Industrial Relations Research Association.

ten years of employment, as is done in some industrial pensions schemes. If this were done any substantial unforeseen rise in wages and salaries would upset the actuarial calculations of the scheme and create a deficit, which would have to be made up by some kind of subsidy.

It is often objected that a system similar to the American one must be complicated and expensive to administer. In the American scheme about four million employers have to keep and return wage records and over one hundred million accounts have to be kept for periods of anything up to the length of a man's working lifetime. But the administrative costs of the scheme in 1952 amounted to no more than 3·5% of benefits and 2·2% of contributions.

The American scheme of O.A.S.I. appears to have several advantages. It is more equitable in incidence than the regressive flat rate of contribution used in British social insurance; and the benefits are more realistic as a contribution towards preserving living standards in old age, because they bear a more direct relationship to former earnings. Benefits and contributions increase up to a maximum but what is earned beyond that is not taken into account, and there is no disincentive created by further tax above the named maximum. Actual contribution records were strictly adhered to in the early development of the scheme, with the inevitable use of assistance for those who were ineligible; but the scheme now is increasingly covering the elderly on an insurance basis, and the assistance services are decreasing in importance. O.A.S.I. pensions cannot be wholly protected from rising costs, but the percentage method of calculating contributions and benefit affords a partial protection. The O.A.S.I. fund is solvent and there is no anxiety in the foreseeable future about its ability to balance its account without requiring any subsidy from public funds. Though there are features of the American scheme for income maintenance in old age which might not be acceptable in Britain, the difficulties of our own insurance scheme, especially the obstinate refusal to contemplate differentials in either contribution or benefit, might be re-examined with some profit in the light of American experience.

PENSIONS

There is a widespread feeling that present methods of financing old age are unsatisfactory, but as yet little agreement about the kind of changes which ought to be made in existing pension schemes. Proposals for reform range from minor amendments to complete abandonment of social insurance.

THE STATUS QUO

In examining the dissatisfactions expressed about National Insurance pensions we must distinguish between those which are focused upon the current level of pension benefits, and those which reject the whole concept of social insurance as a suitable provision for income-maintenance in old age.

Demands to restore the purchasing power which pensions had in 1946 and to make them truly subsistence pensions adjusted automatically to the cost of living, involve a re-examination of pension financing but not necessarily an abandonment of social insurance. The most recent pension increases (December 1954) raised payments about 55% above the 1946 level, which corresponded to changed living costs in the period 1946–54 as measured by the 'working class' index of the London and Cambridge Economic Service.[1] This has not however wholly met the objections of those who want a full 'back to Beveridge' policy. They question whether the level of payments initiated in 1946 and to which subsequent increases have been geared, was ever a true subsistence level in the sense which Beveridge intended, that is, just sufficient to live on even if the pensioner had no other means. 'Subsistence' they would argue has been too narrowly defined to correspond realistically to the pattern of expenditure of social pensioners. This is especially true of old age pensioners who draw their benefits not as a short-term 'tide over' payment, but as a sole means of living for the rest of their years. Also items in the cost of living index would need to be weighted differently for pensioners if pensions are to keep their full value in the face of rising prices.

To provide for all pensioners, except for a small minority with special needs, by way of insurance pensions at subsistence level, would require a further substantial increase in the level

[1] *The Economist*, 4th December 1954.

of pensions. To remove 806,000[1] (80%) of retirement pensioners from the clientele of the National Assistance Board would have required in December 1954 an addition of about 20s. to the then standard pension (32s. 6d.). Some saving would be made on National Assistance if the Board's function were limited to meeting exceptional needs, but the pensions bill would have to be greatly increased immediately and corresponding increases would be added in the future. As it is, the much smaller increases in pensions which in fact were granted in December 1954 of 7s. 6d. single and 11s. for a couple, are estimated to cost £80m. in the first full year, rising to £130m. in twenty-five years' time. This latter estimate is somewhat unrealistic in any case because no one can suppose that there will be no further increases in pension benefits before 1979.

In so far as such increases only reflect upward movements of prices and do not represent in real terms improved benefits, the burden upon the Exchequer is no greater since the inflation of benefits is matched by the inflation of taxable income. If, on the other hand, as seems likely, pensions are allowed to rise with changing notions of what constitutes 'subsistence' in a period when living standards are rising for the rest of the working population, the added cost will be a real one, enlarged each time uncovered benefits are conferred upon present and future pensioners.

The allocation of more real resources to the needs of the elderly does not necessarily mean that a greater proportion of the national income is transferred to them. If at the same time as the claims of the old grow, the national product can be increased at the rate experienced in recent years, and if the needs of the old receive priority in allocating social expenditure, it should be possible to meet the real cost of pensions and other services for the elderly without any undue strain on the economy. But these are very large assumptions both about future prosperity and the determination of social priorities, and the Phillips Committee while accepting them was at pains to point out the magnitude of the commitments now being entered into on behalf of future generations of tax-payers. Already, before the last[2] increases in pension rates were made, the

---

[1] Appendix VI, National Assistance Board Annual Report, 1954, Cmd. 9530.

[2] December 1954 to take effect from April 1955.

Government Actuary estimated that the expenditure of the National Insurance Fund will rise from £535m. in 1954–5 to £917m. in 1979,[1] by which time if the contributions of the Exchequer supplement is unaltered, the deficit which will have to be met to balance income and expenditure will amount to £364m. About two-thirds of this expenditure will be on retirement pensions, and indeed already, while the total fund still shows a small surplus, expenditure on pensions is substantially more than that part of the insurance contribution assigned for this purpose.[2] Even if the proportion which the claims of the elderly make on total resources is not increased, the magnitude of the transfer payments which will have to be made to them will involve heavy fiscal burdens. Not only will the cost of National Insurance pensions have to be met, but also expenditure has risen, and will no doubt be further enlarged, by the cost of civil service pensions and the assumption of deficits in superannuation schemes (e.g. that of the teachers). This expenditure together with the spread of tax concessions to occupational pension schemes, may generate formidable budgetary problems, not least of which will be conflicting claims for different kinds of social expenditure.

While we are enjoying an expansion of national income, and while the ratio of pensioners to workers is more favourable than it will be in future, it would seem prudent to try to do everything to encourage a greater volume of saving and investment to strengthen the economy to meet future claims. Can this be done by continuing the present National Insurance scheme of retirement pensions?

BACK TO BEVERIDGE

In favour of the retention of social insurance it may be said that it is established, familiar, and acceptable and that contractual rights have been created which it would be hard to revoke. By linking contribution and benefits it imposes some restraint on unreasonable pressure for higher payments, and the personal contribution record brings home to each individual his responsibilities in helping to provide for the foresee-

---

[1] These estimates may be too high if little or no unemployment is experienced, and constant rather than declining mortality at high ages takes place.
[2] Cmd. 9333, para. 161, p. 42.

able risks to continuity of income which he may encounter. The compulsory collection of weekly contributions probably adds to the net volume of savings and is a tax to which every-one is accustomed. The adoption of a flat rate of benefit in-volves neither the cost nor the unpopularity which arises from detailed inquiries into individual circumstances. The use of the concept of insurance, though in fact the National Insurance scheme departs materially from the practice of private insur-ance, can be held to be psychologically important in establish-ing a right to claim benefit without an investigation of means.

One of the principal justifications of the National Insurance scheme is that its comprehensive and compulsory nature serves an important social purpose apart from its practical value in conveniently gathering an ear-marked tax. The Beveridge Report stated, 'It has been found to accord best with the senti-ments of the British people that in insurance organized by the community by the use of compulsory powers each individual should stand in on the same terms.'[1] Social insurance schemes, because their conditions are 'the same for all', may be supported along with 'free'[2] social services as an instrument for reducing social barriers as well as relieving want.

DISADVANTAGES OF SOCIAL INSURANCE

What are regarded as the disadvantages of social insurance will depend upon how far some of the claims made above in its favour are accepted as true. Some of the advantages claimed could be maintained under a different system. For example, the link between contribution and benefit could be secured by a special social security tax collected through the existing machinery of P.A.Y.E.

The flat-rate system of benefits and contributions was ad-mitted in the Beveridge Report to be a very blunt instrument. In the case of uniform benefits the cost of subsistence, especially in relation to rents, varies widely between individuals and dis-tricts and has been particularly distorted by the operation of the Rent Restriction Acts. A flat-rate benefit can never pro-vide a subsistence payment for every beneficiary without an

[1] The Beveridge Report, p. 13.
[2] 'Free' that is in the sense of not being paid for at the use of or in relation to the amount used.

extravagant use of available resources since it must 'over-provide' for some in order to provide adequately for others.

The flat rate of contribution is equally unsatisfactory. It is a regressive tax which bears most hardly upon lower paid workers, and any move to raise contributions to help to finance better benefits is limited by this consideration. An increasing proportion of the total cost of insurance benefits will have to be made from general taxation in any case to take account of back-service charges created by paying the full rate of pension to those who have had no opportunity to make the corresponding contributions. Already, therefore, the resemblance of the National Insurance scheme to what is ordinarily meant by insurance has become rather faint. Is it worth preserving the façade of insurance by using the terminology associated with private insurance where contributions are funded and bear a direct relationship to risks covered?

Mr. Alan Peacock[1] and others have demonstrated the misunderstandings which arise from a policy that appears to treat National Insurance finances as though they could be separated from the rest of fiscal policy. Also apart from economic consequences, the methods used to present the financial position of the National Insurance funds creates what Dr. Abel-Smith[2] has called 'an accounting smoke screen', which misleads the public about the realities of benefit costs and the resources available to meet them. A specific contribution may be useful (though an ear-marked tax would serve the same purpose) in making contributors appreciative of the fact that there is no bottomless public purse to finance benefits, but the present method of presenting National Insurance accounts is likely to have an opposite effect, since it may appear that there are large reserve funds available to underwrite benefits.

There are other disadvantages in using the concept of insurance. Detailed contribution records have to be kept for every insured person and claims checked against them and this involves an elaborate and quite expensive piece of administrative machinery absorbing scarce manpower. Since by definition the National Insurance scheme is meant to include every citizen and national assistance payments are available to meet the needs of anyone who renders himself ineligible for benefit, it

---

[1] *Economics of Social Insurance*, A. T. Peacock.
[2] *Reform of Social Security*, B. Abel-Smith.

may be questioned whether individual record keeping in a uniform benefit scheme is a profitable exercise.

A social insurance scheme tends to be less flexible than a system of social benefits financed by a social security tax or from general taxation. 'Rights' have been created to a named level of benefits or age of retirement and it is difficult to make very frequent adjustments of the scheme to meet changing circumstances and to avoid binding future generations to provisions which may become inappropriate.

These disadvantages however may be outweighed by other considerations. Beveridge[1] and others have insisted that the British people are attached to the contributory principle. Dr. Hagenbuch[2] says, 'People have got it into their heads that insurance benefits are something they can claim unashamedly; they have a right to them because they have contributed. They have also got it into their heads that free benefits are immoral.' If this is so, the British people are certainly not consistent in their attachment to these views. There has been no general outcry against the immorality of free cash family allowances, for example, quite apart from free health and education services.

Does the provision of National Insurance pensions irrespective of means really do much to equalize social status and income among the retired? The existence of occupational and private pension schemes still creates as great a range of incomes among the retired as among the rest of the population. In the case of sickness or unemployment insurance there are both practical and social reasons for including everyone in one scheme. 'Good' lives (i.e. those not likely to draw benefit frequently) as well as 'bad' need to be enrolled to spread risks more widely than would be the case in a scheme confined to contributors in the lowest income groups. In the payment of sickness and unemployment benefits also there is a lateral redistribution of resources as between the sick and the well, the employed and the unemployed among all income groups, and it is socially valuable that there should be this pooling of risks and assumption of responsibility for the less fortunate. It is doubtful whether these arguments apply with equal force to old age benefits where the

---

[1] The Beveridge Report, para. 21, pp. 11–12.
[2] 'The Rationale of the Social Services', W. Hagenbuch, *Lloyds Bank Review*, July 1953, p. 14.

intention is that each man should build up by his contributions a certain future claim to benefit for himself which is then drawn as long as he lives.

Whether or not the National Insurance scheme is maintained in its present form, the commitments already undertaken for current and future pensions are ineluctable. Once persons of older ages were admitted to full pension rights in a scheme in which contributions were only adequate for future benefits for age 16 entrants, a heavy deficit was bound to emerge and grow with every increase in pension rates. There is nothing unexpected about this. Present retirement pension claims could only be reduced by letting pension rates lag behind rising prices, thus decreasing their purchase power. Such a reduction of living standards for the elderly is unlikely to be acceptable to public opinion and the votes of six million pensioners could be exercised against it. But it might be possible, if it were thought desirable, to try to limit pension liabilities so that they are not increased beyond commitments already undertaken. To find ways of effecting this the amendment or even total abandonment of social insurance may be advisable.

The amendments which have been proposed to improve the National Insurance scheme are of two kinds, those which seek to reduce costs either by increasing contributions or limiting benefits, and those which aim at a greater incentive to earning and saving. The Phillips Committee,[1] for example, suggested that when an improvement in benefits is made the higher contribution demanded should not only be appropriate to an age 16 entrant into the scheme, but also a further sum should be required, sufficient on the average for contributors of all ages, to meet part of the cost of the increased benefit. Suggestions to limit the cost of benefits have included raising the minimum retirement age by three or more years, making the retirement age the same for women and men, and paying differential benefits to pensioners over 70 (65 for women).

HIGHER MINIMUM PENSION AGES

To raise minimum retirement ages to say 68 years for men and 63 years for women would not significantly reduce costs unless it could be assumed that most workers of these ages could

[1] Cmd. 9333, pp. 45–6.

remain in or find alternative employment. Half a million are postponing retirement already, but what of the rest? As pointed out above[1] many of the remainder, probably between 50–60%, being unfit for continued employment, would draw a sickness benefit equal in value to a retirement pension. Others, willing to work, might not be able to find suitable employment and would receive unemployment benefit, which would have to be extended indefinitely for them if necessary. It may be possible to change radically the pattern of working and retiring among older employees over a period of years, but all the present indications are that full-time employment cannot easily be made available for a very much larger number of older persons than are already postponing retirement. Though any voluntary postponement of retirement is valuable both by reducing pension costs and by adding to the national output, only a limited relief to insurance funds can be expected by compulsorily raising pension ages, and it would be difficult to avoid some hardships as a result of such a change. A compulsory lengthening of working life in order to reduce pension costs would be regarded by some workers as a reduction in their standard of living since they would have to work and contribute longer for their pension rights.

EQUAL PENSION AGES FOR MEN AND WOMEN

Restoring parity between pension ages for both sexes has everything to commend it except that it would not make substantial savings to pension funds. There is no reason why there should not be equality between the sexes in this respect, especially as women have the longer expectation of life. By reason of the allowance for a dependent wife of any age which men pensioners may draw, and which is payable at the same rate as a married woman's retirement pension on her husband's insurance, the same payments would have to be made to married women even if they did not work between the ages of 60 and 63 or whatever other minimum pension was fixed. The only small savings which might be made would be at the expense of spinsters and married women insured in their own right.

[1] See Chapter III.

PENSIONS

The over-seventies (over sixty-five for women) have always been treated differently from pensioners under seventy in the National Insurance scheme and in other pension arrangements. Non-contributory pensions (1908) were paid only to those satisfying conditions of residence and limited means who were over seventy, and have thus remained up to the present time. Pensions for the over-seventies in National Insurance have never been retirement pensions since no condition of ceasing work or reporting earnings has ever been applied during more than the first five years after minimum pension age. In 1951 an attempt was made to raise pensions only for those over-seventy, but the proposal was extended during debates to include those who had already reached 65 (60 for women) by October 1951, and finally pensions and other insurance benefits were restored to a uniform level in 1952.

Any proposal to raise pension ages or to discriminate between the over-seventies and under-seventies evokes a protest from men who work in trades where continued occupation in later years is unlikely and which leaves men often physically impaired for alternative employment. There is certainly something to be said for applying any improvements in pension benefits to the over-seventies, whose capacity for self support is in general likely to be less than that of younger pensions. But individual adaptation to the process of ageing is so widely varied that if lower pensions were paid to the under-seventies, more of them might have to seek supplementation of their pensions from the Assistance Board.

The possible savings which could result from a differential pension for the over-seventies is limited by the fact that the greater part of pension expenditure (3,269,000 out of 4,310,000 pensions at December 1953) is already paid on account of those who are more than five years older than minimum pension ages.

PENSIONS AND INCENTIVES

The field for savings to pension funds which might be made by varying minimum pension ages is thus somewhat narrow. An alternative approach would be to try to redraft pension regulations to give maximum incentive to all kinds of employment beyond pension ages without withholding pensions from those who seek work in the five years following retirement. The cost of paying pensions to those at present working after pension ages would initially increase costs, but if the increments scheme (which would have no further purpose) were abolished, future saving would nearly balance the increase over a period.[1] If the effect were to be a stimulation of voluntary postponement of retirement this would obviously be desirable. Unfortunately there is little evidence to show whether this would happen or not. In inquiries made into reasons for retirement those interviewed have volunteered few comments on the incentive or disincentive effects of the retirement condition and the increments device. If fixed retirement rules were relaxed so that fit older men had a genuine choice of retiring or continuing, and if more suitable jobs could be made available for older workers, generally, the abolition of the retirement conditions might be a useful development. Because of the limits to extending employment for the old which exist at present, however, there is no certainty that removing the retirement condition attached to National Insurance pensions would result in any immediate widespread increase in post-pension age employment. A stronger argument for paying pensions to all on reaching the minimum age is that to withhold them discriminates unfairly against the National Insurance pensioner as compared with those who belong to other kinds of occupational pension schemes. The need for a retirement condition to get older workers out of the labour market is totally inappropriate in a period of over-full employment, and trade unions are quite strong enough to deal with any dangers, should they arise, from the competition of the pension-subsidized labour of older workers.

Two objections continue to be raised against the removal of the retirement condition and the abolition of any earnings limit for pensioners. The first is that it is wrong in principle to pay wages and pensions at the same time, quite apart from the practical difficulties which may arise, the idea being that those who can work have no need of pension partly financed by the

[1] There is another objection to the increments scheme. In so far as those who postpone retirement create some savings for pension funds, they subsidize those who retire promptly. If early retirement was always due to poor health this might be reasonable, but those who retire at conventional retirement ages are in many cases those who have an occupational pension also.

taxpayer. It is difficult to believe in this as an inviolable principle when it has already been discarded in the case of retirement pensioners over seventy (over sixty-five for women) and when freedom is allowed to pensioners of other schemes to have both pensions and earnings at the same time. The connection between contribution and benefit has become somewhat tenuous in these other schemes as well as in National Insurance pensions, so that it cannot be said that in the case of occupational pensions beneficiaries have a right to their pensions irrespective of retirement, simply because they have 'paid' for them.

Arising out of this reluctance to pay pensions and wages simultaneously is the further objection that people might be better off in the years immediately after pension age than at any other period of their lives; their family responsibilities are over, and they have their full earnings augmented by a pension. Would this necessarily be undesirable? If during the period of say 65–70 years a man could have basic pension and earnings, this would give him a valuable last opportunity for savings to make adequate provision for his remaining years. It might reduce the numbers of over-seventies who have to go at present to the Assistance Board.

The second objection is that far from acting as a stimulus to full-time employment the right to draw a pension without retirement would lead older workers at present in full employment to take part-time employment and a pension. The same fear has prevented the raising of the present earnings limit for pensioners. Part-time employment is not very widespread for older men, but if more older men did take part-time employment and a pension, would this be an unsatisfactory trend? If part-time employment became customary for most older workers as the accepted way of matching lessening powers to reduced exertion and earnings, the more gradual exit from industry which resulted might well be more satisfactory than the present alternative of full-time work or complete retirement. Professor Cairncross has suggested in a reservation about some of the recommendations of the Phillips Committee, 'From the point of view of a happy and prosperous society it is desirable that men of 65–70 should be free to choose not whether to retire but how much to retire; far more desirable than that every able-bodied man should postpone retirement until the last possible moment.'

128

If part-time working became a widespread habit for older workers, the total volume of employment and earnings might be certainly no less and possibly greater than the sum of full and part-time employment among older persons at present. The temptation to evasion of the earnings limit would be removed and the administration of pension benefits would be greatly simplified.

Thus amendments to National Insurance pensions regulations could mitigate to a limited extent the cost of benefits and make the provision work more equitably, but they cannot be counted upon to alter very significantly the major financial burdens. Can anything further be done by encouraging those below pension age to provide more effectively by taxes, contributions or other savings for their own old age?

The expansion of occupational pension schemes has shown one way. A supplementary scheme associated with employment can enable people to have more than the basic retirement pension in old age and can reduce the need to raise pensions or pay National Assistance grants. At present these pension schemes are confined to certain occupations and business enterprises only, and since they are favoured by tax concessions some provision seems indicated for those as yet uncovered by this type of scheme.

It would be difficult to enforce the organization of occupational schemes to cover all kinds of employment. But no less favourable terms could be offered in some kind of National or Joint Pension Fund available to those willing to contribute for more than the basic insurance pension, and who had no facilities for this type of saving through their place of employment. Employers not able or willing to provide their own schemes could pay contributions on behalf of their employees into the Fund. Apart from these occupations which present difficulties for the organization of pension schemes, and for whom the National Pension fund could be a substitute, occupational pension schemes could be encouraged to become as general throughout industry as other forms of welfare provision are already. Subject to the approval of the Inland Revenue authorities, employers could be free to vary the conditions of their own scheme, and some would provide more generously than others, thus retaining pension provision as an asset to man-power recruitment. If most firms had some kind of pension scheme, with a minority providing through a National Pension Fund, the contributions set aside from current income in so far as they represented additional savings would put future generations in a stronger position to pay pension claims as they fall due without too great a strain on their resources.

The Millard Tucker Report did not question the value of occupational pension schemes and recommended extension of tax concessions to pension provision for other groups (e.g. the self-employed) at present excluded. The Phillips Committee also gave its blessing to the expansion of occupational schemes. Doubts have been raised however in some quarters about whether the savings accumulated in occupational schemes really create any net addition to savings or whether they only replace savings which might otherwise have been made in a different form. It has also been questioned whether it is true, as the Phillips Committee maintained, that 'normally there is some equivalence between the benefits enjoyed by the pensioner and the income which his savings have allowed to be generated'. This is not true of non-contributory pensions in public service or in industry. Even in contributory schemes some unfunded deficits may be met by the employer and passed on to the public in the shape of higher prices. An objection may be raised in relation to all occupational pension schemes viewed as a method of providing pensions other than through national finances, which is that a substantial part of their cost is shifted through the manipulation of wages and prices on to the employees concerned and on to the community at large.

On balance the growth of approved occupational pension schemes appears to be a useful way of collecting present savings for investment to meet future pension claims, but the wider economic implications of such a development need to be more closely studied and assessed before it can be claimed that this is the best way of making provision for old age, on the ground that it is at once more adequate for pensioners and less onerous for the rest of the community.

An alternative to encouraging the erection of a superstructure of occupational pensions on the basic retirement pensions would be to recognize frankly that in a scheme which seeks to cover the whole population, wide differences in income during working life call for a pension scheme which broadly relates contributions and benefits to varying levels of income. The

National Insurance scheme with its flat rate of contribution and benefit results in a heavy tax on the lowest paid worker and a benefit inadequate for subsistence. A proportional contribution from both employer and employee would allow higher contributions to earn higher benefits and yet avoid the hardship of demanding higher contributions from the poorest workers. When prices and wages rose contributions would rise automatically and this would afford a partial protection against inflationary pressure. If a gradual transition were made from the present insurance scheme to a national superannuation scheme with differential contributions and benefits, no one would have to be left worse off than under the former scheme. It would be necessary therefore, as is the case in the American O.A.S.I., to mitigate the strict proportionality of the scheme with a basic minimum benefit and a maximum limit for earnings on which a tax or contribution would be levied. Some supplement from the Exchequer would be needed to guarantee the basic minimum for those with poor earnings records and insufficient contributions.

The pay-roll tax on employers would probably have to be higher under this type of scheme (a ratio of 5% to 3% for employers and employees has been suggested) than their present contributions, and it is doubtful whether either employers or employees would want also to continue their occupational pension schemes. If participation in a national superannuation scheme were voluntary some workers who felt adequately covered already would exercise their option to stay out of the scheme. If it were compulsory it is probable that some occupational schemes would have to be wound up as neither employers nor employees might be willing to set aside so much current income.

Employers might object that the heavier cost involved for them, and which they expect to pass on in prices, would adversely affect the competitiveness of their prices in overseas markets. Nor do employees collectively as yet look with any favour on percentage schemes; the Trades Union Congress had already registered a firm rejection of the idea of differential contributions and benefits. Nevertheless such a proposal merits further examination and it seems regrettable that the Phillips Committee did not explore this possibility and offer some calculation of its possible cost. If a proportional superannuation scheme led to a very much larger subvention from the Exchequer than is contemplated for existing schemes, or if it laid so heavy a compulsory levy on employers that their costs were seriously affected little would be gained, but it appears likely that some variant on a proportional scheme such as the Swiss or American schemes could be evolved to meet British needs more satisfactorily than the present inadequate flat-rate insurance scheme. If a proportional insurance scheme were adopted which enabled us to seize the opportunity at present afforded by full employment and rising living standards to set aside a greater volume of savings, the accumulation of new capital assets thus made possible would put taxpayers of the future in a better position to meet the obligations which our present policies will inevitably lay upon them. No pension programme can be wholly protected from inflationary trends, but such a scheme while it might make greater demands upon the present working population by way of taxation and contributions, would be preferable to an indefinite future prospect of inadequate pensions buttressed by National Assistance. If a larger proportion of the cost of insurance benefits has to be met in future from contributors rather than from the Exchequer, there is every reason for distributing the incidence of these costs more equitably. A proportional scheme with minimum and maximum limits of benefit or a scheme financed by direct taxation, would be fairer than a uniform level of contributions as under National Insurance.

Since this chapter was written, the recommendation of the Millard Tucker committee to remove the distinction between employed persons providing for pensions out of untaxed income, and the self-employed who are unable to benefit from schemes sponsored by employers, has been accepted. By the Finance Act of 1956, those who are not members of a pension scheme to which employers contribute can set aside a fixed proportion of current income, which may be deducted from gross earnings before tax liability is calculated, provided these sums are irrevocably invested in pension provision.

The percentage of earnings which can be set aside is strictly limited, but the conditions can be varied for older men who have only a short period in which to make provision for retirement. Retirement may be at any time between 60 and 70 years, or even before 60 years in special cases, e.g. ill-health or where it is customary in certain occupations to retire before 60.

These new arrangements have everything to commend them in so far as they remove the indefensible disadvantages to which the self-employed have been subjected as compared with members of occupational pension schemes. But the flexibility of the proposed schemes and the generous tax treatment offered to those who elect to participate emphasizes again the inadequacy of the rigid and limited National Insurance pensions which is all that is available to many workers.

CHAPTER V

HOUSING

THOUGH the poverty experienced by the elderly as their
earning capacity fails has been greatly reduced in recent years
by pension schemes, there are other kinds of needs the lack of
which impoverish the elderly, even when their cash resources
are sufficient to purchase a modest standard of living. They may
become destitute of care and accommodation. The Public Assistance institutions of local authorities took into their care increasingly after 1929 old people who were frail or sick. Apart
from those who needed nursing and medical care there were
others who, though technically 'ambulant', were unable to live
independently in a household of their own, and lacked relatives
to care for them. By 1939 these institutions had become largely
infirmaries for the elderly sick who were chronically ill, and
they admitted not only rate-aided patients but those for whom
relatives were able to pay. For frail old people without homes
and care the authorities endeavoured to provide accommodation of a permanent kind outside the institutions, though some
part of those old buildings often had to be used for emergency
and residual care. Before the war it had become part of the
accepted duties of local authorities to provide, wherever possible, separate Homes for old people. At first there were mainly
large Homes with perhaps up to two or three hundred residents,
but subsequently converted properties and new Homes have
been designed to provide a more congenial atmosphere for very
much smaller numbers. The criterion for admission to these
Homes now is not need of money but need of care.

Whether older people can continue to maintain a separate
household or whether they must rely in whole or in part upon
accommodation and services provided for them by others, is
another important aspect of dependency which must be

considered in relation to the increasing numbers of older persons in our population. Some older people can continue to live quite independently in their own homes or with relatives and need no special help. Some may be able to continue to maintain a household only if they have either specially suitable housing, or domiciliary welfare services taken to them, others who find the housing and domestic arrangements which are available to them beyond their capacity to manage, may have to be provided for in some kind of group care. It is important to consider housing, domiciliary services and communal care together because a co-ordinated policy in the provision of all three is the only way to make the most effective use of them all, both from the point of view of the needs of older householders and from that of the cost to the community.

At present the great majority of older people remain in private households, either their own or those of relatives, and only a very small minority live in any kind of group or communal care.[1] It is difficult to calculate precisely how many live in any kind of Home, because in addition to Homes provided by local authorities, some national and local voluntary organizations maintain small old people's Homes.

In 1946 just over 1% of the population of England and Wales of pensionable age were in Public Assistance institutions.[2] Of these 62,957 persons thus maintained, over 60% (39,208) were in wards or establishments for the sick or mentally infirm, so that only a very small number (23,749) of older persons who were not sick were accommodated in Public Assistance institutions. Dr. Sheldon found in Wolverhampton in 1947 that among a random sample of persons[3] of pensionable age, 98% were living in a private home and only 2% in some form of group care. The proportion appears to vary in different parts of the country but is nowhere likely to be more than 5%. The 1% sample tables of the 1951 Census record 67,000 persons in Great Britain as living in Homes for old people or as permanently disabled persons. The elderly sick or mentally ill are not included in this figure since they are now shown separately as hospital inmates, but the number is

---

[1] Separate accommodation within one building, as for example in flats or almshouses, is included here as forms of private households, and by group care is meant the kind of provision where all meals and domestic services are common for a group of residents.

[2] Rowntree, *op. cit.*, p. 18.   [3] Sheldon, *op. cit.*, p. 16.

increased by the inclusion of some younger disabled persons. Even so this only represents 1% of persons of pensionable age, or if a further 49,500 persons of pensionable age resident in hotels and boarding houses (with more than ten rooms) are added, the total is still less than 2% of all people in this age group. It appears that a slightly higher proportion, though still a very small percentage of all old people, are being cared for in Homes now than formerly. The present numbers do not measure the full need, however, since most Homes, both statutory and voluntary, have a waiting list of would-be residents. The type of accommodation provided, the relaxation of irksome rules, and the different atmosphere in which residential care for old people is now provided in small Homes, have undoubtedly removed most of the old terrors of being 'taken away'.

The need for communal care is likely to be greater among the more elderly, but even so it seems to be a very limited demand. In an inquiry among 2,230 persons over 70 years of age in Birmingham in 1947,[1] 374 (18%) expressed an urgent desire to move from their existing accommodation, but only 2% of these inquired for a Home or Hostel. A more recent inquiry into living accommodation among a hundred old persons aged over 70 and living alone[2] elicited unprompted inquiries from nine old ladies about the possibility of entering a Home, though five other persons volunteered adverse opinions about this kind of care. The inquiries and waiting lists for existing Homes show that more residential care probably needs to be created for some very frail elderly persons who are without relatives to care for them. It seems reasonable to assume, however, from the many studies and enquiries already made, and from the unanimous opinion of those constantly working with older people,[3] that old persons in general prefer to remain in their own homes wherever this is possible and that many of them struggle to do so under circumstances which might well daunt younger householders.[4]

In some cases the desire to go into a Home arises from inability to cope any longer with unsatisfactory housing. Old people, like other younger householders, can be found in accommodation which is on the top floor of three- or four-storey

---

[1] Appendix III below. [2] *Over Seventy*, *op. cit.*, p. 87.
[3] See, e.g., 'Memorandum on Housing Elderly People', National Old People's Welfare Committee.
[4] *Op. cit.*, p. 142.

buildings or which has shared outside sanitation and other in-conveniences. In these circumstances suitable housing rather than a place in a residential Home may be the older person's true need.

HOUSING CONDITIONS OF OLD PEOPLE

There is no evidence to show that older people are in general any worse housed than the rest of the population, but local conditions in this respect vary widely. After an inquiry in seven different areas into housing conditions among old people, and the length of time which they had lived in the same house, the Rowntree Committee[1] concluded: 'The committee are of the opinion that in spite of some evidence to the contrary it would on the whole be wrong to assume that old people are worse housed than the average of their class and that the many cases quoted of bad housing conditions are a criticism of general housing conditions in the areas investigated rather than an in-dication that old people occupy an unduly high proportion of unsatisfactory houses.' In the inquiry in Birmingham,[2] 46·2% of old people's household had no bath as compared with 37% of all households without baths,[3] but this reflects the type and age of housing occupied by the elderly. A comparison of sharing kitchen facilities (stoves and sinks) showed that 14% of all households lacked the exclusive use of these according to the 1951 Census, while 15·8% of older persons were to be found sharing kitchens in the Birmingham inquiry. This latter inquiry was among persons aged 70 and over, among whom there is a higher proportion of widowed persons and fewer married couples than in the whole group of men and women of pension-able age, and thus there is more sharing of accommodation and fewer independent households in separate dwellings. In so far as this inquiry is representative it does not seem to indicate very much more inconvenience among the old from having to share amenities than that suffered by the rest of the population except in relation to bathing facilities. There are of course wide regional and local variations in housing amenities for old people; far more old people in London for example live in tenements, flats and single rooms, and in some areas old people may be

[1] Rowntree, *op. cit.*, p. 1. [2] Appendix III below.
[3] Census of Great Britain, 1951, One Per Cent Tables.

suffering worse housing than the average for their area. Among a hundred old people over seventy and living alone in the inquiry referred to above,[1] 80% had no bathroom provision and 9% shared a bath, as compared with 62% of all households in the borough with no exclusive use of a fixed bath. 53% of the old people were sharing lavatories and in 33 instances they were outside the house, as compared with 36% of all households sharing in this area.

The lack of a bathroom may not be so important to some old people who have never enjoyed this amenity, but certainly outdoor and shared sanitation is a cause of constant discomfort and inconvenience and constitutes a real hardship. In the Birmingham inquiry, where 46·2% of households visited had no bathroom, this was not so often complained about by the old themselves, though it occasioned unfavourable comment from children and relatives living in those households, but the inconvenience of outdoor sanitation which was all that was available in 59·9% of old people's homes, was cited very frequently as a problem. Clearly second- or third-floor accommodation and shared kitchen or sanitary facilities, though by no means exclusively the housing problems of older people, press more hardly upon them than upon younger persons who are physically more able to cope with these inconveniences.

UNDERCROWDING

Some older persons however are over-provided with housing in the sense that they have more room than they need[2] and the upkeep of their accommodation may impose an onerous and unwanted domestic burden. Fitting the numbers and size and structure of households to the existing dwellings available is an ever present housing problem.[3] Families have different needs at different periods of time in their history, and if a family

[1] *Over Seventy, op. cit.*, p. 87.

[2] The Ministry of Labour Budget Inquiry (Cmd. 933, p. 71) found that the average number of rooms occupied by old people living alone was 3·6, and by elderly couples 4·5. See also the Annual Report of the National Assistance Board, 1954, which gives the results of an inquiry into circumstances of persons over 80 and living alone. The Board reports 'Among persons over 80 and living alone the great majority were over-housed rather than under-housed' (p. 17).

[3] Even sub-letting spare rooms is discouraged by the fact that the receipt of income from this may result in a man's assistance payment being reduced.

sized house has been the dwelling used, there is likely to come a time when married children establish their own households and the old parents are left with more living space than they need.

Whole areas of new housing estates are experiencing these circumstances now in some districts. These estates were developed to accommodate young families, many of which were moved from unsuitable housing in slum or near-slum properties in the central areas of our cities. Not only was family housing provided but other kinds of expensive community equipment, all related to the needs of young families, were developed in these areas. Older couples are now left under-using the much-needed housing but with a right, since housing authorities are loath to use compulsion, to remain where they are. Many housing authorities try to persuade such tenants to accept transfers if they have other more suitable accommodation to offer them. Unfortunately, the number of bungalows or maisonettes built so far is limited and this alternative is not always available. Even if it were, there is the difficulty that people may not want to move. They may have become attached to their district by all kinds of associations which are important to them, and some very considerable inducement would have to be offered to persuade them at their age to embark upon the inconvenience and expense of moving,[1] and to accept the disruption of social life which may be involved in transferring to an unfamiliar district. The inducement most likely to be effective would be the offer of accommodation with an equal standard of amenities, but which was smaller and cheaper and not very far from the tenants' present home. Unfortunately the high cost of post-war building means that an old person's bungalow costs nearly as much as a house to erect, and even a subsidized rent is not particularly cheap compared with the rent which may be paid for a pre-war house.

Local authority housing departments moreover are not the landlords of many old people, who are not in property owned or constructed by the authority, since many of them set up house before much local authority building took place. (Though it is true that as some cities have taken over for re-development large central areas within their boundaries they have become

---

[1] Some Local Housing Authorities contribute to removal expenses in order to encourage the transfer of tenants.

the owners of a good deal of older property and hence land-lords of many elderly tenants.) Where older persons are in private property as tenants they may have no incentive to move from housing which is larger than they need. Their rents are probably controlled at lower levels than those of the local council's old people's bungalows and they are protected tenants, an element of security which is particularly reassuring to elderly householders. Moreover, some older tenants have their rents paid in full by the National Assistance Board, and even if it were offered to them, a cheaper rent would simply mean a reduction in their assistance grant. The power of the National Assistance Board to pay rents in full has been a potent factor in making it possible for many old people to keep an independent household, but it is not a wholly unmixed blessing since it sometimes keeps them in a family sized house long after they need it.

MOBILITY OF OLDER HOUSEHOLDERS

However some old people are found to be willing to move, a number which, bearing in mind their circumstances, is perhaps surprisingly high. In the Birmingham inquiry[1] 18% of the over 70's visited urgently wanted to move from their existing housing, and this percentage was as high as 28% among old people living in the inner rings of the city. The most frequent single reason given for their wanting to move was that the house was too large (27%) and a further 4·3% said that their house was too expensive. 7% wanted to move because they were overcrowded and sharing accommodation. Whenever they have suitable smaller units of housing available local housing authorities are very willing to re-house older persons who can give up family sized accommodation. Very often, however, the landlord is only waiting for the old tenant to die in order to get possession of the property and sell it. Authorities find it difficult to disturb existing arrangements and rehouse older persons, if they are unable to secure at the same time a tenancy for a family on their waiting list. The economies of house space which can be effected by transfers[2] have been demonstrated and are well known, but there are these very considerable difficulties in the

[1] See Appendix I.
[2] A close of 34 cottages each consisting of one room, a large bed alcove with window, kitchenette and bathroom was built by Hornsey Borough

way of moving tenants more freely, quite apart from the reluctance to move of tenants themselves.

A second major problem which has to be faced in housing programmes is that the siting both of family housing and of any special housing for old people must take into account the fact that families need to be near each other, even though they may not wish to live under the same roof. Families tend to cluster in districts if housing is available. Dr. Sheldon[1] found in Wolverhampton that many old people who might be classed as living alone, since they were alone in a separate dwelling, actually lived in a web of close family care and help. Defining living near as the 'distance within which a hot meal can be carried from one house to another without reheating it', Sheldon found that 29·7% of his sample had relatives living near. In 4% of cases relatives actually lived next door, 5·9% had relatives within three houses away, 4·0% lived in the same street, and 7% within five minutes' walking distance.[2] In no less than 20·5% of this group of old people, the old and their relatives had really fused their households so that, although living in separate houses, they functioned as one household. This eminently satisfactory state of affairs, where families can render reciprocal services during illness and other family crises and during old age, can only be maintained with great difficulty if physical proximity is destroyed. Housing development in the last twenty years has tended to move the young and their families out to the periphery of towns and to leave the old at some distance from their families.[3] Now that their turn comes to move the old may be offered a bungalow or maisonette on the opposite side of the city from where their children live. Time and the cost of bus fares intervene to make it less easy for daughters to slip round and do some cleaning or washing for their mothers, or send children to tea at granny's when they have to be out themselves. In these circumstances a new well-equipped bungalow may seem attractive until the prospective older tenant is taken

Council. Of the tenants chosen, 6 left 6-roomed houses, 11 left 5-roomed houses, 11 left 4-roomed houses and 4 left 3-roomed houses. The cost was £27,000 and the rents are 12s. 6d. including rates.

[1] Sheldon, *op. cit.*, p. 16.

[2] See also Peter Townsend, 'The Family Life of Old People', *The Sociological Review*, Vol. 3, No. 2, December 1955.

[3] The development of New Towns also tends to separate families. See, e.g., The National Corporation for the Care of Old People Annual Report, 1955, p. 10.

to see it. Then the distance from relatives, the unfamiliar district, the unmade road, the remoteness from shops and post office chills enthusiasm, and, returning to all that is familiar, the older person accompanies his or her refusal with some such reflection as 'You can't transplant old trees'.

Mixed development, that is the siting of individual or small groups of dwellings suitable for older persons among other kinds of houses and flats for families, might do much to secure a limited but effective mobility of tenants. It is one thing to ask a tenant to give up a house and move to an entirely new district and another to move him a few streets away in the same district so that many social habits can continue undisturbed. There also is the possibility of keeping families near each other in a district which has a variety of types and sizes of dwelling. Some housing authorities who have developed large estates of three-bedroom houses, are trying now to diversify these areas and to introduce, among other things, some smaller dwellings suitable for old people. The possibility of adding to some existing housing a 'granny plus' flatlet (for example, there is room for these to be attached to corner houses) is being considered by some authorities. The difficulty is that the family whose position on the waiting list gives them first claim to the next house vacant may be a family with no grandmother. Though, if having an elderly relative living with a family increased its 'points' and became an asset in securing a house, perhaps grandmothers might become more in demand! At best mixed development may facilitate the more economical use of living space. At least it will avoid on the one hand creating colonies of old people who feel segregated from the rest of their community, or on the other isolating them at a distance from their relatives.

HOUSING DESIGNED FOR OLD PEOPLE

Between the two Wars very little housing was built specially for older persons. Of the 1,163,000 houses built by local authorities in England and Wales about 4·2% were small dwellings suitable for old people. Hardly any special housing was built privately and thus of 3,150,000 houses built in Great Britain between 1919 and 1939, less than 1·5% was specially designed for the elderly.[1] Out of a total of 42,066 houses and flats built

[1] Rowntree, *op. cit.*, p. 18.

HOUSING

in Liverpool[1] by the local authority up to 1943 only 350 were specially for old people, and a further 389 small flats were suitable though not specially reserved for old people. The whole 739 dwellings amount to 1·7% of all the dwellings built by this local authority, and this was typical of most larger cities' housing programmes.

In the post-war period there has been more building both of bungalows and maisonettes which are suitable for any kind of small household. In view of the very high cost of building and bearing in mind that once constructed this durable capital has to last for a substantial time, it is important to avoid creating single-purpose dwellings. As much flexibility as possible will be needed in housing programmes and it will be an advantage if some smaller dwellings can be used for younger childless couples and other small households where necessary,[2] as well as for old persons.

Between 1945 and 1953 in England and Wales 22,038 permanent one-bedroom houses and 50,846 one-bedroom flats were built by local authorities and New Towns, which represents 6·5% of all their new building in this period, and this proportion has subsequently been raised to about 8%. About 38% of the flats are in London, which reflects the pattern of accommodation for all age groups in that area. These figures are very approximate. All single-bedroom dwellings will not in fact be allocated to old people and a few older persons may have two-bedroom bungalows. In one large Midland city, for example, of approximately 20,000 new municipal properties constructed since 1945, 687 bungalows about half of which are of the bedroom-recess type, have been built for old people, and about 1,256 maisonettes have been constructed which are suitable, though not necessarily exclusively designed, for older tenants. As in most areas there are also almshouses and flatlets and hostels provided by Housing Associations and other voluntary bodies, which in this city provide about another 500 dwellings. It was estimated in 1953 that Housing Societies had provided at least 1,180 flats, flatlets and bungalows in Great Britain[3] and nearly 18,000 people are in almshouses, cottages and flats administered by charitable Societies.

[1] *Old People's Welfare on Merseyside*, E. I. Black and D. B. Reed.
[2] One of every ten households consists of a single person (1951 Census).
[3] 'Housing Memorandum', National Old People's Welfare Committee.

Table XVII shows the number of specially designed and otherwise suitable dwellings for old people in local authority areas in the West Midlands. When this information was given in 1949 fifteen authorities reported plans for future building, and these were again asked to report progress in 1952. Thirteen authorities had begun building and between them had built or were in the course of building another 500 dwellings. Almost all of these were bungalows, except in the case of one large city which had built 1,256 maisonettes some of which will be let to older tenants.

If this development is typical it appears that local authorities are increasingly including in their housing programmes some special provision for elderly tenants, but the provision so far is not nearly sufficient to meet the demand. It is interesting to note, however, that some authorities report a very high rate of refusal among older applicants even when they have been sorted into 'rent-paying capacity'. If their desire for a bungalow in a specified district cannot be met many older tenants will not accept any alternative. As already noted their desire to be near relatives or in a familiar district may be so strong as to offset the attraction of a more suitable type of dwelling in a new district.

No authority in this area reported any attempt to convert large property into flats, a course frequently undertaken by voluntary bodies. The cost of such conversions varies a great deal according to the type of property available, but the average *per capita* cost is £500–700. If no special staff are employed other than a cleaner for stairs and passages, and a reduced rent is allowed to one middle-aged tenant in return for some small services, this kind of conversion can be solvently managed on rents ranging from 15s. to 20s. (For tenants able to pay more some schemes require rents between 30s. and 35s.) Some of the voluntary bodies undertaking this work have been able to secure substantial loans from local Housing Authorities[1] but the Housing Committees of local authorities generally have not been very ready to arrange this kind of conversion of older property. They have argued that the amount of scarce building resources involved in such alteration of existing properties is out of all proportion to the results obtained, and that the same resources which produce eight or ten flatlets for old people could

[1] Housing Act, 1936.

TABLE XVII

Provision of specially designed and suitable dwellings for old people in various authority areas in the West Midlands

Type of local authority area	No. in this area	No. supplying information	Total population 1951	No. of dwellings specially designed for old people				No. of dwellings suitable but not specially designed for old people		No. of authorities which have provided no special dwellings
				Local Authority Housing	Alms-houses *	Other Voluntary bodies *		Local Authority Housing	Voluntary bodies *	
County Boroughs	9	9	2,258,616	Bungalows 1,219 Flats 132	548	Flatlets 158		Flats and maisonettes 1,212	Bungalow and small dwellings 66	0
Non-County Boroughs	20	19	617,774	Bungalows 460 Flats 46	183	Flatlets 38		Flats and maisonettes 264	Flatlets 41	3
Urban District Councils	20	18	487,560	Bungalows 310 Flats 23	75	Bungalows 18		Prefabricated Bungalows 408	Bungalows 68	4
Rural District Council	23	21	507,097	Bungalows 138 Flats 8	132	—		Prefabricated Bungalows 258	Cottages 73	5
All local authorities	72	67	3,871,047	Total Bungalows 2,021 Total Flats 197 Total dwellings 2,218	938	214		2,142	280	12

* This information was provided by local authority housing departments and some voluntary provision may not have been known to them.

be applied to traditional family type house building on new sites to produce accommodation for larger numbers of people urgently in need of it. Much of the detailed planning and subsequent arrangements of a small conversion is undertaken by the unpaid voluntary help of a committee in the case of voluntary bodies, but local authorities cannot count upon such help or delegate their responsibilities once undertaken, and they tend to feel that too much of expensive skilled manpower has to be devoted to planning and managing converted property to make it worthwhile. However, in view of present costs of new building,[1] and of the experience which the voluntary bodies have found of an unsatisfied demand for simpler types of flatlets in small groups, local authorities might look again at the possibility of converting existing house space to the needs of single or widowed older tenants.

Another type of housing suitable for older people are almshouses, where more than 12,000 elderly tenants are still accommodated. Many of these buildings are old and in bad condition but they can be, and are being improved and modernized. With a change of name and some repairs this traditional form of help for old people can still serve a useful purpose.

When we consider special housing for older people we have to remember that our heterogeneous group of older persons will have varying housing requirements which will need to be met by several different kinds of provision.[2] All types of provision, flats, bungalows, hostels, and maisonettes, have some drawbacks. Flats are unsuitable for old people above the first, or at most, the second, floor, unless a lift is provided, which add considerably to costs. In maisonettes older tenants like the ground floor for convenience but almost always complain about the noises which disturb them from overhead. Bungalows are expensive and as the most uneconomical form of horizontal development they add to the problem of the urban sprawl of our larger cities. Hostels may involve problems of reduced independence and privacy.

If, however, old people are consulted about their preferences in housing it is most likely that they will choose 'a nice little bungalow'. This is, of course, a clear case of like choosing like. Most old people are familiar with living in a house and the idea

[1] In 1954 the average cost of one-bedroom flats was £1,344.
[2] See Table XXII.

of something the same, only smaller and with no stairs, seems most suitable to them. In the provinces at any rate the present generation of older people are not yet very familiar with the idea of flatlets or hostels and are unlikely to indicate them as a choice; although in fact this kind of accommodation in independent units within a building always has a waiting list, and there is little evidence of any serious dissatisfaction among those who choose this kind of living arrangement.

One large city tried to get some estimate of the demand for bungalows for old people by public notices requesting those in need of this accommodation to apply to their Housing Department. Between 1946 and 1948 the replies were collected and in all 2,328 applications from persons of pensionable age were completed and registered. Half of the applicants were private tenants, 38% were lodgers, and 9·7% were owner occupiers. 45% of the tenants were in five-roomed houses or larger and 77·8% of the owners also had larger sized houses. This may have been an important reason why they wanted to move. 53% wanted a one-bedroom bungalow as against 47% who inquired for a two-bedroom dwelling. Nearly 40% of the applicants were paying under 10s. a week rent in their existing accommodation, and a further 37% were paying between 10s. and 15s. 49% of the applicants were aged over 70, and of this over 70 group 10% were over 80. About equal numbers of applications were from married couples and single or widowed females, with a very small number from single or widowed old men. Among the over 70's a substantial number (46% of tenants and 56% of owners) had houses of five rooms or more, but among this group a quarter of owners and tenants also wanted to move from three- and four-bedroom houses. In 1953 this same authority had on its waiting list for old people's bungalows 703 applicants of whom 74% were householders and 26% in lodgings and rooms, and the number was much greater a year later. It appears that there are numerous older people not likely to be prevented, either by their age or by the fact of being a protected tenant or even a house owner, from wanting to move if suitable housing is offered to them.

Bungalows on the whole probably prove most suitable for fairly active married couples. They want, and are usually capable of maintaining, an independent household, and a garden or small tasks concerned with the care of property may provide a welcome interest for the retired man. But for the single or widowed elderly it may be questioned whether bungalows are not an unnecessarily lavish way of providing suitable housing.

For many elderly persons living alone a bed-sitting room, or living-room with bed recess, together with very modest arrangements for cooking and storing food and fuel, is all that they require, and indeed all that many wish to have to look after. In separate bungalows not much further economy could be made than at present, except to have smaller rooms and more bed recesses, since each dwelling must have separate bathroom and toilet facilities. But certainly where flatlets or bed-sitting rooms are used, either in a converted property or a newly constructed block, it would not seem to be a very great hardship to have some sharing of facilities, for example, bathrooms. When building costs are so high and nearly 5,500,000 households have no bath at all, it may not be a wise use of scarce resources to insist that all old persons given any specially designed accommodation must have a bathroom to themselves.[1] There is a danger of creating a very small number of very expensive and ideally planned old people's dwellings which are allocated to a rather haphazardly chosen and very small number of old people, the rest being forced to continue to make the best of whatever housing they happen to have.

Old people's housing should have a standard of amenities and comfort which is at least as good as that which is currently the basis for house building for other groups in the community. But the over-riding considerations must be that it is small and that rents and running costs can be kept at a very modest level. The old cannot afford high rentals out of their reduced incomes, and expensive buildings will involve a very heavy subsidy to support uneconomic rents. If electrical equipment is installed it may prove too costly for the pensioner to use very frequently and means of heating which is so important to the older tenant must be planned with a view to maximum warmth from a limited expenditure on fuel. The bed-recess type of bungalow, for example, obviates the chilly bedroom and the cost of trying to warm it. Kitchens and larders need not be planned on the

---

[1] The policy of making grants in respect of self-contained units only (section 15, Housing Act, 1949, and Circular 50) formerly hindered the development of flats where it was not practicable to provide separate toilet facilities for each self-contained flat. These requirements for grant-aid have now been amended to avoid some of these difficulties.

assumption that a family wash and cooking for several children is likely. The quantities of food stored and prepared are very small in most pensioners' households and elaborate facilities are not necessary. Over-lavish provision is not only expensive to the community but creates additional domestic upkeep for the older tenant. More careful design to eliminate awkwardly placed fixtures like high shelves and to facilitate easy cleaning are more important than a large floor space. It is true that old people often bring with them large pieces of furniture but these are usually of the kind that can be placed against the walls round the room. The effect is to make the room rather cluttered with possessions but many older people like it that way; it feels more cosy to them, and moving slowly they do not seem to be unduly impeded by what, in the eyes of younger tenants, might seem an excessive amount of furniture.

A small number of two-bedroom bungalows mixed among one-bedroom and bed-recess types is useful since, however fit a couple may be when they become tenants, by the simple effluxion of time one partner only may be left in a frail state of health and it may be necessary to have a relative living with them. The same consideration applies to temporary illness. A report of the Royal College of Physicians went so far as to suggest that every old person's bungalow should have two bedrooms so that there was a spare room for a relative to visit or, when necessary, to help to look after an elderly tenant. It is very expensive to provide for every possible need in this way, needs which in some cases will never arise at all, and the provision of a second bedroom in at most every tenth bungalow is probably sufficient.

FLATS AND CONVERTED PROPERTIES

For single or widowed elderly persons flatlets in a small block or hostel have much to commend them. This development has been mainly pioneered and sponsored by voluntary bodies, especially Housing Associations[1] and local Old People's Welfare Councils. Some old property has been converted to this use, and some new buildings erected. The cost can be kept down where the project can be managed with voluntary help

---

[1] About 3,400 old people are living in flatlets, flats and bungalows provided by Housing Associations.

and without paid staff. If a caretaker and/or a warden has to be employed, this adds appreciably to costs. Many schemes providing these bed-sitting rooms or flatlets find one tenant who is a little younger, perhaps a retired nurse or a person with similar experience. In return for accommodation she renders small services to the other tenants when this is necessary and she can act in any emergency or accident. From flatlets in converted houses some housing schemes shade imperceptibly into the provision of Homes. In some, one main meal a day is provided and a common dining-room and sitting-room is available, though residents have complete privacy in their own rooms and are of course surrounded by their own furniture and possessions. An infinite number of variations on this theme have been worked out by voluntary bodies to meet the needs of different groups of elderly tenants or residents and it may be asked why the local housing authorities have done little in this way to extend suitable accommodation for the elderly.

Under Section 40 of the 1949 Housing Act authorities were enabled to provide hostels, by which was meant residential accommodation with board, either by new building or by altering the use of suitable existing property. A special supplement to the Housing Manual for 1949 gives details of the kind of accommodation recommended[1] under this section of the Housing Act. This provision has not been used by local authorities because the subsidy is only £5 per bedroom compared with the full subsidy for old persons' bungalows of £22 10s. 0d. Since all subsidies are pooled by housing authorities towards the cost of every kind of housing, most of them are unwilling to forego the higher subsidy available for separate dwellings. There seems to be a case here for a higher subsidy for hostels and more encouragement to local authorities to build or convert. This would produce more very small dwellings where some facilities can be shared conveniently by the tenants.[2] Provision of services like meals or laundry in connection with such hostels is a more questionable policy. Such services involve expensive staff costs and destroy the idea of cheap but independent living arrangements. Moreover, where common dining- and sitting-rooms have

[1] 'Housing for Special Purposes', Ministry of Local Government and Planning, 1951.
[2] One bathroom and two lavatories are suggested as a minimum provision for ten residents.

been provided they sometimes have not been very much used by the tenants. It would be best for local housing authorities to concentrate on providing a group of 25–30 bed-sitting rooms with some shared facilities in one building and to leave tenants to attend to their own domestic needs. Certain services like the delivery of hot meals, chiropody, or laundry could, if required, be delivered more cheaply to a small group of old people rather than to 25 or 30 scattered homes. But true residential care involving continuous personal services should be left to the social welfare departments of local authorities and to voluntary bodies to make provision under the National Assistance Act of 1948. The function of the housing authorities is to provide sufficient small units of accommodation to meet the needs of older persons who can, in ordinary circumstances, manage their own domestic arrangements.

OLD PEOPLE'S HOUSEHOLDS

By no means all older people will require separate housing accommodation, since some live with relatives and may prefer to do so. Between 40 and 50% of old people live in the same households as their children (there appears to be some variation in different areas), and probably nearer 60% live with people in addition to or other than a spouse. From the point of view of the independence of the elderly it is very important whether they are the householders or whether they have gone to live in children's homes. At the census of 1951 of the 4,116,100 persons aged over 60 years and married, more than half were the heads of the households in which they lived, and over 40% were heads of primary family units.[1] The great majority of the latter (1,167,200) formed households where there were no children at all, about 70,000 had one or two near relatives living with them, and 361,100 were heads of composite households which included about 205,600 'family nuclei', that is, married children and their children, who may be presumed in most cases to have been families which needed separate accommodation. Only

[1] Primary family units are defined by the Registrar-General as a household containing one or more of the following—the head of the household, the spouse of the head, designated children, that is children of the head of any age except if married or, if widowed or divorced, having children with them. Also children under 16 of the brothers or sisters of the head, or any other children present with no parents, and near relatives of the head, e.g. parents or unmarried brothers and sisters.

15,500 *old* married couples were found living in composite households as family nuclei themselves. Households are not, of course, accommodated in separate dwellings necessarily, more than fourteen million households being found in 1951 in 13,311,900 dwellings; but it does appear that married couples are in most cases the heads of the households in which they live, and where they share with other relatives the latter have remained, or come to live with, their parents.

Of all the groups representing the growth of a new family which the Registrar-General designated as a family nucleus and who share a household, only 1·5% were married couples aged over 60 years in 1951, while over 76% were married couples aged under 40 years and having between them over one million children. The sharing of households presses, as one would expect, harder upon younger couples with children rather than upon older couples, the majority of whom are the heads of the households in which they live. Of all those married and under 40 years of age 7·7% formed a family nucleus in another household while among those of 60 and over only ·3% were in this situation.

Even among the single, widowed and divorced men and women aged 60 years or over, rather more than half are heads of households. In an inquiry in one Midland city among a sample of people of pensionable age[1] 23% lived alone or only with their spouses, 38% were householders having families living with them and only 12% were living in their children's homes. The number was higher, nearly one-fifth, living with their children among those over 70. Among married couples only approximately 7% lived in their children's homes, but as would be expected the figure is much higher among the widowed. 31% of widowers and 18% of widows lived in their children's households. In the Birmingham inquiry[2] among 2,230 persons over 70 years of age, where a higher proportion were widowed persons, 39·8% were found living alone or with their spouses and of the remainder, over 90% of whom were living with relatives, just over one-fifth were living in their children's homes. The proportion living in their children's households rises with age, and at age 80 or 85 about one-third are not heads of their own households, but are living with their families.

[1] Sheldon, *op. cit.*, p. 16. [2] Appendix III below.

HOUSING

The continued capacity to care for a home among even very elderly women suggests that independent living arrangements can be managed by most old people. In the Birmingham inquiry 64·5% of women in the sample did their own housework. These women were all over 70 and some of them over 80 years of age. Of those who did not do all their own domestic work, a quarter were helped by relatives and the rest had some paid help. Only 8% said they needed and wanted domestic help. On the other hand, as Dr. Sheldon suggests, while a surprisingly large number of elderly people manage household tasks and look after themselves there are a small number who ought not to have to try to do so. In 7·3% of the sample he investigated he concluded that the domestic work being undertaken was clearly beyond the capacity of the old people. Even here in over a third of the cases the strain was due to the care of a household too large for the older person to manage; that is, the domestic upkeep of a flatlet might not have been impossible.

Among the same sample of old people medical examinations rated 68·5% as being in a physical state which was normal or better than normal, 63·4% had capacity for unlimited movement, and a further 23·9% had limited mobility outside their homes. More than 80% were considered to be fully normal in their mental state. If this is representative it is likely that the majority of older people can live independent lives in their own households well into their 70's.

It is difficult to make anything but the most approximate calculation of housing needs for the elderly from the meagre data at present available. It does not appear that the elderly have less housing accommodation than younger families. Indeed the numbers of older people who are heads of a household seem to indicate that the contrary is true. Old people who live with their families in some cases clearly do so because they are cared for as well as accommodated in this way, and they do not represent a demand for separate accommodation. Some old people are in housing unsuitable in every way to their needs, but again they do not seem to suffer more of this unsatisfactory housing than other families. In determining the proportion of building resources which should be devoted to special housing for older people, every area would have to make its own estimates allow-

ing for the numbers, age and marital status of its older citizens
and the amount of suitable accommodation already available.
Certain broad <u>conclusions,</u> however, can probably be applied
to most areas. The first is that a substantial proportion of households among old people will only consist of one or two persons.
At present such households form about one-quarter of those of
pensionable age, and about one-third to one-half of those over
seventy years of age, but if some children living at present with
parents were able to secure homes of their own these numbers
would increase. The numbers of elderly widowed and single
women, who form 39·3% of all persons of pensionable age and
who are likely to need small units of accommodation, indicates
the need for some flatlets or hostels in addition to separate
dwellings of the bungalow or maisonette type. Where providing
housing for older persons creates direct competition for building
resources which would otherwise be devoted to housing overcrowded families with young children, it would be unwise to
suggest that more than perhaps 6% or 7% of new building
should be allocated to the special needs of the elderly. Fortunately it is possible to keep the ratio of housing for the elderly to
the total housing provision reasonably flexible, as small units of
accommodation can be created which can be used for all types
of small households. With an allocation of 10% of all new
dwellings to one-bedroom types, the proportion given to elderly
tenants can be raised from 5% upwards as it becomes possible
to put more young married couples directly into two-bedroom
houses. One and two-person households form at present about
38% of all households, and existing dwellings with three or
less rooms about one-quarter of the total. 10% of new housing
allocated to these small units would therefore seem to be a fair
estimate,[1] with at least 6% to 7% devoted to the needs of the
elderly. Bearing in mind also the possibility of freeing family-
sized housing by moving the elderly to smaller accommodation,
the housing needs of the young and old need not necessarily
clash.

This argument is valid only if the dwellings provided for the
old are cheaper than family housing. If there is very little difference in price between an old person's bungalow and a three-
bedroomed house, local authorities faced with long waiting lists

[1] In the last six months of 1953 8·4% of dwellings provided by local
authorities were suitable for, though not necessarily given to, elderly tenants.

of overcrowded families may well feel it is their duty to concentrate on houses.

The following list of comparative building costs is for dwellings erected or contracted for in 1954.

1 bedroom bungalows	£1,506
1 bedroom flats and bed-recess flats (average)	£1,344
1 bedroom flats in multi-storey blocks	£2,200
2 bedroom houses	£1,800
2 bedroom flats in 3 storey blocks	£1,900
2 bedroom flats in multi-storey blocks from	£2,200–3,000
3 bedrooms (4 persons) houses	£1,912
3 bedrooms (4 persons) flats in 3 storey blocks	£1,911
3 bedrooms (4 persons) flats in multi-storey blocks	£2,900
3 bedrooms (5 persons) houses	£2,059
3 bedrooms (5 persons) flats in 2 storey blocks	£1,985
3 bedrooms (5 persons) flats in 3 storey blocks	£2,001
3 bedrooms (5 persons) flats in multi-storey blocks	£3,150

If some accommodation were created more cheaply by flatlets or hostels than by special old people's dwellings, the most urgent housing needs of some elderly people unable to manage in their present domestic circumstances might be met, though many more would have to continue to tolerate housing which is anything but ideal. Any kind of housing provision is costly but providing suitable accommodation for the frail, solitary elderly often prevents yet another application for a place in an Old Person's Home or another claim for an expensive hospital bed.

The provision of small dwellings for the elderly, especially by means of converting existing property, may receive a considerable impetus from the Housing Repairs and Rents Act (1954). Lettings made by Housing Trusts and Associations and Development Corporations will in future, as has always been the case with Local Authority lettings, be excluded from the Rent Acts. Freedom from rent restriction will make possible further development in all kinds of housing by the non-profit making Housing Societies, many of which are especially concerned with provision for elderly tenants.

Further, the conditions with regard to conversion and improvement grants have been made less rigid, and this together with relaxation of the licensing system will enable more conversions to be undertaken. By this recent legislation the period

HOUSING

during which a converted building must continue to provide
satisfactory accommodation has been reduced from thirty to
ten years. Also, the limit on the amount that can be spent on
work which qualifies for a grant has been removed, and the
maximum grant, half the cost of conversion up to £400, may
be increased. In place of the old controlled rents, the Local
Authority will fix a rent appropriate to the type of property and
the cost of conversion. But the standard laid down as necessary
to attract a grant and the maximum contribution towards the
cost can be varied by consent of the Minister, and these pro-
visos ought to be used in making a more flexible and realistic
approach to the use of existing houses. This should be especially
valuable in the provision of small households suitable for old
people.

CHAPTER VI

RESIDENTIAL CARE AND DOMICILIARY
WELFARE SERVICES

OLD PEOPLE'S HOMES

HOWEVER successful the provision of suitable small dwellings
can be in making it possible for older people to stay in a home
of their own, there are inevitably some frail, elderly people who
will need residential accommodation with full care. Small residential Homes for the elderly began to be provided by religious
organizations and charitable trusts more than forty years ago,
but the total accommodation in small Homes provided either
by voluntary bodies or local authorities was very small until
the period of the last War. During this emergency bombing and
evacuation drew attention to the plight of the old people unable any longer to look after themselves, and organizations
like the Friends' Relief Service and the British Red Cross
Society opened residential hostels. In 1941 this development
was encouraged and extended into permanent residential
accommodation by an arrangement with the National Assistance
Board. Supplementary pensioners entering Homes approved by
the Board were given a special allowance to enable them to pay
substantially towards the cost of their maintenance, while retaining a small part of their pension for personal needs. Many
voluntary organizations took up this work aided by grants from
the Lord Mayor's National Air-raid Distress and both old and
newly formed Housing Societies devoted much of their efforts
to the need of the elderly.

Some small Homes had been provided by local authorities
before the war and in 1947 the Ministry of Health reminded
them[1] of the need to go forward with the creation of Homes

[1] Ministry of Health Circular 49/47.

which would provide for about 30 to 35 elderly residents. Where this was not immediately possible authorities were encouraged to divide into small and more homely units the existing large institutions, and to operate them with the minimum of restrictions in regard to visiting, clothing and similar matters.

These developments were embodied in legislative form in the National Assistance Act of 1948. Under Section 21 local authorities are charged with responsibility for providing residential care for any old person in their area who is in need of care and attention and this is to be provided as 'a substitute for a normal home'.[1]

The need to use the experience and continued efforts of voluntary bodies in this matter was emphasized by the provision in the National Assistance Act that local authorities can make use of voluntary bodies as their agents (Section 26) and a subsequent circular from the Ministry urged the closest co-operation between the voluntary agencies in planning the provision of homes. Local authorities are able to contribute to the funds of voluntary bodies, including Housing Associations, which provide suitable accommodation for the elderly. This can be done either by a grant towards the funds of the organization, or by paying for the maintenance of residents less the amount they can pay for themselves. These grants may take the form of contributions toward the capital cost of establishment and equipment of voluntary homes, but where substantial financial aid is required towards the setting up of a voluntary Home, and where the voluntary body has constituted itself a Housing Association, help is more readily arranged under the Housing Acts. Local authorities already had the power to aid Housing Associations by loans and guaranteed mortgages (Housing Act 1936), and under Section 28 of the National Assistance Act a Housing Association which provides a Home by arrangement with the local authority is able also to receive, through that authority, an Exchequer subsidy towards the cost of new premises or conversion of existing property. The provision of homes and hostels by both statutory authorities and voluntary bodies assisted out of public funds, has been almost without exception carried out under Part III of the National Assistance Act. Altogether local authorities in Great Britain (1953) were accommodating about 50,000 old people in Homes, and voluntary bodies of various

[1] Ministry of Health Circular 87/48.

kinds have provided about another 600 small Homes. Few of the buildings are new and most have been created by the conversion of existing large houses.

Where local authorities pay for maintenance of elderly persons in voluntary Homes the amount has to be agreed with the voluntary committee responsible. This is usually the actual cost of maintenance including staff and overhead expenses. The contribution of the voluntary body being the provision of the Home and its administration. Where a resident can pay the full charge no question of assistance from the local authority arises; otherwise the older resident is assessed on his capacity to pay towards his keep. No resident will have less than 32s. 6d. a week (that is a pension of 40s. less 7s. 6d. to be retained for personal use). Anyone who does not have a pension of this amount will have his resources made up to this level by the National Assistance Board.

In making an assessment of capacity to pay the local authority uses a similar calculation of means in regard to both capital and income as that normally applied by the National Assistance Board.

The cost of care in residential homes provided by voluntary bodies averages between £3 10s. 0d. and £3 15s. 0d. per week, though there is naturally a great range of cost depending on considerations like the staff-resident ratio which may be higher, for example, if there are more very infirm old people accommodated. The charges for renewal and repairs to both buildings and furniture will vary according to the type and condition of property converted and how far residents bring their own furnishings. The charges quoted above do not allow for extras like the issue of sweets and tobacco, such as are commonly given in local authority Homes, or for any repayment of capital costs. 20 residents appear to be about the smallest number which can be catered for and 30 to 35 is usually found to be a more economical number. The National Old People's Welfare Committee in consultation with the National Corporation for the Care of Old People suggest in their handbook[1] that the cost per resident may be as much as 6s. higher where there are 20 residents than where there are 30. Local authorities' Homes also vary in cost but are mainly run at about £4 per week per resi-

[1] See 'Age is Opportunity', National Old People's Welfare Committee, April 1954.

dent. Lacking voluntary help their staff and administrative costs may be higher and certain amenities like tobacco, newspapers, etc., are included in their charges. They are also more often involved in the provision of clothing for their residents who may have fewer personal resources than the old people entering some of the voluntary Homes. Voluntary Homes more often than local authorities encourage residents to bring their own furniture and other personal possessions within the limits of room available, and though this is not advocated primarily for reasons of economy, but rather to help elderly residents settle down in new surroundings, it does help to reduce the cost of furnishings in a Home.

The number of residential Homes in existence is certainly not enough to meet the present demand for such care and accommodation. Probably less than a fifth of those seeking a place in a Home are able to find one.[1] All kinds of Homes have waiting lists which have usually been carefully examined to establish some order of urgency in allocating the few vacancies which become available. Often a Home is able to take a discharged hospital patient only if one of their own very infirm or acutely ill residents is admitted to hospital care in exchange, and only deaths are likely to create new vacancies to be filled from the waiting list. In areas where residential accommodation and hospital beds for elderly patients are more than usually scarce, the transfer of older persons to suitable care in accordance with their condition becomes almost impossible to effect.

As was pointed out when the post-war pattern of health and welfare legislation was being designed,[2] the dichotomy in the administration of services for the old, which left the treatment of the elderly sick to the Regional Hospital Boards and the provision of residential accommodation to the local authorities, assumes a convenient dividing line between the healthy and sick aged, which in practice is not easy to determine. In a period when every kind of housing, residential Home and hospital bed has been fully occupied, there have been unfortunate and distressing cases of old people in need of care who have been unable to get themselves accepted as the responsibility of any authority.

[1] The National Old People's Welfare Committee estimate that in London and Greater London the prospects are much worse, and only 8·5% of those known to wish to enter Homes are successful. See p. 61 'Age is Opportunity', 1954.

[2] See *The Aged and the Nation, op. cit.*, p. 34.

Since 1948 much progress has been made in the co-ordination of services for the elderly at a local level, including in some areas the setting up of liaison committees and in one area joint appointment of a Medical Officer, i.e. by a Regional Hospital and a local authority. Whether it would have been better to have made special appointments of local Old People's Welfare Officers, rather on the pattern of Children's Officers, who could have had well-defined responsibilities to co-ordinate all service for the elderly in their areas is open to question. Certainly with so many agencies concerned including Local Authority, Health and Housing and Welfare departments, Regional Hospital Boards, the National Assistance Board, and many voluntary organizations, there does seem to be a case for something more than exhortation to local bodies and officers to consult each other. In some areas this consultation does work successfully, especially where good personal relationships are established between responsible officers, but this is by no means so general that we can feel that we have solved the problem of finding the most efficient, economical and *humane* use of limited resources for the elderly within local areas. However, the problem is now very widely recognized and the term 'comprehensive care' for the elderly has come into use to describe just this kind of mobilization of local resources.

THE DEMAND FOR RESIDENTIAL CARE

Only a very small minority of old people are in residential Homes though more may seek this kind of accommodation. Part of the increased demand arises because modern local authority Homes are much less forbidding than the old institutions. Smaller Homes with a greater degree of privacy and more homely and attractive furnishings, and with rules and regulations reduced to a minimum, are more acceptable to frail elderly persons in need of care. They are also more acceptable to the consciences of their relatives. Even larger old Homes which will have to continue to be used until they can be replaced have been modernized by redecoration and the sub-division into cubicles of sleeping accommodation, so that they have lost some of their grimmer features. These can provide shelter for those needing a considerable degree of care, including the mildly confused, and those old persons passed over from the Poor Law who are by this time often badly 'institutional-ized'. It has been estimated that not more than 20% of these latter old persons could be transferred to a more independent way of living. Some of these people ought never to have been allowed to accumulate in old people's Homes; they have fallen to the care of local authorities through some handicap or lack of family help, or they have been transferred after sickness from a Public Assistance Infirmary into a Home. It is now too late to do more than continue to give them support and care, but they are a group whom it is hoped modern social services will largely eliminate. More 'respectable' old persons are prepared now to enter local authority Homes; though since local authorities, un-like voluntary bodies, have a statutory duty, they tend to col-lect a more mixed group of residents in Part III accommoda-tion. Voluntary Homes cater for all types of residents also, but some frankly provide for old people from a professional and middle class background and are able to charge more.

A voluntary body is able to impose more conditions on those applying for residence in its Homes, but the local authority must provide residential care for some old people whose habits and behaviour would be difficult to fit into a small group of resi-dents from a better social background. The greatest degree of tact and skill is needed in the selection of a group of old people likely to be set in their ways, some suffering from various degrees of disability, and all with time on their hands, if they are to be able to settle down happily together.

Very few new local authority Homes have been built since the last war, but like the voluntary bodies welfare authorities have converted existing large houses. These have sometimes been criticized as a little lavish in contrast to the meanness of some former Poor Law provision. While the standard of fur-nishing and equipment should be comfortable, the decor of some recently opened Homes, both statutory and voluntary, must be strangely unfamiliar to old people from simple homes, and it may not represent their idea of comfort. Similarly, con-verted country houses can be positively intimidating in their grandeur, and have the added disadvantage of being a long way from familiar surroundings, and an expensive bus ride away from relatives. In such cases it is almost impossible for residents to participate in any social life outside the Home, except by means of outings organized *en masse*. Where voluntary

Homes allow elderly residents to bring some of their own furniture this helps to make the old people feel at home, though the appearance of the Home as a result may not be so pleasing to the eye as the chintz and cream paint beloved by Committees designing Old People's Homes. Nomenclature also is changing, and what used to be known as 'The Old People's Home' is now more likely to be 'The Cedars' in deference to the feelings of residents who may prefer a title which has no association with what was formerly mainly charitable provision.

At the moment there is such a demonstrable shortage of places in small residential Homes of all kinds, that there is no danger in the immediate future of over-provision. But what is the future of this kind of accommodation? Ought we to think in terms of a continuous expansion of this fairly expensive kind of substitute home for elderly persons? There are and will continue to be more old people in the population. If only 5% of old people need residential accommodation when their numbers total 8 million, 400,000 places in Homes will be required. Since there is not, however, a larger proportion of very elderly people in the higher age groups who are more likely to need residential care than formerly, what we want to know is whether more old people will choose residential accommodation in future. Because this type of accommodation is different now, because it can be accepted by the self-respecting, and because families are small[1] and married daughters likely to be employed, will a larger proportion of the elderly seek residential Homes in future and ought they to be encouraged to do so?

The three factors most likely to bring old people to desire a place in a Home are lack of any other suitable housing, inability to live independently without a certain degree of care, and loneliness. The first reason ought to be eliminated in time by increased provision of simple small units of accommodation of the kind suggested earlier. Many more people could continue to live in their own homes to the end of their lives if they were not exhausted by excessive domestic duties or made uncomfortable by the lack of simple amenities. Residential Homes ought not to be a substitute for suitable housing for older per-

[1] The effects of this trend in the size of families upon the care available to old people should not be exaggerated. A smaller number of children may nevertheless sustain a very close supportive relationship with elderly parents. See Townsend, *op. cit.*, p. 140.

sons. Surveys have shown to what advanced years women continue to do their own housework. Sheldon found in Wolverhampton that up to the age of 74 years, half the women were responsible for all their housework and this often meant caring for a husband and sometimes children too. Even at 79 years 40% of women coped with their domestic chores and over a third of the men in the survey helped with the housework. Comparatively few homes are found where the old persons are unable to keep their housing reasonably clean and where they are manifestly failing to look after themselves. This capacity to manage their own care on the part of large numbers of elderly people indicates that given nearby shopping facilities, not too many stairs and some help either by family or towards the cost of heavy work like laundry, most old people in suitable housing accommodation are unlikely, unless becoming very infirm, to need a residential Home.

FAMILY CARE FOR THE ELDERLY

Some old people, of course, can only be kept in their own or their relatives' homes if their families are able to devote to them a good deal of care and nursing. The constant care of frail old persons, especially if they become confused or need attention during the night, can be a very heavy burden on the younger generation. It is often shouldered cheerfully by responsible relatives, and though isolated cases of neglect can be found there is no evidence to show any marked diminution in family care for elderly relatives.

A difficult problem is sometimes created where an unmarried daughter has to undertake paid employment and the care of an aged parent, and this is also a problem for married daughters with their own family duties, as well as employment. Some daughters looking after parents may suffer ill-health and strain themselves, and are frequently prevented from enjoying activities outside the home or taking any regular holidays. The more women, especially married women, are drawn into employment, the more likely it is that alternative care may have to be found for elderly relatives needing a good deal of attention. Whether in these circumstances it is always right to say that it is better for an old person to stay in his or her own home is by no means certain. Sometimes the strain created leads to reproaches and unhappy relationships and increases the feeling of helpless dependence experienced by an infirm old person. The knowledge of being a heavy burden on younger relatives may cause more unhappiness to the old than if they were encouraged to enter a Rest Home providing a substantial degree of care. For most families placing an old relative in a Home is still regarded as a last desperate resort, and at present it tends to be those who have no close relatives at all who choose this. Whether attitudes to residential accommodation will change so that it becomes increasingly popular is hard to predict; many middle-aged women, who have helped to plan and administer pleasant old people's Homes, can be heard to say that they would not mind ending their days in one, though their ideas may well change when they are actually faced with such a prospect. It is certain, however, that in the foreseeable future residential Homes should only be provided for the really frail and infirm elderly, who must have a substantial degree of care. There is no reason why active older persons, who are lonely and prefer communal living, should not also enjoy this type of accommodation, but in the immediate future their need is not so great and can be met to some extent by simple communal facilities associated with flatlets or groups of old persons' bungalows and by all-day clubs.

THE CARE OF THE INFIRM ELDERLY

If residential Homes increasingly take only those needing a good deal of care and attention their costs are likely to rise, and they will experience in an acute form the problem which any residential Home at some time has to face as residents become enfeebled—how are they to be nursed? While it would be clearly uneconomic to create fully staffed sick bays in residential Homes, some provision must be made for simple nursing, and in an emergency for more serious cases. Immediate transference to hospital will not always be a practical possibility in view of the shortage of hospital beds, and it is generally agreed that it is more humane to nurse illnesses known to be terminal in the Home where the patient has resided when possible. If voluntary bodies setting up residential Homes confine their care to those who most need it, the frail elderly, they will increasingly find themselves with very heavy responsibilities as their residents inevitably grow older and weaker. It is not surprising that some have felt unequal to such responsibility and have limited themselves to taking the more healthy and active residents into their Homes.

One way of approaching this problem is to create what have been called 'half-way houses', half-way between hospital care and living at home. For some the half-way house is a temporary measure. An early discharge from a much needed and expensive hospital bed, is followed by convalescence before returning the patient to his family or to a Home. These half-way houses, first sponsored by the King Edward Hospital Fund, are closely associated with geriatric units, and only suitable patients are sent from the unit. In these long-term convalescent Homes patients are able to get both physical and mental rehabilitation and plans can be made for their future. But they must have a future, that is, there must be a reasonable possibility of getting them well and home again or into a Home or Hostel. Only a well-established geriatric unit can supply a stream of patients of this kind for convalescence. This type of half-way house must not find all its beds blocked by permanently infirm old people. For other old people the half-way stage is fairly permanent. They do not need the expensive services of hospital care but they do need constant attention and help of a simpler kind and could not manage to live alone.

For them some kind of permanent Rest Home is needed where they can be received for an indefinite period unless they need hospital treatment. Again admission to such Homes ought to be through a geriatric unit where the resident has been selected as suitable for his kind of care and which will take the patient back if he needs such nursing care as can only be properly supplied in a hospital. The provision of long-stay annexes for the irremediably sick must remain a responsibility of the Hospital Boards and the half-way house or rest house is not intended to provide for the true chronic sick. The National Corporation for the Care of Old People has established Rest Homes of the type described, and the development of this work will be watched with great interest both by voluntary bodies considering embarking upon the provision of new Homes for the elderly infirm, and by those who are already finding many of their residents beginning to fall into this category.

The group of old people for whom it is most difficult to find any accommodation at all are the mentally confused. They are quite unable to look after themselves and sometimes it is impossible for relatives to look after them properly. Ordinary residential Homes will not take them and mental hospitals are full. The kind of provision envisaged for them in the report prepared for the British Medical Association, 'The Care and Treatment of the Elderly and Infirm', has never been created. The numbers of such old people are quite considerable, and they represent a serious unsolved problem in the care of the elderly.[1] The future of residential care for those who cannot easily be classified as sick or well is bedevilled by the question of financial responsibility. Where convalescent care only is offered it would seem to be the responsibility of the Regional Hospital Boards, though of course local authorities have duties under the National Health Service Act to provide after-care for those who have been ill. Where long-term residential accommodation is given local authorities certainly ought to be concerned both in planning use and in finance, and a precedent has already been established in this direction by the pioneer efforts of the National Corporation for the Care of Old People in getting both Hospital Boards and local authorities to pay for patients in 'half-way' care.

Residential care is expensive especially in woman-power, and we do not want to provide more than is demonstrably necessary. But it must be remembered also that lack of both suitable residential care and domiciliary services may cause patients to remain blocking even more scarce and expensive hospital beds. An examination of 393 patients seeking admission to a chronic sick hospital revealed that a quarter of them could stay at home if provided with either domestic help, the services of a district nurse or other simple assistance.[2]

DOMICILIARY SERVICES FOR OLD PEOPLE

Whether an elderly person can continue to manage in his own home or becomes an applicant for admission to a Home will often depend upon what help and assistance is available to him either from relatives or from various kinds of welfare

---

[1] For further discussion of this kind of care see p. 188 below.
[2] *The Care of the Ageing and Chronic Sick*, Thomson, Lowe, McKeown. See also Chapter VII below.

services. The need for help may be temporary as in the provision of nursing or domestic help during illness, or it may be more or less permanent owing to the increasing frailty of the old person.

The most obvious need, domestic help, is met to some extent by the services of Home-helps, which are now provided by local authorities, though in some areas voluntary bodies like the W.V.S. administer the schemes. Most areas are very short of this kind of domestic help, which has to be shared with maternity cases and the younger chronic sick, as well as old people. A charge is made for the service from the householder if able to pay, or part of the cost can be borne by the authority. Two or three hours' cleaning help per week is very valuable for old persons who cannot undertake any strenuous domestic work, but who can, perhaps, just look after themselves and get and clear their own meals. But if daily help is needed during long-term infirmity or illness the cost is quite heavy and in any case the old person may not need a lot of cleaning or cooking completed in an hour or two, but rather small services and attention at frequent intervals during the day or night. It is difficult to meet these needs by the home help service as it is usually organized.

Laundry is another problem since it is a particularly strenuous domestic task, and sending out laundry is expensive and requires a sufficient stock of linen. The laundering of soiled linen is a great difficulty and one of the major problems of nursing incontinent elderly persons at home. A number of local authorities, as well as some voluntary bodies, have developed cheap or assisted laundry services, and some supply bed-linen on loan. The National Assistance Board makes discretionary addition to grants for, among other needs, laundry costs. Of 821,000 special needs met by the Board (1953) 314,000 were laundry costs.

As far as cooking is concerned some assistance can be given to older people in catering for themselves by the delivery of hot meals to people in their own homes,[1] or by the organization of luncheon clubs, or facilities at British Restaurants for cheap

[1] The delivery of meals to scattered homes is not cheap and ought to be reserved for the infirm and housebound. More active old people could get meals through luncheon clubs. This is cheaper, it is easier to ensure that the food is really hot, and it encourages those old people who can go out from their homes and meet other people.

meals. Local authorities have powers to contribute to the funds of voluntary organizations engaged in this work. Thus in some areas old people can get help with basic domestic needs like cleaning, washing and feeding through services provided by voluntary and statutory bodies.

What other needs are likely to undermine independent living unless supplied? The most obvious one is illness. The nursing of a sick old person, which sometimes involves heavy lifting and often sitting up at nights, places a heavy strain on relatives. Many old people can be, and are, nursed at home by their relatives. This is done with the help of the Home Nursing Service, and perhaps a home-help or, where this service exists, a night 'sitter-up'. But what can be managed during a short illness cannot always be managed for a lengthy one, or for indefinite chronic sickness.

Keeping old people in their own homes has been strongly advocated as both the right and the cheapest way of caring for them. It is certainly almost always what they prefer, but whether it is cheap or not depends upon the degree of attention needed and the period of time for which this must be supplied. Regular domiciliary services provided over long periods are expensive and may cost as much as six or seven guineas a week to provide in some cases. Night attendance, for example, usually costs 10s. per night and physiotherapy treatment at home may cost £1 per time compared with 8s. if given in hospital. If so much domiciliary help is needed it may be that the time has come to consider temporarily or permanently some other kind of care. Whether this is necessary or desirable will depend both upon the views of the old persons concerned and upon those of their relatives. It may be possible to give relatives a holiday from continuous care by admission of the elderly for a short period to a hospital or half-way house, and this is being increasingly done to help relatives. Hospitals report that they do not have difficulty in getting relatives to accept back the older person after they themselves have had a rest. In such cases it may then be possible for a family to resume domiciliary care for a further lengthy period. Where it is thought possible for an old person to be looked after at home, if there is some younger person responsible, a few boarding out schemes have been successfully tried.

A less ambitious, though useful, variant of this scheme is to put young couples needing housing in touch with an old person who has house space to offer in return for some services such as preparation of meals. Co-operation between Housing Departments and local Old People's Welfare Committees has been successful in some areas in effecting such introductions.

THE COST OF KEEPING OLD PEOPLE IN THEIR OWN HOMES

It is difficult to estimate with any precision the cost of various kinds of care for older persons. The most expensive care is certainly that of servicing hospital beds and the cheapest is probably providing a limited number of domiciliary services to old people living in their old homes. The only way to use services for old people effectively is to see that the services which are *appropriate* are made available for them. So much emphasis has, quite rightly, been placed upon the importance of keeping old people in their own homes that it is sometimes forgotten that this is not invariably a reasonable or practicable possibility. If old persons are so mentally or physically ill that they need constant attention day and night they cannot always be kept at home. Families can rarely manage such nursing single-handed for very long. And it is not sensible to have three people fully occupied in looking after one. Where a twenty-four hour service is needed it must usually be given in group care where a small number of trained people can look after larger numbers in successive turns of duty. If on the other hand the cost of some domestic help and laundry and the visits of the district nurse can, together with family help, give adequate care for a sick or frail old person this is obviously the best and the cheapest way to do so. But the employment over a lengthy period of, for example, a night attendant at a cost of about 10s. per night in order to allow some undisturbed rest for relatives, can make domiciliary care very expensive. It is this kind of problem which has caused some queries to be raised recently about the dictum that old people should *always* be kept at home if possible. Sometimes there may be no alternative since no hospital bed is available, but each case needs to be considered individually with regard to how much family and voluntary help can be mobilized and what demands will be made upon public services. It is not merely a question of direct costs, though this is important enough, but of the claims of the old (already more than 60%) upon scarce services of domestic and nursing help which have to be shared with younger people who also require them.

The following approximate estimates may be made of the average cost of different services for the old.

	Per year £
Hospital bed [1] (Chronic)	400
Residence in local authority Home	200
Stay in a Half-way Home	320–350
Residence in a Home provided by a Voluntary Body .	180–195
Residence in a Flatlet or Hostel	see below
Boarding out with a private family	130–150
Living in own home with some domiciliary services (Home help, laundry, some hot meals, chiropody, visits from the district nurse and/or health visitor, the attention of a general practitioner and use of other general medical services)	80–100

The capital cost of providing flatlet or hostel accommodation is about £600 per room. Where a Housing Society provides this the cost to public funds after allowing for the rents which will be collected, may be no more than the Exchequer subsidy, a guaranteed loan through the Public Works Loan Board at a special rate of interest, and tax exemption if the Housing Association has charitable status.

The cost of domiciliary services is estimated to include regular domestic help, laundering of bed linen, three hot meals delivered per week, four chiropody treatments per year, and occasional medical and nursing attention. If the demand for medical and nursing attention is considerable and continuous the cost will rise very sharply above the estimates suggested here. The full cost of the other domiciliary services also may be understated by those estimates because those provided by voluntary associations are often started from voluntary funds donated for the purpose, and no proper allowance may be made for depreciation of, for example, motor vehicles delivering meals, or laundry equipment. Many of these services have only been in operation for a short time and when accounts can be analysed for a longer period it will be possible to cost them

---

[1] The average cost in a non-teaching general hospital is £750 per year. For patients staying in hospital more than two months some saving on reduced pensions can be deducted from the cost of a hospital bed.

more accurately. Even so, it is most likely that from every point of view it is worth while to spend up to £100 per year to help keep an old person at home rather than in a Home or in a hospital bed, and this can probably be achieved for most old people, if family help is available, for a good deal less. Where, however, old people live alone and have no help from relatives or neighbours the happiest arrangements for them is not simple to decide.

LIVING ALONE. THE NEED FOR OCCUPATIONS AND INTERESTS

The Phillips Report notes that at the last census (1951) there were about 918,000 elderly men and women living alone, and for them and many more, acute problems of loneliness and lack of interesting activities may be added to other difficulties which arise from increasing infirmity. Having a friendly visitor once a week and a home-help for an hour every day still leaves many lonely hours to be occupied. The fact that to-day so many more people are able to afford to maintain their independence in a home of their own is one welcome aspect of the improvement which has taken place in the financial resources of the elderly, but it creates other problems unless old people are able to maintain satisfying social relationships with families and friends which fortunately most of them are able to do. How many old people have no regular visitors is difficult to assess. In the Birmingham Survey, which was made before the present system of visiting old people had been organized by voluntary bodies in the city, nearly a third of old people living alone said they did not anticipate any kind of regular visiting. A later survey, *Social Contacts in Old Age* in Liverpool (1953) in studying a group of 500 old people of whom 17·8% lived alone and 56% were over 70 years of age, found only 5·6% where there was a definite need for regular visiting. The 'Over-Seventy' study in London (1954) found a high percentage of old people who had no regular visitors, but an investigation into kinship ties among old people in Bethnal Green[1] has reported that 72 out of 100 informants were members of an effectively functioning family group.

Though we do not know from this conflicting evidence how many old people feel a severe lack of social contacts, every

[1] Townsend, *op. cit.*, p. 140.

voluntary and statutory organization dealing with the elderly knows that there are quite a number of lonely old people who lack occupation and companionship. Whether in such cases an old lady continues to live alone at home or would prefer to go into a small Home for the sake of care and company will depend as much upon her psychological adjustment to old age as upon her material resources and state of health. Individuals face old age with differing amounts of spiritual as well as financial capital accumulated over a lifetime. Surveys on the use of leisure made by the old reveal a rather depressing picture of the narrow range of interests on which so many people have to nourish vitality in old age.

From information collected in the Birmingham Survey among 2,230 old people over 70, Table XVIII shows something of the way in which they use their leisure time.[1]

TABLE XVIII

Leisure Occupations of Old People

Occupation	% Males	% Females	% Total
1. Reading and listening to wireless	44·5	38·9	41·3
2. Handicrafts other than 3	3	3·8	4·1
3. Knitting and sewing (Women)	—	52·2	—
4. Gardening (Men)	30·6	—	—
5. None *	3·5	5·2	4·5

Activities outside the home	% Males	% Females	% Total
6. Clubs (any kind)	10·2	4·5	6·8
7. None	36·2	34·6	35·1
8. Proportion of those old people in the sample who were unable by reason of infirmity to leave their homes	4·0	13·1	9·0

* 16% of old people in the sample were blind or had serious defects of vision and 21% had some degree of deafness.

The Liverpool Survey[2] found that among old people not at work or housekeeping for someone at work, who formed more than 70% of the sample interviewed, 8% had no occupation and less than 9% had outdoor activities. This report concludes, 'We are concerned not only about the lack of adequate social

[1] For a more detailed analysis see Appendix III.   [2] *Op. cit.*, p. 171.

contacts of some old people in our sample, but about the poverty of their cultural and recreational interest. Among the old people who caused us concern were those who, although physically fit, seldom or never left home, because they had no reason for going out, and moreover had nothing to occupy or interest them within their homes.' Some voluntary bodies who undertake the exchange of library books and of the provision of materials and instruction for handicrafts or the organization of clubs, etc., are already trying to widen the interests and activities for old people, but there remains much to be done in this direction. It requires considerable tact and skill to persuade many old people to use such services when they are available. A limited education followed by fifty or more years of physically strenuous work leaves some old people without the energy necessary to learn a new skill or to make new social contacts. Those who are content to do a good deal of 'just sitting' ought not to be unduly pressed into activity, but lonely and bored old people are likely to welcome new interests.

OLD PEOPLE'S CLUBS

As great a problem as any arising out of health or housing problems therefore is that of loneliness among old people, especially those living alone. Even those who live with relatives may have many hours of inactivity and boredom,[1] especially if their mobility is limited by infirmity or their senses beginning to fail. For the more physically active Old People's Clubs, open either daily or at a weekly meeting, supply occupational interest and sustain relationships. The Clubs have grown in numbers in the last five years and apart from their main social activities other services such as chiropody and the organization of holidays provided by voluntary bodies can be more easily planned around membership of a club. It is true that initially and to some extent still, the clubs tend to attract sociable old people and may not reach the lonely and socially withdrawn older persons. A study of the membership of several old people's clubs[2] in a large city during the first two or three years of their

[1] For old people who live with relatives who must be out at work during the whole day some experiments in providing Day Centres and Day Hospitals have been successfully carried out.

[2] An inquiry among 769 club members attending at sixteen clubs showed that just over a third of the members had other activities outside their

operation showed that a substantial percentage of members had belonged throughout their lives to one or more groups meeting regularly and connected mainly with religion or politics. And then in old age they moved happily into Darby and Joan Clubs. They were distinguishable at club meetings by their readiness to take an active part in arrangements, their insistence upon the 'proper' way to do things—e.g. elect officials, and they showed themselves connoisseurs of coach trips within fifty miles of their native city! Though clubbable old people may have tended to predominate in the early days of the clubs, once established the clubs have been able to draw in some of the more diffident and less easily sociable old people, who now enjoy attending regularly. Failure to attend is often a useful indication of the need for a friendly visit to a club member's home to see whether any special help may be needed in case of illness or accident. This is especially important in the case of old people living absolutely alone and in housing accommodation which does not encourage frequent contact with neighbours.

An interesting and important development springing from the clubs is the way in which in some clubs, older members increasingly manage these organizations for themselves, including the planning in some cases of annual holidays. Some help may be needed from a few younger persons who are able to undertake the more strenuous duties, especially if the upkeep of club premises is involved. It must be borne in mind by those who are concerned in developing clubs that wherever possible they have to be run by, as well as for, old people. For this reason it is important, of course, to have some clubbable old people with experience of active participation in other social groups, for they act as leaven in what may otherwise be a rather passive membership of an old persons' club. It is only too easy to get groups of old people who are quite prepared to sit and have things done for them and who need a good deal of encouragement to take responsibility for their own programmes. Where

homes, apart from belonging to an old people's club. Most of them belonged to well-established social groups, but in new housing estates areas, which had a relatively undeveloped social life, getting an old person to attend a club in a community centre had often been an introduction to other social activities and the development of outside interests had followed rather than preceded membership of an old persons' club. Just over half of these members (that is, those with other outside interests) belonged to another club or social group meeting regularly, and nearly 80% had some kind of hobby.

this is done, however, there is more chance of establishing a co-operative 'self-help' group of older people able to help themselves and each other, and whose self-respect is not injured by being the recipient of well-meant benevolence. The clubs can be a useful channel for disseminating information, assessing local requirements and understanding the needs of old people *as they themselves see them.*

Despite their growth[1] in recent years the clubs still only touch a very small number of old people and very few old people express any spontaneous desire for them.[2]

FRIENDLY VISITING

For the very old who are housebound informal visiting undertaken by interested individuals, i.e. churches and members of certain voluntary bodies, has always been of great value. Increasingly, old people's local welfare committees are organizing more formally a friendly visiting service, with rotas of those wanting to visit and be visited. This kind of sustained interest in lonely older people is a work obviously suitable for voluntary effort and it is disappointing to find that it is often one of their functions which is least well carried out. As always in any kind of social service it is easier to find people willing to help with the creation of some tangible token of their interest in the elderly, like an old persons' Home or Club, or the provision of meals on wheels or a mobile library. It is not so easy to find people who are able to visit regularly old people who had no immediate material needs, and for whom the creation of a meaningful relationship involves a continued and patient

---

[1] The National Old People's Welfare Committee have reported in their 'Progress Report for 1953' that there were about 3,578 clubs in Britain, of which at least 376 meet daily, 155 several times weekly, 2,110 weekly and 68 fortnightly. About 180,000 old people are members. These numbers may well have grown substantially in the last eighteen months but even if the number of members is half as great again this would still mean that less than 5% of persons of pensionable age are in touch with Old People's Clubs.

[2] The Birmingham Survey (see Appendix III) found 6·8% of old people mentioned belong to clubs of some kind, though a larger number inquired about the possibility of joining. In the Liverpool Survey in 1953 after there had been a good deal more publicity about old people's clubs, only 15% of the old people visited were found to belong regularly to any club, and only 3% of those interviewed expressed any wish to belong to a club. 82% of the sample had no knowledge of, or showed any interest in, the idea of clubs for old people.

endeavour to understand and really like them. An easy sentimentality may be dished out with a hot dinner, but it cannot help the old person who wants sustained friendship and interest. It is work which is not easy to arrange since someone must undertake the difficult task of 'matching' the lonely older person to a suitable available visitor, and since it is work undertaken voluntarily by busy people it needs constant supervision to ensure the continuity which is its most important feature. Some Old People's Welfare Committees use some paid help in the organization of this visiting, others continue to struggle with enormous lists of older people waiting to be visited, and hope that through district committees the lists of names handed out will eventually be visited. In some areas long and indiscriminate lists of old people have been collected for one purpose or another, e.g., for the issue of Coronation tea-caddies for all pensioners, or the distribution of food parcels sent from abroad after the War. Unless these lists have been carefully sorted out by subsequent visiting it is impossible to know what kind of needs they represent and whether friendly visiting is appropriate at all. Not nearly enough time and money has been devoted yet by the voluntary bodies concerned with old people's welfare to this unspectacular but important piece of work.[1] It might perhaps be better if voluntary bodies ceased to try and make an inadequate provision of services like chiropody, which manifestly should be part of the National Health Service provision, and concentrated on duties like friendly visiting for which they are in every way more fitted.

THE VOLUNTARY BODIES

The voluntary bodies interested in old people, and there are many apart from those bodies styled as Old People's Welfare Committees, have effected already the most important pioneer work in the field of welfare services for the old. At a time when public social services were being so greatly extended and improved that it could be seriously doubted if voluntary social effort had any major contribution still to make, voluntary organizations have given a brilliant demonstration of their adapt-

---

[1] Voluntary bodies in general are very well aware of the need for this kind of visiting, but in some areas find great difficulty in organizing an effective service.

ability in changing social conditions. They have picked their way through the administrative maze of legislation and circulars, taking advantage of what public funds are available for their work, but retaining their independence of management and with it their all-important function to experiment and make mistakes and to evolve new services. The influence of the more wealthy and influential bodies like the National Corporation for the Care of Old People has been tremendous in developing this work, but the most heartening feature is the mobilization of so much practical voluntary help at local levels, even in the smallest community.

What is needed now after some fourteen years of experience in developing voluntary welfare services for the elderly is a stock-taking and a candid review of what has been achieved and what policies are most likely to prove fruitful in future. Co-operation between voluntary and statutory bodies in providing for old people's needs can be an excellent arrangement, but voluntary bodies should not allow their effort to be a shield for lazy local authorities unwilling to carry out their responsibilities, nor should they develop a vested interest in doing good which keeps an inadequate voluntary service standing in the way of better statutory provision.

Voluntary bodies have to raise money and helpers from the general public and must enjoy its sympathy if they are to get their work supported. It is thus tempting to devote too much of the time of paid and trained social workers to organizing large-scale evacuations of old people annually, to the seaside complete with civic send-offs and receptions. This is excellent in itself, but these old people often may be the most hale and hearty, and the least in need of special help, and their interests might be equally well served by holidays organized through local clubs. Unless the limited numbers of full-time social workers are relieved of some of their duties of this kind, they will never have time to do the careful case-work which is needed among a smaller number of old people who have very difficult personal as well as material problems facing them in their old age. Such old people need skilled counselling of the kind we have developed in social case-work for younger persons.

Of course friendly visiting by interested voluntary workers is all that many older persons may need, and as has been rightly said one does not need a social science certificate to say 'good evening' to an old lady. But training and experience are necessary for the social worker who wants to work with old people at a more profound level, just as much as it is needed in dealing with maladjusted children or frustrated adults. There is still too much of a tendency for those working among old people to accept what they find and to be pessimistic about the possibility of some personality change and development even at later ages. When the psychologists have devoted as much study to senescent psychology as they have done to child psychology, workers with the elderly will be much better equipped to understand the personality and motives of elderly men and women and the range of possible adaptive behaviour. But already much which has proved fruitful in case-work with other age groups, for example, finding what is meaningful in past experiences and linking on to this the advice and help offered in the present, can be used with older persons too. Many general family case-work agencies are increasingly finding old people among their clients, and so their staff, like the case-workers of specialized agencies for the elderly, will need to broaden their knowledge and experience of counselling older clients. It is to be hoped that Social Study students in training will also be encouraged to approach older clients as a challenging but soluble problem in human relationships and to avoid accepting a stereotyped version of old age. The National Old People's Welfare Committee have developed training courses for those who wish to do residential work, or are already working in this way, among old people, and funds from the King George VI Jubilee Trust Fund have been made available to the Committee for further training schemes. With the general acceptance of the idea that every effort should be made to continue to keep about 95% of old people in their own homes, more attention might now be paid to evolving suitable training for those whose jobs it will be to help old people adjust themselves to their domestic environment as happily as possible.

Fortunately the number who need prolonged help are a small minority. As in other age-groups, there are a small number of old people who need more help than most of their contemporaries, but there is no need to suppose that people need extensive welfare services just because they are over pension ages. Families remain, despite the reduction in their size, the primary source of help and care, interest and affection for their older members, though they may be glad to avail themselves of the help of social services in looking after elderly relatives. Social agencies should concentrate their resources mainly on helping the minority of isolated old people without families or friends who need assistance in adjusting to increasing age and infirmity.

CHAPTER VII

MEDICAL CARE

SOME elderly people must be cared for either temporarily or permanently outside their own homes because they are sick, and their illness is of such a character that they cannot be properly treated and nursed at home. But notions about what kind of illness requires hospitalization and the kind of treatment deemed appropriate for old people admitted to hospitals have changed very considerably in recent years. So much so that something of a new specialism, geriatric medicine, has emerged, and special geriatric units have been created in hospitals. Some members of the medical profession, including a number of those directly concerned with the medical care of the elderly, do not favour the development of geriatrics, but suggest rather that our need is 'to restore the study of the aged and chronic sick to the common stream of medical activity'.[1] However that may be, certainly when health services were being reviewed after the War, it quickly became a matter of common agreement that a new approach was needed in treating the aged sick, and that some amelioration of conditions in infirmaries for the chronic sick was long overdue.

These infirmaries were parts of Poor Law institutions handed over to the newly created Public Assistance Departments of local authorities in 1929. In the years which followed they became principally[2] hospitals for the elderly chronic sick, accommodating paying as well as rate-aided patients who were un-

[1] A. P. Thomson, 'The Lumeleian Lectures', *British Medical Journal*, 1949, Vol. II, pp. 243 and 300. The Chronic Sick survey being carried out at present for the Ministry of Health will no doubt throw further light on the most effective way in which the medical care of the elderly can be improved.

[2] These institutions were also providing medical treatment for venereal disease, maternity, skin diseases in children, and other medical needs of the miscellaneous group of persons young and old who fell to the care of Public Assistance.

able to secure treatment in voluntary or municipal hospitals. During this period local authorities were empowered to appropriate some of these old institutions and turn them into municipal general hospitals, and a number were converted for this purpose. Thus at a time when the numbers of old people in the population were rising, the hospitals available for the chronic sick were being reduced.

Their history has to be remembered in looking at the conditions in these infirmaries after the War. They had inherited in many cases the old grim Poor Law buildings. They had more than the usual difficulties common to all hospitals in recruiting staff. Nurses were in short supply for this kind of work which involved much lifting of helpless and incontinent patients, and which had to be carried out in the general air of apathy prevailing in wards of old people who had often lost any hope of getting better and going home. Another heritage from the Poor Law was the comparatively high proportion among patients of solitary old people without families to visit them or homes to which they could, if recovered, be discharged. The pressure on beds was always considerable and these infirmaries had a statutory duty to take in sick old people on an admission order.[1] It is scarcely surprising that in these circumstances these institutions collected a number of bedfast elderly patients, some of whom occupied beds for very long periods, and that a substantial proportion of patients remained there for social rather than medical reasons. Or that numbers of patients became apathetic and that, lacking occupation and interests their personality as well as physical condition deteriorated irremediably.

In 1948 a survey[2] was made of the infirmaries in the Birmingham Hospital Region, including a detailed study of one large infirmary with over 1,000 patients. Of these (1,083) patients, 87% were bedridden, and of the bedridden nearly a half were incontinent. It was judged that all but 5% of the bedridden were beyond rehabilitation, but how far their disablement was due to being confined to bed for long periods it was impossible at that stage to tell. 70% of the patients were over 70 years of age, and 27% of men and 37% of women were over 80. This survey examined the length of stay of patients and drew attention to the fact that the infirmaries were dealing not

[1] See *The Aged and the Nation, op. cit.*, p. 34.
[2] The Care of the Ageing and Chronic Sick, *op. cit.*, p. 166.

only with the chronic sick but with many acutely ill old people. The proportion of those admitted in a year who died (32%), or were discharged (47·1%) within four months, demonstrated this. Only 5% of the total admissions in the year studied survived for 26 months or more, though these long-term cases accumulated to give an impression of a greater amount of very long-term sickness. About 85% of patients had been admitted without adequate prior investigation, and one-third of patients were in hospital for social rather than medical reasons. Marital status appears to be directly related to likely need for hospital care among the elderly. An analysis of the population structure of the chronic hospitals based on the Census of Great Britain 1951[1] has shown that about two-thirds of hospital accommodation for persons over 65 is occupied by the single, widowed and divorced. Among the single and widowed over 65 who need hospital care most of them are likely to be found in chronic or mental hospitals, and they form the majority of all patients in such institutions. The numbers of married men and women in hospital does not rise nearly so sharply as among single and widowed persons with advancing age, and even after 65 the percentage is still small. The authors of this study conclude: 'Marriage and its survival into old age appears to be a powerful safeguard against admission to hospitals in general and to mental and chronic hospitals in particular.'

Since the data were collected for these investigations the demands on available beds for the elderly sick have grown even greater, and have become one of the most pressing problems of the organization of hospital services.[2]

Several solutions have been offered for these difficulties and they all have basically the same objective, to reduce the amount of skilled bedside nursing to the minimum necessary and to use other kinds of care wherever possible to rehabilitate elderly patients. Dr. Marjorie Warren, Dr. Trevor Howell, Lord Amulree and others have demonstrated the possibilities of re-

[1] The 'Cost of the National Health Service in England and Wales', B. Abel-Smith (ed. R. M. Titmuss), The National Institute of Economic and Social Research, occasional papers, XVIII, 1956.
[2] 'Clearly a great deal more of the country's resources would have to be devoted to local authority and hospital services to make them fully "adequate" in this respect (i.e. the care of the aged).' Report of the Enquiry into the Cost of the National Health Service (the Guillebaud Committee), H.M.S.O., Cmd. 9663, paras. 640–2, pp. 214–15.

habilitation and re-activation of elderly patients formerly regarded as incurable. Their work has shown that a new attitude to the treatment of old people is as important as the discovery of new methods to be used by the physicians or physiotherapists. Where there is renewed hope of recovery, a change of surroundings and exercise and occupation, elderly patients are stimulated to fuller co-operation with those responsible for their medical care.

Rehabilitation cannot be attempted successfully for all patients since some have pathological conditions which in the present state of medical knowledge are beyond treatment. Others, whose original condition on admission might have been capable of treatment have by now deteriorated through long confinement to bed, and may have contractures and deformities which are not susceptible to much improvement. For such patients it is necessary to determine the extent of medical and nursing care needed and to see that they receive this from appropriate services. Cosin[1] suggests that a geriatric department ought to be divided into acute geriatric wards, a long-stay annexe for the frail ambulant, and a long-stay annexe for the ambulant. The two latter would provide for some patients' various degrees of temporary convalescent care prior to discharge. In addition he suggests long-stay accommodation for those who suffer from confusional states, and for the permanently bedfast. In whatever way geriatric units or departments are organized, the underlying principle is the same, to avoid getting an undifferentiated group of elderly patients lying in hospital beds for long periods without investigation and periodic review of their medical and social needs.

Even before entering hospital patients seeking admission need careful investigation to ascertain their medical needs, and, in view of the shortage of beds for the elderly sick, to estimate urgency and order priorities. Instead of the registration of long uninvestigated waiting lists, hospitals for the elderly sick now often have their own medical staff making domiciliary visits, and, in consultation with the patient's own doctor, deciding whether and how urgently the patients need to be admitted.[2]

[1] 'The Psychological Significance of Geriatric Rehabilitation', L. Z. Cosin, *Journal of the Royal Institute of Public Health and Hygiene.*
[2] J. Greenwood, 'Development of a Geriatric Service'. *The Almoner*, December 1955.

In the same hospital where the investigation was made by Professor Thomson[1] the position has altered considerably since 1948. Whereas in the earlier inquiry, about one-third of old people had on admission no disability so great as to necessitate a hospital bed on medical grounds, a study of female admissions (963) for 1950–1 showed that only half as many patients were admitted for mainly social reasons. Similarly a waiting list at this hospital of 1,091 between 1953 and 1954 was disposed of by admitting 59·9%, referring to other medical and welfare services 15·4%, while the remainder (24·7%) recovered, were refused admission, or died, leaving an actual waiting list of 19 persons.[2] Cases of old people urgently needing hospital care and unable to secure it come to notice too frequently for the situation concerning hospital care for old people to be regarded as in any way solved,[3] but domiciliary visiting has proved valuable in effecting the economical use of beds. The hospital gets an accurate picture of the need waiting to be met, and is not simply overwhelmed by a long uninvestigated list of elderly patients seeking admission. Moreover the medical staff know something of the patients' home environment both from the point of view of its relevance to treatment and to subsequent discharge.

One way of easing pressure on hospital beds is to make the fullest possible use of out-patient departments.[4] A geriatric clinic in an out-patients' department can enable some old patients to be discharged earlier with continued out-patient attendance, and can do preventive work with old people who might otherwise come to need a hospital bed. Services like physiotherapy, chiropody and the help of a hospital almoner can be given through an out-patient department, and though transport has to be provided, even with this cost it is cheaper if the need for a hospital bed is avoided and older patients are enabled to 'keep going' at home. In a few areas Day Hospitals are organized

---

[1] *Op. cit.*, p. 166.

[2] From information supplied by Dr. L. Nagley, Consultant Physician, Summerfield Hospital, Birmingham.

[3] At the end of 1953 it was stated by the Parliamentary Secretary to the Ministry of Health that although there were approximately 4,800 more beds for the chronic sick, waiting lists had continued to increase and numbered about 9,000 patients. See also 'The Neglect of the Aged Sick', *The Manchester Guardian*, 1953.

[4] See *The Right Patient in the Right Bed*, The British Medical Association, 1948.

where patients are collected and spend the greater part of the day at hospital but return to their own homes in the evening. By this arrangement older patients get any treatment needed, occupation and exercise, meals and company. This is particularly useful for infirm or mildly confused old people who could not stay at home all day alone in the absence of working relatives.

Nursing an old person at home may also necessitate some domiciliary services other than nursing and medical care. The availability of domiciliary welfare services both before and after hospital treatment, and, in some cases, in lieu of it, can help to reduce the demand for hospital beds. Dr. Brooke[1] has shown at St. Helier Hospital, Carshalton, how the effective co-ordination of social and medical services can mitigate the difficulties of an old person while waiting for admission, and may avoid the need for some admissions altogether.

The rate of discharge of older patients from hospital beds will depend not only upon their treatment and powers of recovery, but upon their home circumstances. Some old people have to be kept in hospital because they have no home or could not live alone and have no relatives. Such people can sometimes be transferred to Old People's Homes, but these too usually have waiting lists. Some old people are admitted to hospital from such unsuitable living conditions that it would be impossible to return them, but others come from their own or relatives' homes and it is of the first importance to maintain contact with relatives with a view to the subsequent return home of the elderly patient. Domiciliary visiting of patients seeking admission must be done in the first place by the hospital medical staff since the purpose is essentially to assess the *medical* need for a hospital bed. Later, however, hospital almoners[2] should visit the home to keep in touch with relatives and ensure that living arrangements are not so altered during the patient's stay in hospital that there is no room for the old person to return. Where these contacts are skilfully handled the chance of an old person being left with no home is minimized, and both the old person and his or her family are spared some anxiety and uncertainty. For old people who have no home or relatives

[1] E. B. Brooke, *The Lancet*, 1949, 1, 462.
[2] See 'Medico-social Work for the Aged in the United Kingdom', paper from the Geriatric Almoners sub-committee to the Gerontological Conference, St. Louis, U.S.A., September 1951.

admission to hospital for social reasons can be avoided and discharges facilitated if more housing and Homes with various degrees of care are provided.

Even where, however, the fullest use has been made of domiciliary services to enable older persons to remain well cared for in their own homes, there remain some old people who may not need the full services of a hospital bed, but who need a degree of continuous nursing care which cannot be provided by relatives or by statutory or voluntary welfare services in their own homes. Attempts to meet the needs of such patients without using unnecessarily expensive hospital services has led to the development of an intermediate kind of care sometimes called the 'half-way house'. For the reasons discussed above (see p. 159) there has been real difficulty in deciding who is to deal with the needs of elderly persons who need, either temporarily or permanently, more than the degree of care usually provided by local authority welfare homes, but who do not require a hospital bed.

The Guillebaud Committee[1] examined this problem to decide whether there was a genuine gap in the present structure of welfare and health services which led to the need for half-way care, or whether the difficulty in meeting this type of need arose from the financial limitations which have hindered the full development of services theoretically available under health and welfare legislation. The Committee came to the conclusion that there is no real gap in these services; that special half-way care as a form of long-term provision for older people[2] is not a desirable development as a public service, and that all needs could be met if the respective duties of the welfare and health authorities were clearly demarcated and defined. Though such a clarification of the respective roles of the welfare, local health and hospital authorities is most welcome and valuable, it may appear to those statutory and voluntary agencies which are daily confronted with the problem of providing for old people who cannot be neatly classified as ambulant, frail-ambulant or hospital cases, that the Committee underestimates the difficulties which arise from tripartite administration of the

[1] Report of the Committee of Inquiry into cost of the National Health Service, Cmd. 9663, 1956.

[2] The Committee's conclusions do not apply to half-way homes as a form of transitional convalescent care, which they believe forms a proper part of the hospital service.

health services. To change this pattern of administration, however, despite its generally admitted shortcomings, presents so many practical problems that even those who advocate it as an eventual necessity do not suggest that changes (e.g. the transference of the hospital services back to the control of local authorities) can be effected at present. There seems little chance, therefore, of improvement of services by altering the overall pattern of administration of the Health Services in the immediate future, and such gaps as exist must be closed by some re-organization of functions within the existing structure.

The Guillebaud Committee, in defining the respective duties of welfare and health authorities assumes that 'intermediate accommodation' will be provided by local welfare authorities. In addition to nursing minor and terminal illnesses, the care of infirm old people needing some help in dressing, etc., and who may need to spend some part of their days in bed, is considered by the Committee to be a suitable function for Welfare Homes. They recognize that some nursing staff will have to be employed in the Homes for this purpose (though the Committee expressly rejects any arrangement which would create again the old infirmary wards) and they recommend an Exchequer grant to local authorities to assist in the further development of this work.

It is difficult to see how this recommendation, if accepted, will not produce the very half-way Homes condemned earlier by the Committee as unnecessary. If local welfare authorities are responsible for patients who need skilled nursing supervision for varying periods, but are not suitable for permanent hospital care, they will either have to send them to hospital from time to time or nurse them in their Homes. If transfer of elderly residents to hospital for anything but minor or terminal illnesses is to be strictly carried out, some residents of Homes would be frequently in transit between a Home and a hospital bed, which seems neither a practical nor a humane way of meeting their needs.

If they are not so transferred, they will need intermittent nursing care in the Homes, and to make the best use of existing buildings and trained nursing staff it is likely that some Homes will be specially organized to deal with this kind of resident rather than the more active elderly. These Homes will thus become half-way houses.

To accept that, among other provisions, the statutory services should include a type of more permanent half-way care for old people, would be to recognize the range and variety of elderly persons' needs, and not necessarily, as the Guillebaud Committee suggests, to create 'yet another category of aged patients, adding to the difficulties of defining borderline cases'.[1]

The problem of institutional care for the elderly who are mentally ill presents great difficulties. The shortage of beds in mental hospitals is acute, and in any case the elderly who are only mildly confused or suffering from simple senile dementia, do not need mental hospital care. Even when beds are available it is not always possible to get a confused old person to understand and give consent to being a voluntary patient, and unnecessary certification is offensive to relatives and may be prejudicial to their interests in other connections. Sometimes certification is made in order to get a confused elderly patient admitted to some kind of care, and this is highly undesirable from every point of view. Abnormal mental conditions among old people need to be distinguished and investigated with a view to treatment just as much as any other conditions from which they suffer. The report of the British Medical Association in 1949[2] stated that 'only after expert assessment by a psychiatric consultant in this (i.e. geriatric) department should a patient be sent to a long-stay annexe as irremediable or to a mental hospital as likely to benefit from the active treatment provided in modern hospitals of this kind'. This remains a pious hope. Moreover those suffering from some degree of senile dementia are not a group which can be easily looked after in accommodation provided by voluntary bodies, though the latter have been much concerned with this problem.[3] It is to be hoped that the Royal Commission at present sitting to inquire into the detention and certification of mental patients will direct special attention to the needs of elderly psychiatric patients.

Fortunately the majority of old people do not need hospital beds and they will receive such care as they need from the general practitioners. It seems to be a matter of common agreement that an increasing amount of the time of general prac-

[1] Cmd. 9663, *op. cit.*

[2] See 'The Care and Treatment of the Elderly Infirm', Report of the British Medical Association, 1947, p. 10.

[3] See Memorandum to the Board of Control, submitted by the National Old People's Welfare Committee, 'Progress Report', 1954.

titioners is taken up with elderly patients. There are more older patients at risk, they may need more domiciliary visiting, and they must be dealt with more slowly. A sample of eight practices in England believed to be representative[1] showed that patients who were 65 years or older had on the average significantly more consultations per patient than younger patients. More extensive representative studies need to be undertaken, however, before the demands of older patients upon general practitioner services can be accurately assessed.

It is sometimes suggested that general practitioners have not the time to deal adequately with the old and that local authority health services should now play a similar part in providing health care for the elderly to that which they have so successfully undertaken in the care of mothers and children. Local health authorities were of course given very wide responsibilities under the National Health Service Act to provide preventive health measures and after-care for all age-groups including the elderly. There is no doubt that the work of the domiciliary nurse and health visitor and other local health officers will increasingly be concerned with the very old as well as the very young. The primary function of the general practitioner is to secure for his patient adequate medical care, and his work will be greatly assisted if, through the local authorities and voluntary bodies, there are domiciliary welfare and nursing services available to his patient. But to set up special clinics for the elderly,[2] as has sometimes been advocated, would be a retrograde step since it would tend again to take the treatment of the elderly out of general medicine. The development of special local health services for mothers and children preceded by many years the concept of a free and comprehensive health service, and to encourage the proliferation now of geriatric clinics when the National Health Service is established would surely be a wrong use of available resources.

The National Health Service is not yet, by any means, fully comprehensive in design (quite apart from the inadequacy of provision in the services theoretically available), and there are some lacunae in its structure which are particularly unfortunate

[1] See R. C. Walsh, 'Medical Care of Old People at Home', paper presented to the Gerontological Congress, London, July 1954.

[2] See W. F. Anderson, 'A Clinical Study of the Patients attending a consultative Health Centre for old people at Rutherglen, Scotland', paper presented to the Gerontological Congress, London, 1954.

for the elderly. An obvious gap is the failure to make sufficient provision for chiropody. Chiropody is provided under the National Health Service where it is necessary in connection with hospital treatment and there are also a very small number of foot clinics which were in existence before the Act began to operate, and which have been allowed to continue. Chiropody is also usually given to elderly residents who need it in local authority Old People's Homes, but this does not help the very much larger numbers of old people living at home, who need this kind of treatment. Some voluntary bodies make provision for this need but it is a fairly expensive service for them to provide for large numbers of people continuously, even if the organization is receiving a grant towards its funds from the local authority. It is also an expensive service for old people themselves if they need fairly frequent treatment. Even a subsidized chiropody service requires a contribution from the old person of sometimes as much as 3s. 6d., though 1s. 6d. and 2s. are more usual. Needy old people may not be able to afford the charge, especially as it is not a purpose for which the National Assistance Board may make grants. So far about fifty schemes are reported, by the National Old People's Welfare Committee, to have been developed by voluntary bodies, and the hindrance to further development is undoubtedly the cost.[1] A subsidy of from 3s. to 4s. per patient may have to be made for each treatment at a clinic and more for domiciliary visits. Foot troubles are very common among old people and a voluntary body may find itself very quickly with three or four hundred old people requesting a subsidized chiropody service. To set this up may involve an expenditure of £500 or £600, of which not more than a third is likely to be recoverable from the old people treated. This voluntary effort is admirable and deals with a very real need; but it can do no more than nibble at the problem which is obviously one which should be dealt with through the National Health Service.

Representations to the Minister of Health have not so far elicited any early intention to include chiropody in the National Health Service and it remains to be seen whether the further recommendation about the need to include chiropody in pre-

---

[1] The National Corporation for the Care of Old People has recently set aside a fund for grant-aid towards chiropody services provided by voluntary bodies.

ventive health services which has been made by the Guillebaud Committee[1] will be accepted.

Much anxiety has been expressed about the effect upon the total cost of the National Health Service and upon the distribution of available resources within it, which may be created by the increasing numbers and proportions of old people. A recent study of the cost of the National Health Service made for the Guillebaud Committee[1] has paid particular attention to the effect of likely population trends upon the future cost of health. The conclusions which emerge from this inquiry should dispel some of the earlier alarming predictions about the 'medicated survival' of rising numbers of very elderly persons.[2]

Changes in age-structure are not expected by themselves to increase the cost to public funds of the service by more than $3\frac{1}{2}\%$ by 1971–2. At present about one-fifth of expenditure is estimated to be due to the use made by old people of the health services, though this does not include, as it undoubtedly should, the cost of the heavier demands of the elderly on the general practitioner service. If this could be accurately costed, and if a more adequate expensive service for old people (e.g. in chronic and mental hospitals) is provided in future, the increase in health costs due to a rising proportion of old people in the population might be substantially larger than this estimate of $3\frac{1}{2}\%$. This study strongly confirms by its lucid analysis of health service costs what has long been surmised by those who have to try and secure appropriate health care for old persons, namely that social factors like marital status, family relationships, and occupation, are of paramount importance in determining whether old people have to resort to hospital care; social and medical needs are not distinct but directly related to each other. The results of such a study show that much research will need to be conducted to assess more fully the influence of changing social habits in, e.g., marriage rates, the size of families, the employment of married women, etc. on the health care of older men and women. The findings of such inquiries may well cause us to change considerably our present conceptions of the best way to provide satisfactory care for physically frail old people.

[1] *Op. cit.*, p. 17.
[2] See, for example, *The Cost of Health*, Ffrangcon Roberts.

...some considerations which will have to be the full-kind Committee will be accepted.

Much anxiety has been expressed about the effect upon the future of the National Health Service and upon the disparity between available resources within it which may be created by the increasing numbers and proportions of old people. A recent study of the cost of the National Health Service made for the Guillebaud Committee has paid particular attention to the effect of likely population trends upon the future cost of health. The conclusions which emerge from this feature stand clearly point of the cost, the changing population, about the immensely small of change amount or over elderly persons.

Chances in the way which are not occupied by themselves to increase the way in number node of the world. In fact, their gladly the elderly. At present about one tenth of expenditure is estimated to devote to the use made by old people of the health service; though this does not include cost unfortunately, should the cost of the service. If this were to demands in the elderly on the general operation of this would be appreciably raised, and so their non-particular expensive part the old people. So, in chronic and mental institutions is provided by society, the greater. In health care due to a rising proportion of old people in the population would be substantially larger than this, perhaps 3½%. This study strongly confirms by us held analysis of health care workers has long been stressed by those who have to try and secure appropriate health care for old people, namely that social factors like marital status, family relationships and occupations, are of paramount importance in determining whether old people have to resort to hospital care; social and medical needs are not distinct but directly related to each other. The results of such inquiries show that until research will need to be conducted to assess more fully the influence of changing social habits in, e.g. marriage rates, the size of families, the employment of married women, etc., on the health care of older men and women. The findings of such inquiries may well cause us to change considerably our present conceptions of the best way to provide satisfactory care for increasingly aged people.

See, for example, The Cost of Health, Chapman, London.

APPENDIX I

Post-War Trends in Employment of Older Workers, 1945–48

(Nos. of workers of pensionable age in employment in the Midland Region 1945–48 and the percentage they formed of all workers employed) *

	Dec. 1945		June 1946		Dec. 1946		June 1947		Dec. 1947		June 1948	
	No.	%	No.	%	No.	%	No.	%	No.	%	No.	%
Manufacturing Industries:												
III. Non-Metal products other than Coal Mining	1,849	4·1	1,954	4·9	1,736	3·3	1,691	3·1	1,739	3·0	1,931	3·1
IV. Chemicals	692	3·4	562	3·7	526	3·0	492	2·8	509	3·2	469	2·9
V. Metal Manufacture	3,810	4·2	3,673	4·0	3,390	3·8	3,165	3·2	3,338	3·2	3,477	3·5
VI. Engineering	6,814	3·4	6,234	3·1	5,836	2·9	5,732	2·8	5,887	2·7	6,362	2·9
VII. Vehicles	4,377	3·6	3,849	3·2	3,932	3·2	3,180	2·5	3,245	2·7	3,149	2·6
VIII. Metal Goods	8,684	4·6	8,477	4·3	8,418	4·4	8,000	3·9	8,515	3·9	8,491	3·9
X. Textiles	1,292	5·1	1,492	4·8	1,446	4·5	1,433	4·3	1,596	4·3	1,609	4·2
XI. Clothing	638	4·4	602	3·7	602	3·4	543	2·9	585	3·1	591	3·2
XIII. Food, Drink and Tobacco	1,799	4·6	1,598	3·9	1,453	3·5	1,324	3·1	1,319	3·0	1,441	3·2
XIV. Cork and Wood	685	5·5	683	4·8	706	5·1	623	4·5	626	4·1	703	4·4
XV. Paper and Printing	768	5·2	725	4·4	686	4·3	675	3·5	714	3·6	750	3·8
XVI. Other Manufacturing Industries	700	2·6	739	2·8	725	2·4	744	2·4	801	2·5	805	2·4
Total	32,108	3·9	30,688	3·8	29,476	3·6	27,602	3·2	28,874	3·2	29,715	3·3
Non-Manufacturing Industries:												
XVII. Building and Contracting	19	0·8	16	0·6	21	0·6	24	0·9	26	0·9	27	0·8
XVIII. Gas, Water and Electricity	352	5·2	334	4·6	266	3·7	245	3·2	266	3·1	282	3·5
XIX. Transport and Communications	213	2·6	425	1·5	356	1·3	293	1·0	345	1·2	428	1·4
XX. Distribution	998	3·8	881	3·3	843	3·0	792	2·8	815	2·8	803	2·8
XXI. Insurance, Banking and Finance	23	7·3	19	5·9	24	6·5	24	5·6	18	4·4	18	4·4
XXIII. Professional Services	100	4·8	110	5·0	81	3·7	92	4·1	91	3·7	93	3·6
XXIV. Miscellaneous Services	515	3·8	568	4·3	515	4·0	501	4·8	596	4·4	633	4·7
Total for non-manufacturing industries	2,220	3·6	2,350	2·9	2,106	2·6	1,971	2·5	2,157	2·5	2,284	2·6

* Source, Ministry of Labour.

APPENDIX II

INQUIRY INTO EMPLOYMENT POLICIES TOWARDS OLDER WORKERS IN 57 FIRMS

57 firms in and near Birmingham were asked to give some details of their experience of employing older workers. This was not a representative sample of all firms in the area, but the firms in question ranged in size from 28 to 24,000 employees and fell within twelve of the standard industrial classification groups. The inquiry, therefore, which was intended as the basis for some further study of the problem of employing older workers, included a wide variety of occupations. Compared with the national distribution of the working population (Ministry of Labour Manpower Statistics) firms in the industrial grouping, including engineering, electrical goods, metal goods, precision instruments and jewellery, were heavily over-represented, which is characteristic of Birmingham and industrial South Staffordshire. No workers in the building industry, in transport and communications, or in gas, electricity or water undertakings were included, and the groups mainly represented here were industrial factory workers.

A questionnaire was circulated to firms agreeing to co-operate in this inquiry, followed by personal interviews with managers, labour officers and foremen. In most cases someone representing the highest level of management discussed the firm's employment policy with the interviewer.

A statement of personnel was obtained divided into three age groups, viz. those born before 1st July 1883, those born between 1st July 1883 and 30th June 1893, and those born after 1st July 1893, and these groups were again divided by sex and industrial status. An analysis was also requested of the length of service of these three groups and their experience of time lost by lateness and absence during the period January to June 1948. These data, together with the answers obtained to a further series of questions (Form II), formed the basis of the inquiry.

APPENDIX II

INQUIRY INTO EMPLOYMENT OF OLDER PERSONS

1. How many older employees are retained on their former job?
   - (a) How many transferred to special jobs and at what age were they transferred?
   - (b) On what types of work are these older employees successfully engaged?
   - (c) Describe very briefly any types of work that have been selected as specially suitable for older workers.
   - (d) Where older workers are transferred, give details (e.g. Medical Officers' reports) of the more common disabling defects, e.g. loss of eyesight, rheumatism.

2. Dividing these older workers into
   - (a) i. Those who remain in their old jobs

     and
     - ii. Those who are transferred to selected suitable work, what is the method of remuneration, time or piece rates, bonuses, etc., for each group?
   - (b) Are the earnings of Group 1 appreciably less after pensionable age?

3. (a) Do older workers take part in any form of team work?
   - (b) Are they able to contribute their fair share to the output of the team?
   - (c) Are they 'carried' by the other workers and is this resented?
   - (d) Are there any teams composed entirely of older workers?

4. (a) Are there any special conditions created for older workers, such as—

1. Lighter jobs.	5. Different piece rate.
2. Reduced pace.	6. Relaxation of any rules, e.g.
3. Less responsibility.	lateness.
4. Reduced hours.	7. Any other special concessions.

   If so, please give particulars.
   - (b) Do you think being placed in such special categories would be resented by older workers?

5. Make some comparison of behaviour of older workers under the following heads:
   1. Need for supervision.
   2. Respect for employers' tools and property.
   3. Keeping general rules.
   4. Influence on behaviour of other workers.
   5. Attitudes towards management, sense of loyalty to the firm.

6. Give details of your pension scheme and any ways in which this will be affected by the new National Insurance Scheme.

7. Give details of special welfare schemes for pensioners either remaining with or retiring from service with the company.

8. Detail the views of your Company on compulsory retirement (dividing this into staff and manual, men and women, etc.).

9. Give details of any experience you have in training older workers and their ability to learn new methods.

10. Give the views of your Labour Officers on the extent to which there is any friction between younger and older workers, e.g. resentment about delayed promotion. Is there lack of co-operation of elder workers, especially in positions of authority, e.g. foremen, in accepting new techniques?

11. Can you give any indication now if these older workers participate in Workers Organizations, e.g. Trade Union activity or in Employee-Employer Committee, etc.? Do they find their way into the positions of responsibility and leadership?

12. (Where applicable)
Apart from the problems of deciding whether to retain or dismiss workers who have reached either your own or the State Insurance retirement age, do you find that there is the problem of the worker on very heavy manual work who is physically impaired at perhaps 50 or 55? How do you deal with these employees? Would it be practical to consider schemes of diversion and retraining at this age rather than allowing them to continue on this heavy work at substantially less than their former efficiency until retirement age?

13. (Where applicable)
Could older persons be used to replace
   (a) juveniles
   (b) married women
on some jobs if they were paid a correspondingly lower rate?

In this study of 104,638 employees of whom 73.3% were men, 2.7% were men over the age of 65 years and 0.7% were women over the age of 60 years. A further 11% of men were between the ages of 55 and 64 years, and 4.2% of women were between 55 and 59 years.

Dividing workers into those over 65 years (60 for women), those 55–65 years and those under 55 years, there was not a great variation in the numbers classed as skilled and unskilled manual workers and clerical workers in the different age groups. These were, of course, very approximate divisions, but it was not found possible to evolve a more precise division which could

APPENDIX II

TABLE I

Age and Industrial Status

MALES

65 years and over				55–64 years				Under 55 years			
% of all Males	% Skilled	% un-Skilled	% Clerical	% of all Males	% Skilled	% un-Skilled	% Clerical	% of all Males	% Skilled	% un-Skilled	% Clerical
2·7	27·0	64·1	8·9	11·0	26·9	63·2	9·9	86·3	24·6	64·1	11·3

FEMALES

60 years and over			55 to 60 years			Under 55 years		
% of all Females	% Manual	% Clerical, etc.	% of all Females	% Manual	% Clerical, etc.	% of all Females	% Manual	% Clerical, etc.
0·7	92·7	7·3	4·2	92·7	7·3	95·1	82·7	17·3

'Clerical, etc.' included clerical, technical and administrative employees.

adequately cover all the processes involved, and the category skilled or unskilled depended therefore on the subjective and customary judgments of individual employers.

Individual firms showed some variation on these proportions, in some cases a higher percentage of the oldest age group being

TABLE II

Range in the proportions classified as skilled, unskilled and clerical workers among individual firms

	MALES			FEMALES	
	% Skilled	% Unskilled	% Clerical	% Manual	% Clerical
Men aged 65 Women 60 years	22–47	57–100	0–15·4	87–100	0–12·2
Men 55–65 years Women 55–60	12–37	66–94	0–17·5	68–100	0–11·4
Men and Women under 55 years	27–48	62–84	0–18·6	61–96	3·1–38

skilled workers than among the general body of workers, in other cases the reverse being found. But the impression often gained that chiefly skilled workers are retained in employment can be corrected by looking at the older men doing unskilled and miscellaneous tasks not in the direct line of production.

Work on which older persons were successfully engaged

Only one firm thought older workers not suitable for any employment, and a wide variety of suitable jobs was mentioned. Some firms indicated up to ten different types of work which were being successfully undertaken by older workers in their employment. Six firms thought all kinds of work could be successfully carried on except very heavy work, and eleven said the most important point was to let older workers go on in the jobs with which they were familiar and in which they could exercise their accumulated experience and skill. Supervisory work was not mentioned by many firms. Eight gave examples of light inspection, two used older foremen successfully and one older manageresses.

TABLE III

Work being successfully undertaken by older workers, and work suggested by employers as specially suitable for older workers

Type of Work	No. of firms where this was successfully done	No. of firms who suggested this as specially suitable for older workers
Factory, directly on production:		
General	33	13
Supervisory	11	10
Factory, but not directly on production:		
Clerical	9	7
General labouring	44	19
Stores and warehouse	12	13
Cleaning and shop-sweeping	12	14
Canteen	4	—
Porters and attendants	19	16

When employers were asked to suggest specially suitable work they did not mention many kinds of skilled factory work (e.g. sheet-metal work) which, in fact, older workers could be found doing successfully. They tended to think of very light work and miscellaneous jobs, for example porters, cleaners, and the like. Not many firms suggested clerical work, probably because few older clerical staff want continued employment and there are obvious obstacles to the transfer of the older manual worker to such employment. Although two firms successfully employed older foremen no firm suggested this as especially suitable for older men. There seemed some evidence that employers tended to divide older workers into two groups, those who continued at their old job without anyone really noticing their age, and the others who needed to be found more suitable employment because of age. For the latter there was a tendency to look automatically for light labouring or miscellaneous service jobs out of the main stream of production. This may in fact be the best use which can be made of some older workers, but more consideration might be given to other possibilities before transfers are made.

TABLE IV

Retention of older workers on former jobs

23 firms stated that they retained					ALL	on former jobs
20 ,,	,,	,,	,,	,,	MOST	,,
5 ,,	,,	,,	,,	,,	SOME	,,
1 ,,	,,	,,	,,	,,	NONE	,,
8 ,,					NO INFORMATION	

Of the 19 firms who gave details of transferring older male workers, 5 had moved workers between 50 and 60 years, 11 had transferred workers between 60 and 64 years, and 3 firms had made this adjustment for those over 65 years.

A number of firms commented on the difficulty of finding suitable light work to which older workers could be transferred since so often the light work available involved a greater degree of accuracy and speed, a higher degree of mental concentration, and good eyesight.

Of the commonest disablements necessitating a transfer of older workers to other employment 35% of firms mentioned rheumatism, 22% cardio-vascular conditions and 19% respiratory diseases. Less specifically 10 firms mentioned failing eyesight, 14 general physical fatigue, and 3 had made transfers because they suspected accident proneness.

APPENDIX II

One large metal manufacturing firm (employing 6,167 workers, of whom 788 were over 55 years) who kept careful medical records, analysed their transference of older (i.e. 55 and over) workers for certified medical reasons as—

	%
Rheumatism and allied complaints (fibrositis, etc.) .	20
Respiratory diseases	25
Peptic Ulcers	12
Cardio-Vascular diseases	8
Accident	8
Miscellaneous conditions	27

Methods of Remuneration for Older Workers

The majority of older workers who had been transferred were paid time rates because they had been moved to the type of work normally paid in this way, but they continued to earn the same amounts as any other workers on similar processes. Only 7% of firms mentioned any drop in earnings associated with transference. Among older workers remaining on their former jobs there was no reduction of earnings since their retention presumably meant that they could maintain the same standards of performance as they did before reaching pensionable age.

Old Workers in Team or Group Work

Employers were asked if their older employees took part in any form of team work and whether any difficulties arose out of this, where older workers had to keep pace with younger men. Information was also requested about any team work done by groups composed only of older workers.

TABLE V

Use of older workers in team or group work

19 Firms	.	.	.	.	Yes
21 Firms	.	.	.	.	None
9 Firms	.	.	.	.	Rarely used
8 Firms	.	.	.	.	Question not applicable

Only 3 firms thought that older workers failed to contribute an equal share to the team's output along with other workers, and only one thought that there was any evidence of resentment among younger workers. Firms gave isolated examples of older workers being 'carried' to some extent by the rest of the team, and 'the reaction to this varies from good-natured quipping to open and strong resentment'. If the slowness of an older worker so dislocates the work of a team that their wage packets are affected, the other workers without openly stating their reasons will ask for transfers. Failing this they will certainly complain.

In answer to a further question about the possibilities of friction between younger and older workers, very few examples were offered of this, though some firms did mention 'the dead man's shoes' problem caused by retarded promotion. Younger charge hands found they needed to be especially tactful in handling older workers and some younger workers complained that they got all the heavier jobs. Such friction as there was, however, seemed to arise from the well-known difficulties of youth and crabbed age living together and did not arise particularly out of the work situation. For instance, in a department of women workers the complaints of the older women were vaguely about the way the young girls 'carry on'.

On the other hand many firms said that the older worker, steady, reliable, and experienced, was often the backbone of the group. Of the 19 firms actually using older workers in teams, 13 said they thought older workers contributed their fair share and were never carried by younger workers, and a further 3 firms thought that their older workers were very rarely carried by their younger team-mates.

Only 4 firms had special teams of older workers, 3 of these being firms with over 5,000 employees. The general opinion was that, apart from the practical difficulties of arranging such work, it was undesirable to segregate older workers and likely to be much resented by them. Special workshops may become quickly labelled 'old crocks' shops' and by drawing attention to the age of the workers in them cause anxieties and embarrassment.

Training Older Workers

37 firms had had no experience of training older workers, 12 had had some experience, and 5 gave no information on this point. The firms without experience had a very negative attitude towards teaching older workers, 'we have never tried', 'we do not train', 'we do not put elderly people to learn new methods', 'not necessary', 'impractical', were typical comments.

Of the 12 firms which had tried training older workers 5 had found it fairly easy and 7 very difficult. The 3 firms who had trained them successfully for manual work said it was for simpler tasks and semi-skilled work in the main, while the other firms had trained them successfully for clerical work. The firms which had experienced difficulty mentioned the longer time taken to learn a process by older workers and their strong conservatism. 'There is no harder job in the mill than to try and sell an older worker a new method', one firm commented.

Diversion and Re-training of Workers at 50–55 years

Firms were asked about the problems of finding suitable employment for the man of 50 or 55 years whose powers, perhaps ten years before normal retirement date, are physically impaired and who needs to be transferred to other work. Could schemes of earlier diversion and training make it possible for more older men to continue afterwards beyond normal pension age?

39·3% of firms said the question was not applicable and a further 10·7% said they did not think the problem would arise. Only 12·5% of firms recognized this problem while the remainder thought that the situation might arise very occasionally. Most firms transferred such workers to lighter jobs if they had them available, and some had found that men left if this involved any drop in earnings. Most firms were suspicious of the idea of retraining well before retirement ages, considering it impracticable and unnecessary. A few firms did welcome the suggestion though they had no ideas about how to implement it, except by continuing to transfer their prematurely aged workers to such lighter jobs as they had available.

Replacement of (a) Juveniles (b) Married Women by Older Workers

Employers were asked whether, in the event of a shortage of labour of the kind they normally used, they could substitute the labour of older workers.

A quarter of the firms did not feel able to give any information on this question and a further 13% in the case of juveniles, and 11% in the case of married women, were doubtful. A quarter of the firms, however, thought juveniles might be replaced and about 16% thought it possible to substitute for married women.

TABLE VI

Substitution of Older Workers

No. of firms	%	JUVENILES %	No. of firms	%	MARRIED WOMEN %
14	25·4	Yes	9	16·4	Yes
20	36·3	No	26	47·2	No
7	13·0	Doubtful	6	11·0	Doubtful
14	25·3	No information	14	25·4	No information
55	100·0	—	55	100·0	—

The figure is higher for juveniles since they also are often employed, at any rate in their initial period, on miscellaneous service jobs, such as older men might do. On the other hand, married women are likely to be engaged in quick deft repetitive work at a pace which older men would find difficult to sustain. The majority of firms did not favour this idea, no doubt because they would have to pay more (an adult man's rate) for the job formerly done at the wage rates of women and juveniles, unless they carried out some substantial re-arrangement of their work.

TABLE VII

Special Conditions for Older Workers

Concession	No. of firms giving this	%	No. of firms not giving this	%
Lighter jobs	29	53	26	47
Reduced pace	11	20	44	80
Less responsibility	13	24	42	76
Reduced hours	25	45	30	55
Different piece rates	3	6	50	94
Relaxation of rules	9	16	46	84
Any other special conditions	10	18	45	82

General opinion among employers on concessions was divided fairly evenly into three schools:

(a) those who were willing to extend all reasonable concessions in order to keep the older worker at his maximum usefulness.

(b) those who considered that in the interest of general discipline it was dangerous to relax conditions in any way.

(c) those who would treat every case on its merits but appreciated that they would then have to face the problem of establishing precedents which might prove embarrassing.

TABLE VIII

Number of Concessions given by 55 Firms

(Two firms gave no information)

No. of firms	% of all firms	No. of special conditions permitted
12	22	NONE
17	31	1
12	22	2
7	13	3
5	9	4 and over
2	4	ALL concessions mentioned in inquiry

The Type of Concession Granted to Older Workers

While about half the firms were prepared to give lighter jobs and reduced hours, concessions involving reduced pace, different piece rates, and relaxation of rules were not given by approximately 80% of firms. Nearly as many rejected the idea of reduced responsibility, but that may have been because many firms thought this a concession unlikely to be often needed. One firm stated that 'the mental characteristics required for shouldering responsibility do not deteriorate as do the physical faculties, and therefore this concession is seldom called for. If, due to loss of manual dexterity, an older worker cannot cope with a fast automatic or semi-automatic machine, it is obviously essential to reduce his burden of nervous tension by transferring him to a slower machine.'

14 firms gave concessions which involved arriving later or leaving earlier than other workers. One firm which did not permit this stated, 'Rather than permit the older worker to slip away early or clock on late if he is not sticking the pace, it would be preferable to institute set reduced hours of work for

part-time workers, though part-time employment has a number of attendant complications.'

Firms were asked if they thought that older workers might resent special conditions because it categorized them as elderly.

Assessment of Attitudes of Older Workers to Special Concessions

There was a marked division of opinion among managements as to whether special concessions were welcomed or not by older workers. 19 firms (35%) thought they were likely to be resented, but 24 firms (44%) thought that concessions were likely to be acceptable. Those firms who gave this latter opinion added that the granting of such concessions needed to be tactfully handled, that they should be given at the workers' request, and that they should not be such as would very adversely affect the wage-packet. If these conditions were not fulfilled they agreed that 'Older workers may not want special conditions'.

TABLE IX

Attitudes and Conduct of Older Workers compared with Other Workers as judged by Employers

	Less	Same	More	No information	Good	Bad	Negligible
Need for supervision	64%	26%	2%	8%	—	—	—
Respect for employers' tools and property	—	22%	67%	11%	—	—	—
Keeping general rules	18%	18%	—	11%	71%	—	—
Influence on behaviour of others	—	13%	—	16%	60%	—	11%
Attitudes towards management	—	9%	—	7%	84%	—	—

43·6% of all firms gave favourable answers to all questions and all firms commented approvingly on the punctuality of older workers.

Participation in Workers' Organizations, Trade Union Activity, Employer-Employee Committees, etc., of Older Workers

Only 11 firms said that older workers were active in such matters, mainly dependent upon whether they had been interested and active in these organizations in the past. The majority of firms felt that their older workers were not very interested and tended to leave positions of responsibility to workers younger than themselves. Some commented upon the way the older man seemed interested only in looking after himself. This is another example of the way in which the natural inclinations of the elderly to introversion may be interpreted as selfishness by younger people around them.

Time lost by Older Workers owing to Lateness, Sickness, Accidents and other causes

Hardly any firms kept sufficiently detailed records to make a valid comparison between older workers and other employees in the matters of absenteeism and lateness. 21 firms were able to give information about employees over 55 years, but were unable to compare this with any records for younger workers. From these figures and from comments offered by many firms, it is apparent that in general older workers are good timekeepers, and were often described as the best group in the factory in this respect. Similarly, apart from absence due to sickness or accident, older workers took very little time off with or without permission. The figures given for time lost owing to sickness or accidents by the 21 firms who had this information available, showed that workers over 65 years lost less time for these reasons than those between the ages of 55 and 64 years. This may be because in most cases the man over 65 years has already moved away from work involving any accident risk, and he may have light work not demanding much physical exertion or strain. Or it is possible that the men who continue in employment after pensionable age are a highly select group having greater physical stamina and being in general more efficient and careful workers. In any case the numbers over 65 years are much smaller than those aged 55–64 years and it would be unwise to draw any definite conclusions from such limited evidence.

One large metal manufacturing firm employing 6,167 workers gave a detailed analysis of time lost owing to various causes,

APPENDIX II

TABLE X

Older Workers. Comparison of Lost Time Rates in one Large Firm
(Period—6 months, January–June 1948)

(Proportion of shifts lost to shifts called for, expressed as a percentage)

| Age group | Reason for lost time | | | | Total lost time | No. of workers involved |
	Sickness	Accident	Absence with leave	Absence without leave		
MEN:						
Over 65 *	6·6	·4	·2	·2	7·4	38
Over 65 †	4·0	·4	·2	·2	4·8	36
55–65	4·9	·1	·2	·1	5·3	471
All ages	3·4	·3	·5	·4	4·6	3,836

* Includes two men whose large amount of sickness distorts the overall picture.
† The figures for men over 65, excluding the two men referred to above.

TABLE XI

Older Workers. Comparison of Lost Time Rates in one Large Firm
(Period—6 months, January to June, 1948)

(Proportion of shifts lost to shifts called for, expressed as a percentage)

| Age-group | Reason for lost time | | | | Total lost time | No. of workers involved |
	Sickness	Accident	Absence with leave	Absence without leave		
WOMEN:						
Over 65 *	1·1	—	7·8	—	8·9	7
Over 65 †	1·3	—	1·9	—	3·2	6
55–65	6·7	—	1·0	·2	7·9	100
All ages	5·0	·1	2·5	1·9	9·5	2,331

* Includes one woman worker whose absence with leave to nurse a sick sister accounts for 56 of the 71 shifts lost under this heading.
† The figures for women over 65 excluding the woman referred to above.

APPENDIX II

which is shown in Tables X and XI. Even including individuals whose bad record distorts the general picture, the superiority of the older worker in punctuality is very marked, and less time is taken off with or without permission. For men sickness rates are higher. The accident rate is also higher but this is a severity rate which is likely to be higher among older workers. Older women show a considerably lower incidence of lost time in all categories than the average for women workers of all ages. For older men the higher rates of sickness and accidents experienced is balanced by less absenteeism due to lateness or time taken with or without permission, so that in total their record departs very little from the normal figures for lost time for workers of all ages.

Length of Service of Older Employees

46 firms gave information about the periods of service completed by their older workers, covering 10,836 employees (Table XII). It is interesting to note how many older men and women had obtained their present employment in the previous ten years. A quarter of men aged 55–64 years and a fifth of men aged 65 and over had no more than five years' service with their

TABLE XII

Length of Service of Employees over 55 years of age

	MALES		FEMALES		TOTAL	
	55–64	65 and over	55–59	60 and over	Males 55–64 Females 55–59	Males 65 and over Females 60 and over
No. of Employees	7,507	1,975	1,062	292	8,569	2,267
Years of Service in Factory:						
0–4	25·5	21·0	43·4	34·2	22·6	27·5
5–9	20·0	21·0	28·0	25·7	21·6	20·9
10–14	10·8	10·5	6·6	5·8	9·9	10·9
15–19	8·3	8·2	5·0	6·9	8·0	8·0
20–24	8·4	10·2	2·7	4·4	9·5	7·6
25 and over	27·0	29·1	14·3	23·0	28·4	25·1
	100·0	100·0	100·0	100·0	100·0	100·0

present employers, and the proportion of women with shorter periods of service was even higher. Thomas and Osborne[1] report rather similar findings in their survey, 26% of manipulative workers, 17% of operatives and 30% of unskilled workers having less than five years' service in the firms employing them, and women again having shorter periods of service. Mobility, at any rate between different firms, is greater than is often assumed to be the case among older workers.

Special Welfare Provisions for those of Pension Age either still working or after leaving employment

Firms in general in this inquiry did not provide any special welfare services, older workers participating in such welfare provision as was made along with other workers. It was clear, however, from the comments on this point that many firms kept a special eye on the needs of older employees in the same way that they felt some extra responsibility for young recruits to their pay-roll.

11 firms mentioned special provision for pensioners. These included continued membership of social clubs, regular visiting to collect pensions, tea parties, Christmas presents, encouragement to seek advice, including legal advice from the firm's staff, and various kinds of discretionary financial assistance. One firm had all its pensioners visited by a welfare officer if they were unable to collect their pension in person. Many more firms who had no special schemes indicated that they would view sympathetically any appeal for advice or help from old employees with long records of service, even after they had left the firm's employment.

Retirement Policies for Older Employees

Firms were questioned about the attitude which they adopted towards retirement for older workers and especially if they operated any compulsory retirement regulations. The answers were requested separately for staff and works employees since the policy of a management often differs as between salaried and manual workers. Firms operating a compulsory retiring age were few, 1·9% for manual workers, 11% for staffs.[2] These

[1] *Older People and Their Employment, op. cit.,* p. 60.
[2] It must be emphasized that this information about retirement policies is given to illustrate attitudes which were found among employers, and since

figures are lower than those found in the Ministry of Labour Survey,[1] which were 8% for manual workers, and 14% for others. This is because the group of manufacturing industries

TABLE XIII

Policies relating to Retirement of Male Employees

Policy relating to retirement	Works			Staff		
	No. of firms	%	% of all employees covered	No. of firms	%	% of all employees covered
Compulsory retirement enforced	1	2	6	6	11	14
Retirement at fixed age expected and preferred	13	25	37	14	26	33
Older workers definitely encouraged to remain as long as they wish	10	19	5	7	13	3
No compulsion ever used	21	40	43	18	34	48
No definite policy, at discretion of management	8	15	10	8	15	2
	53	100	100	53	100	100

studied here did not include any transport workers, who are included in the Ministry's survey and for whom there is a good deal of compulsory retirement (see p. 194). Again the staff considered here that was clerical, administrative or technical consisted of those found mainly in manufacturing industry, distributive trades and miscellaneous services, and did not include the staff of banks, insurance companies, Building and Friendly Societies included by the Ministry, who are commonly subject to fixed retirement ages.

It must not be assumed that an absence of compulsory retire-

it is not based upon a representative sample it can only indicate *very approximately* the likely proportions of workers who may be subject to the policies described.

[1] *Ministry of Labour Gazette*, Vol. LVII, No. 4, April 1949, 'Age of Compulsory Retirement from Work'.

ment rules means that men are encouraged or in all cases permitted to go on working as long as they feel fit and able. The Ministry of Labour survey reported 86% of firms having no compulsory scheme for male manual workers and none for 76% of male staff, but this ignores the pressures which amount almost to compulsion where men feel they are expected to retire by their employers and fellow workers. Firms were therefore asked in our inquiry to define their management's general attitude and customs and conventions prevailing in their undertaking with regard to retirement, quite apart from any precise rules. It then appeared that there was a further number covering (37% of works employees and 26% of staff) which did not operate fixed rules but which stated clearly that they expected and preferred their employees to retire at a fixed age. The combination of compulsory retirement rules and a strong convention of retirement at a fixed age gives a rather different picture. 26·4% of firms employing 43% of manual workers would regard working beyond retirement age only as very exceptional. 37% of firms employing 46·5% of staff expected to retire these employees at a fixed age. This is nearer to the report made by Osborne and Thomas that about a third of men aged 55–74 interviewed by them said that their employment was subject to compulsory retirement. In our inquiry nearly 40% of firms employing 43% of manual workers did however state definitely that they did not use, and did not approve of, fixed ages for retirement. 34% of firms employing 48·4% of staff also adopted this attitude.

In our study of Midland firms only a small proportion of workers (4·5%) or staff (3%) was in firms whose management stated that they actively encouraged older workers to remain in employment and made it possible for them to do so. One of the discernible differences in retirement policy between the smaller and larger firms was that no firm with over 700 employees pursued a policy of active encouragement to older workers to remain on, though firms of all sizes stated that they did not use compulsory retirement provisions. The relationship of the size of firm and its policy towards older workers is difficult to interpret. It may be the type of work done in small firms, for example skilled precision work, or the type of craftsman needed, which causes the small firms to have a higher proportion of older workers than the bigger firms and to retain them longer. Size of firm and the percentage of older workers used were found to be in inverse ratio in our study but the type of work and the age of the business may be more relevant than the scale of the undertaking in determining its policy towards older workers.

Some firms (15%) preferred to avoid having any definite and stated policy on retirement since they felt that this was a matter for discretion and a consideration of each case on its merits when the occasion arose. They wished to be free to vary their decisions for individual workers and, more important, to adjust policy to their current demands for labour. As one company expressed this—'the company's policy must remain flexible and conditioned by trade and the employment market. Political considerations *vis-à-vis* the general society of management and workers play a larger part in the decision (i.e. to retain or retire older men) than do the financial aspects of employing older workers.' This firm and others expressed clearly the concept of the older worker as a marginal worker.

All but one of the firms which enforced compulsory retirement, all the firms who expected their staff to retire at a fixed age, and nearly two-thirds of the firms who expected their work people to retire at 65 years, had some kind of pension or superannuation provision. Some firms stated that they had instituted pension schemes expressly in order to be able to operate a retirement age without undue hardship. One firm operating a compulsory retirement age defended their policy on the ground that compulsory retirement permitted the promotion of able younger men and painlessly removed older workers whose efficiency had lessened. They admitted that at times they regretted losing a good man, who was still an effective worker, because he had reached the age limit, but they felt that in view of the difficulties of demonstrably measuring efficiency especially on the staff and management side, and the dissatisfaction likely to follow discrimination, a fixed retirement age was the most satisfactory policy. It should not be overlooked that discretionary policies can be very damaging to the self-respect and confidence of older workers. To be retired at a customary age along with others who have reached the same birthday may be more acceptable (though strongly protested against at the time) than a policy in which some employees are retained and some retired. The latter are made more inescapably aware of their

APPENDIX II

failing powers by this rejection than if they had been subject
to an arbitrary rule based on chronological age and applied to
everyone.

It is interesting that the firms which operated compulsory
schemes or those which expected employees to retire at fixed
ages found it necessary to defend and justify their policy from
some supposed suggestion of harshness towards old and faithful
employees. Firms which did not operate a compulsory scheme
took satisfaction in reporting this, and many adopted a slightly
scandalized tone, 'we should not think of compulsorily retiring
loyal older servants of the company', and so on. Many emphasized the fact that the decision had to come from the
employee himself or herself, and it was obvious that '*compulsory*
retirement' was a loaded term. Consideration for elderly employees, whether by prolonged employment or pension provision, was clearly ranked alongside training for juveniles,
works canteens, and adequate toilet facilities, and the like, as
evidence of the 'good' employer and the 'progressive' firm.

TABLE XIV

Provision of Pension Schemes

MALES

	Works			Staff		
	No. of firms	% of all firms	% of employees covered	No. of firms	% of all firms	% of employees covered
No scheme for works or staff	10	19	5	10	19	9
No scheme	17	32	40	3	6	5
Contributory scheme	15	28	29	32	60	71
Non-contributory scheme	4	8	21	4	8	13
Ex gratia payments	7	13	6	4	8	2
	53	100	100	53	100	100

In 53 firms giving details of their provision, if any, for retired
employees, over half of male manual workers (55·4%) and over
four-fifths of male clerical and administrative staff were covered

by some kind of payment derived from their employment. Just under 30% of firms had contributory schemes including all male workers irrespective of status, but many firms differentiated between manual workers and staff. Nearly a quarter of firms, employing 13·6% of male staff, made no pension provision for them, and a much larger number, over a half of firms and nearly a half of male manual workers, had no provision of pension schemes. Ex gratia payments at the discretion of the management was a device used more frequently for manual than staff employees. No clear relationship emerged between size of firm and pension provision. Some of the larger firms (over 2,000 employees) had no pension provision for their operatives, but no very large firms failed to provide a pension scheme for its staff. Ex gratia payments were more frequently used in smaller firms, but non-contributory schemes were in being in firms of all sizes.

With two exceptions, those firms who had no pension provision allowed older workers to continue in employment as long as they felt fit and able to do so. A number of firms stated their intention of reviewing their policy in this matter in future, and it is likely that there has been an increase in pension provision for manual workers in the last five years.

Most schemes fixed 65 for men or 60 for women as the expected retiring age and were calculated with reference to length of service. Employers could be divided into two main groups by their attitudes towards pension provision. Some thought of it as a reward for long and faithful service in rather the same category as awarding gold watches to employees who had been with the company twenty-five years, while the rest regarded a pension scheme as one of the conditions of employment which, along with other amenities and rates of pay, enabled them to attract and retain the labour they needed. The older and smaller firms, especially those using a non-contributory scheme or ex gratia payments tended to fall into the first group, while larger expanding firms competing for young labour and suffering from higher labour turnover rates thought of pension schemes as one of the advantages which could be held out in recruiting their labour force. In both groups there were employers who had found that a regular pension scheme saved them the heart-searching which otherwise took place when an old employee, with many years of service, was unfit to continue

APPENDIX II

in their employment and no one could contemplate retiring
him without some further financial assistance. The view that
contributory pensions for manual workers should be, like those
for clerical and administrative staff, a condition of employment
normally offered has gained ground steadily in recent years;
though the greater mobility of the manual worker as compared
with the 'white collar' employee presents some difficulties in
attaching pension rights to place of employment.

APPENDIX III

NEEDS AND PROBLEMS OF OLD PEOPLE

A Sample Survey of Old People over seventy in Birmingham[1]

THIS was essentially a local survey and the topics covered in the questionnaire were mainly those which it was felt might be tackled at a local level, e.g. visiting, a hot meals service, holiday arrangements and, to some extent, accommodation. No questions were asked about income or the adequacy of pensions, though where such information was offered it was recorded. The general impression was that very acute poverty among the elderly had virtually disappeared though old people were found who were unaware of the services to which they were entitled, for example, a supplement to their pension from the Assistance Board. Those living alone who had to meet the full cost of rent and fuel were very frequently those who complained of financial difficulties.

This inquiry was not concerned only with the aged poor. It covered a number of old people of all income groups in different parts of the city, and indeed one of its purposes was to discover the non-financial needs of older people. Problems of loneliness or infirmity in old age are not confined to any one social class or income group.

The investigation was carried out by the author in collaboration with the Birmingham Old People's Welfare Committee who recruited a number of voluntary visitors in addition to paid investigators. The experience of these voluntary helpers, who were used to visiting old people, was most valuable both in collecting and assessing the replies to the questionnaire. Two

[1] This inquiry was carried out in 1948 but it seems useful to present the results here since, as is confirmed by later studies, many of the problems revealed still exist despite the development of various welfare services for old people in the past seven years.

thousand five hundred visits were completed in 1948, and the information here presented [1] is based on the reports made of these contacts with old people.

The Sample

The old people visited were a random sample of old persons of both sexes taken from the records of the Birmingham Food Office. The number of old people aged seventy years or over who were drawing an extra tea ration was approximately 50,000. This list did not include every person over 70 years in Birmingham living in private homes, but it was likely to include[2] almost all of them. Careful inquiries and observation led us to suppose that irrespective of income groups there were very few men and women who did not apply for their extra tea ration. Those who did not want it for their own use arranged to dispose of it to people who did. From the tea list a completely random sample of one in twenty was extracted, giving 2,500 names.

In comparing the figures given below with the results of other investigations it should be remembered that this survey covered only the over-seventies, not all those who have passed the conventional retirement ages of 65 years for a man and 60 years for a woman. The figures are not therefore directly comparable with those reached in the Rowntree or Wolverhampton inquiries.[3]

Of the 2,500 old people visited we were not able to collect information from 270 of them for various reasons, such as deaths, removals, severe illness or refusals. The number of refusals was not high (3%), most old people being glad to have a visitor. The refusals tended to come from the higher income group households where sometimes domestic problems and certainly financial problems were not so acute as in poorer districts. Information was recorded for 2,230 households, mainly in one interview, but sometimes a second or third visit was necessary.

[1] The results of this inquiry were presented as an interim report to the Old People's Welfare Committee in December 1949 and have been used by them in planning some of their work.

[2] No persons over seventy in hospitals or institutions were included, and this affects the proportion of single old people and those without any relatives who were interviewed.

[3] See 'Old People', *op. cit.*, p. 18.

APPENDIX III

TABLE I

The Sample

(a) Composition of the sample by age and sex

Age	Males	Females	Total
70–74 years	62·1	59·4	60·1
75–79 years	30·7	23·9	27·0
80–84 years	5·1	12·6	9·6
85 years and over	2·1	4·1	3·3
Total	100·0	100·0	100·0
Total all ages	39·8	60·2	100·0

(b) Sex and Marital Status of Sample

Status	Males	Females	Total
Married	24·7	13·3	38·0
Widowed	14·1	40·7	54·8
Single	1·0	6·2	7·2
	39·8	60·2	100·0

Compared with the age and sex distribution in the Census taken three years later (1951) those aged 70–74 years were over-represented and those aged over 80 years were under-represented.

Widows formed the largest single group and by comparison with investigations based on samples of old people of pension ages, there was, as one would expect, a lower proportion married and a higher proportion of widowed persons. Of all male subjects in the sample 62·1% were married, 34·1% widowers and 3·8% single. Of all female subjects 66·7% were widowed, 23·0% were married and 10·3% were single.

Domestic structure

Nearly 40% of the old people interviewed were living alone or with a spouse only, and the remainder lived with relatives, a landlady or communally. Of those not living alone 93·4% lived with relatives. The sample did not include old people living in Public Assistance institutions, but it did include some small voluntary Homes.

The answers to that part of the questionnaire which inquired about immediate domestic needs were examined separately for old people living alone because we formed the general impression, confirmed by the experience of statutory bodies, like the National Assistance Board, as well as by the voluntary bodies, that it was this group who were likely to be in the greatest need of welfare services.

Those living alone were 889 out of 2,230 (39·8%). This group contained a higher proportion of males to females, and a higher proportion of married subjects than in the whole sample.

TABLE II

Sex and Status of Old People Living Alone

Sex	Those living alone	Total sample
Males	47·2	39·8
Females	52·8	60·2
Total	100·0	100·0

Status		
Married	59·4	38·0
Widowed	33·3	54·8
Single	7·3	7·2
Total	100·0	100·0

A larger percentage of this group asked for various kinds of domiciliary services especially the single and widowed living alone.

TABLE III

Services Requested

Help Requested	Living alone or only with spouse	Living alone (widowed and single only)	Total sample
Hot Meals	36·5	42·3	30·7
Domestic help: Males	9·7	12·8	7·3
Females	13·9	14·0	8·0
Shopping	5·4	7·2	5·2
Club membership	31·6	31·5	29·0
Nursing care	3·7	5·0	4·2
Holiday arranged	30·3	36·0	44·0

These figures, especially those relating to the numbers who might join a club or take a holiday, must be treated very cautiously. Such services sound attractive and some old people may say they would like these things but cannot in fact make the effort to use them or cannot afford them when the service is offered. Following this survey it was found that there were many old people in the city who welcomed the chance of a cheap holiday arranged for them and several large parties of old people now have such holidays annually organized by voluntary bodies. But not all the people in the sample who *said* they would like a holiday did in fact take advantage of the arrangements to have one.[1]

Housing

The majority of old people over seventy in Birmingham were living in houses, mostly of the non-Council type.

		%
Living in Non-Council Houses		75·9
,,	,, Council Houses	11·7
,,	,, Rooms or Flats	10·0
,,	,, Alms Houses	·5
,,	,, Hostels or Homes	·2
,,	,, Other Accommodation	1·7
		100·0

Of those living in houses, 82·6% were themselves, or with their families (with whom they lived as one household), the sole occupiers, and 15·6% shared with other than family.

State of Repair of Old People's Dwellings

The kinds of signs our visitors looked for were leaking roofs, dilapidated brickwork and defective pointing, broken stairs and doors, swollen and warped doors and windows, and very extensive dampness. 'Good' was applied to sound property which could be made comfortable accommodation for old people and this was applied even where painting and decorating needed doing as was the case with so much property at that time. The standard taken therefore was a fairly low one, and of course the figures related to housing all over the city, including good

[1] See also p. 230 below.

property in the residential districts. Classed as in good, average and bad state of repair the accommodation of old people was as follows:

$$48\cdot2\% \ (1075) \ \text{Good}$$
$$39\cdot0\% \ (\ 870) \ \text{Average}$$
$$12\cdot8\% \ (\ 285) \ \text{Bad}$$

Our general impression was that, while we found individual cases of bad housing, and especially of housing not bad in itself but unsuitable for old people, older persons were not worse housed than the rest of the population, but were on the whole probably slightly better, having regard to the acute housing shortage in the city.

As far as household facilities were concerned, the majority, over 70%, had their own kitchens, but 15·8% had to share and 3·7% had no kitchen at all. In 91·9% of cases the old person had a bedroom to himself or herself (and spouse) but only 53·5% had their own sitting room, and 33·8% shared. The sharing of living rooms was however rarely complained of by the old people who seemed to like being in the midst of the family's activities. Such complaints as we heard were rather from younger members of the household who did not want to have the old people always with them. A substantial proportion of dwellings had no bathroom (46·2%), which is a reflection of the fact that so many of these old people live in older types of housing without this amenity. This figure, and indeed all these figures of housing conditions, were for the whole city, i.e. they included 'good' as well as 'bad' housing areas. If these figures are divided into districts according to the type of property which predominates, wide difference in housing amenities appear.

For example, of the old people's dwellings visited over the whole city 40·1% had inside sanitation, and 59·9% had outside sanitation. But if a good class residential district is compared with a poorer one the following differences are seen.

	All Districts	Residential Area with some poor parts	Poorer District
	%	%	%
Inside sanitation	40·1	69·7	4·3
Outside ,,	59·9	30·3	95·7
	100·0	100·0	100·0

APPENDIX III

These poor housing conditions will have been to some extent improved since 1948 but by no means eliminated. An inquiry into living conditions among persons over seventy in London found that of 100 homes studied, 22 were very unsatisfactory, 8 needed structural repairs and 34 obviously needed re-decoration; 33 had outside sanitation and in 53 cases it had to be shared.

Housing Needs

The old persons visited were asked about their present accommodation, and this was usually a subject about which they were very willing to talk. Of 2,230, 374, i.e. 18%, said definitely that they wished to move, which is quite a high figure for over 70's in a sample covering all parts of the city. In the outer areas of the city fewer older people wanted to move, more of the old people had the kind of housing they wanted and only 7% expressed a desire to move. In the more central areas, the numbers rose to 28%.

Those who expressed a definite wish to move were further questioned about their reasons, and what sort of dwelling they would like.

TABLE IV

Reasons given for desiring to move house

Reason	Numbers	%
Didn't like house	70	18·7
„ „ sharing	26	7·0
„ „ district	43	11·5
„ „ town	2	·5
House too large	101	27·0
„ „ expensive	16	4·3
Other Reasons	116	31·0
All Reasons	374	100·0

The interesting result here was that the largest single reason distinguished was that their dwellings were too large for many old people, that is, theirs was a problem of 'undercrowding' rather than overcrowding.[1] This view was expressed to many of our visitors, often in the better residential districts, where a large house often imposes an unwanted domestic burden for a

[1] See also Sheldon, *op. cit.*, p. 16.

single old person or couple, especially for those over 70 years of age.

The answers to parts of the questionnaire relating to housing amenities and needs were examined separately for this group of persons (374) to try and ascertain further why they found their present accommodation unsatisfactory, and why they were prepared even at 75 years or more to face the upheaval of moving their home. Analysed by age, there were more (4%) of old people under 75 in this group than in the whole sample, but since 8% of these ready to move (30) were over 80 years it does not seem as if age was particularly significant; it was not necessarily the younger ones who were ready to leave and the older ones who would not. Of those wanting to move, a larger number than in the rest of the sample were in rooms, 5·1% more, and correspondingly fewer in houses.

There was a marked difference between the state of repair of property which its occupiers desired to leave and that recorded for the whole sample, as one would expect. Those who wished to move had in every way less housing amenities and household facilities than those interviewed in the general sample.

TABLE V

Sex and Marital Status of Old Persons wishing to move (374)

Status	Males	Females	Total
Married	106	68	174
Widowed	28	141	169
Single	6	25	31
Total	140	234	374

Thus 46·5% were married couples, 45·2% widowed or single old ladies, and 8·3% widowed or single old men.

The preferences expressed for new dwellings by those who wanted to move were closely related in most cases to what they had known before. They preferred in the main to have the same type of accommodation again. It was difficult to convey the idea of a Home or Hostel to many old people whose idea of a Home tended to be connected with the old Poor Law.[1]

---

[1] Old People's Homes have become much more widely provided and appreciated since this inquiry in 1948.

APPENDIX III

Married couples who wanted to move, numbering 174, expressed the following preferences:

Bungalow	House	Flat or Rooms	Hostel or Home	Alms House	No Opinion
99	45	5	1	—	24

and of the 99 wanting a bungalow 88 were living in houses, and of the 45 wanting a house 39 were living in a house.

TABLE VI

Housing preferences of those old people who stated they wanted to move from their present housing

	Bungalow	House	Flat or Rooms	Hostel or Home	Alms House	No opinion
Married couples	99	45	5	1	—	24
Single men	2	2	1	1	—	—
Widowers	7	9	3	—	1	8
Single women	14	3	3	1	1	3
Widows	66	29	17	5	6	18
Total	188	88	29	8	8	53

56·2% of married couples wanted a bungalow and a further 25·9% a house. Only 2·9% mentioned a flat or rooms. Although many wanted some smaller dwelling, they wanted an independent separate dwelling, not anything communal. Widows had a marked preference for bungalows too, 47% asked for a bungalow and a further 20·6% for a house. But 12% asked for a flat and 3·5% for a Home or Hostel. Of the 6 single old men who wanted to move house two wanted a bungalow and two a house, one asked for a flat and one for a Hostel.

It was impossible in this kind of inquiry to discuss rents or even the district an old person would wish to live in, and obviously these preferences might be very much modified if a choice could really be presented to each old person. On the other hand most of these old people had very fixed and definite views about what they wanted and these figures probably indicate the general trend of their likely choices.

APPENDIX III

Domestic Arrangements

A number of questions was put by our investigators to ascertain how old people managed their shopping and cooking and domestic work and, as other surveys have shown, it is remarkable how many of these older people well into their 70's do in fact manage to run their homes and cope with problems of shopping and queueing and lack of domestic assistance.

Shopping

Nearly 60% of the old people did their own shopping, the rest getting this done for them mainly by relatives and in a smaller number of cases by neighbours. Most of the people we interviewed (1,722 out of 2,230) were within easy distance of a shopping centre and only 5·2% said they would like help with their shopping. This is not an easy need to fill. Few women like the idea of delegating their shopping, at any rate not to anyone outside their own family, as long as they can manage to do this themselves.

Meals

64·4% of the old people we interviewed cooked their own meals, and a further 27·4% had theirs prepared by others. Very few stated they ever ate meals out in a café or restaurant, and only 4·2% used a British Restaurant regularly for some meals while 78·8% said they never used them. The idea of having a hot meal delivered once or twice a week was popular with 30·7% of all those visited but it varied considerably between districts. Again in this case the question of cost could not easily be discussed as at the time of interviewing no hot meals service existed. Some of those who said they would like this might therefore find it too expensive if it cost more than perhaps 1s. per meal. Our visitors remarked on what seemed to them a good deal of voluntary malnutrition on the part of old people because they did not feel they could make the effort to cook for themselves and because they often accepted unsatisfactory diets for fear of being a nuisance.

Domestic Work

64·5% women subjects stated that they did their own housework, and we found older women of up to 80 years old managing quite strenuous domestic tasks. Some of them also helped their families by looking after children or keeping house while a son or daughter went to work. Of those who did not do their own housework (36·5%) 24·4% were helped by relatives and 12·1% had some paid help. Only 8·7% said they would like some domestic help. Among the men subjects who were married in almost every case their wives did the housework, but where help was needed a higher proportion, 16%, had paid help, and 33·4% were helped by relatives. Men subjects did not ask for domestic assistance to a greater extent than women (7·3% compared with 8%). But in comparing these figures it must be remembered that the numbers of men interviewed contained a high proportion (62·1%) who were married and whose wives were over seventy themselves. The larger number of women interviewed contained more very old people, since women's expectation of life is longer in the higher age groups, and there are more solitary elderly women likely to need help with the heavier domestic tasks.

Infirmity

Owing to the nature of this kind of inquiry it was not possible to make more than a very approximate inquiry about matters relating to health, but questions were asked to try and ascertain the degree of mobility normally enjoyed.

The following table shows the proportions of men and women who were active and able to leave their homes. The higher percentage of active old men is again due to the fact that the total number of old women in our sample included a greater number of very elderly women.

TABLE VII

Mobility of old people interviewed

	Active	Able to leave the house	Bed-ridden
Men 70 and over	73·5	13·5	3·0
Women 70 and over *	55·9	31·0	2·1
Women 70–74 years	55·7	27·5	1·3
Women 75–79 years	40·1	36·3	1·5
Women 80 years and over	32·4	27·9	6·6

* There was a higher proportion of very elderly persons among women than among men. Table I (*a*), p. 218.

The remainder (10% of men and 11% of women) were classified as able to move about one room or to move about their house. Thus 75·1% of these old people over 70 were able to leave their homes and 51·1% could be described as active.

1,430 out of 2,230 said they left their houses regularly and this corresponds approximately to the 1,316 who did their own shopping, noted earlier. Those who were infirm, and most of them were suffering from what they themselves and their relatives considered to be more or less permanent infirmity, were looked after almost entirely by relatives, in most cases by daughters. Some inquiry was made about eyesight by asking whether the old person was able to read or sew, and those unable to do so together with those who were blind and those who had very defective sight were 16% of the whole. Some of these were the oldest persons visited in the inquiry. Those who informed us, or whose relatives informed us, that they suffered some degree of deafness numbered 21% of those visited. Those persons we visited who were still in employment were especially active, and the over-70 men who remained in work seemed to derive considerable satisfaction from their ability to continue in employment. They, like the active older women who ran their own households, appeared often to have made a good psychological and physical adjustment to old age. They may very well have been a selected group endowed with better health than those who retired as soon as they reached pension age.

Loneliness and Visiting

During the inquiry some information was collected about the problems of loneliness and occupational interest for old people. The problem of lack of occupation was more marked among men rather than women. Women were to some extent occupied with housework but men who had retired and thus suffered a sharp jolt in the rhythm of their working lives were often bored. Our investigators were sometimes drawn aside by old ladies and begged, 'If only you could find him a job, miss—something regular to do!' Our inquiry bears out the results of the Wolverhampton survey, that having a job to do, or an absorbing hobby, appears to strengthen the will to live in old people. Older women who were obviously the mainstay of the household and had to cook and shop and mind grandchildren, were less troubled by their physical infirmities, and too busy to dwell on a sense of being a burden or unwanted. But solitary older women with no families did complain of loneliness, especially where defects like deafness made social contacts difficult. There is obviously room here for voluntary personal service, for this is essentially a task suited for voluntary effort. Loneliness was found among older people of all social groups, and those who had no request for any kind of financial or material help did express their appreciation at being visited.

Of those old people living alone 59·2% were visited by relatives, 2·2% by the Assistance Board, 6·7% by a Church or voluntary body, and 31·9% did not anticipate any kind of regular visiting.[1] Of those who were visited with some degree of regularity

41·1% were visited weekly
8·8%   ,,   ,,   monthly
5·1%   ,,   ,,   3-monthly
2·1%   ,,   ,,   yearly

and a further 11% said they received irregular visits mostly from relatives. A number of old people living alone had of course a pattern of family relations round them either in the shape of regular visiting and assistance or family who could be called on in the case of illness or other emergency.

Occupational Interests and the use of Leisure

Old people were asked about the way in which they spent their leisure time and were asked especially if they would use a club if there was one in the district. 70·1% said No, though some old people (mainly men) expressed interest in this suggestion. Others, a smaller number, said they would be glad of books and handwork materials.

5·3% would have liked a Radio
8·4%   ,,   ,,   ,,   Books
4·3%   ,,   ,,   ,,   Handwork materials

An examination of leisure pursuits of old people both inside and outside the home was made in the course of the survey. Reading and listening to the wireless were the most popular occupations. 9·4% said reading was their only occupation, and

[1] In the inquiry 'Over Seventy' (1954) 52 out of 100 old people had no regular visiting.

8·6% said they only listened to the wireless. Reading and listening to the wireless were among the occupations of 41·3% of old people interviewed. Reading, listening to the wireless and knitting was the most popular combination of home interests for old ladies, and reading and wireless for old men. More old men than old ladies liked reading and the numbers fell off among the very old which may have been due in part to failing eyesight. 16% of old people in the sample were blind or had serious defects of vision, and 21% had some degree of deafness.

Nearly a third of men mentioned gardening and the extent of this hobby of course corresponded to some extent to facilities; for example there were fewer men in the central city area who gardened than in the outskirts of the city. This occupation was mentioned mainly by men and women in the 70–74 years age-group. Keeping pets was most popular among old women living alone and knitting was a common occupation among this group also. More single or widowed old women did knitting and handwork than married old women, which is probably due to a greater amount of leisure. 4½% of all old people in the sample said they had no occupation at all.

Outside interests were mainly found among the 70–75 group as would be expected, though one old man of 76 told us his hobby was dancing! Church is still the most common outside interest for older people; 36·8% mentioned this as one of their outside interests. The cinema came next in popularity (22·2%), while visits to a public house were mentioned by 8·2% (mainly men). Allowance here must be made for the fact that more people are willing to say they go to Church than that they use a public house. Clubs were mentioned by 6·8% of old people.

35·1% of old people said they had no outside interests of the kind mentioned in our inquiry, though of course some of the interests examined under the heading of home interests do take old people outside their homes, i.e. reading may mean for some old men visiting the reading room of a public library.

Holidays

All the old people visited were asked when they last had a holiday or any kind of stay away from home. 27% had not been to stay away from home for 9 years or more. Asked whether they would welcome any help in arranging a holiday, a fairly large number (32%) said Yes to this question and no doubt meant it at the time (especially those old people who were visited in the depths of winter!). But of course all these generally expressed desires have to be translated into definite alternatives and choices before we can estimate the effective demand for such a service. When arrangements were made for a holiday some of those who had expressed a desire for a holiday did not avail themselves of the opportunity. The time, the place or the cost may not have been suitable for them, and some of them probably faced with a real choice and not a doorstep inquiry could not in fact make the effort required to go away from home. This kind of experience has a valuable lesson for the interpretation of results obtained by the survey method.

As we noted earlier, except in the case of holidays, there is a higher number of solitary old people needing welfare services. The exceptions in the case of holidays is probably due to the numbers of very old people in this group who feel unable to face the change and movement involved even in having a holiday arranged for them.

No doubt some of the needs revealed in this survey have been met and difficulties mitigated by the improvement since 1948 in the development of both statutory and voluntary services for old people. It is interesting to note however from more recent inquiries[1] that the proportion of elderly people in touch with and using special services for old people is still not very large, if this inquiry is in any way representative. In this group, in which 33 were aged 70–74, 40 aged 75–79 and 27 aged over 80 years, 87% did not belong to any kind of club, though in 44 cases there were obvious reasons, e.g. infirmity; 43 had no knowledge of the local Old People's Welfare Committee, and 93 had had no contact with it in the current year. 23 of the men and 29 of the women, that is just over half of the old people, had no regular visitors. The Report also states, 'The housing conditions of people in the sample were little or no different from those found in 1947 in the two London Boroughs included in the Nuffield survey.' On the other hand 27 old people were getting some help with domestic work from the home-helps service, which reflects the extension in recent years of this very valuable domiciliary aid for the elderly.

[1] *Over Seventy, op. cit.*

230

INDEX

Abel Smith, B., 17, 85, 108, 122, 182
Abrams, M., 25
accidents, 49–51, 206–8
Almoner, The, 183
almshouses, 145
American Association of Social Workers, 115
Amulree, Lord, 34, 182
Anderson, W. F., 189
Appointments Bureaux, 70, 74

Bacon, F. W., 87
Barron, M. L., 74, 78
Belbin, R. M., 48
Benjamin, B., 87
Bethnal Green, 171
Beveridge Report, 1, 96–7; assistance, 87–8, 97; deferred retirement, 21; estimated pension costs, 98; flat-rate benefits, 121; retirement condition, 21, 104–5; social insurance principles, 120–1, 123; subsistence benefits, 104, 118; transitional pensions, 96, 99–100; voluntary provision, 86, 109
Birmingham Food Office, 217
Birmingham Hospital Region, 181
Birmingham and Midlands Employment Inquiry, 194–215; jobs opportunities, 45; suitable work, 45
Birmingham Survey, 216–30; housing, 135–7, 220; households, 151; leisure, 172, 228–9
Bismarck, 103
Black, E. I., 142
Board of Control, 188
boarding out, 168
Booth, Charles, 89
British Association, 48

British Journal of Industrial Medicine, 28, 51
British Journal of Physical Medicine, 52
British Journal of Social Medicine, 19
British Medical Association, 166, 184, 188
British Medical Journal, 180
British Red Cross Society, 156
British Restaurants, 167
British Transport Commission, 108
Brooke, E. B., 185
Brown, G. W., 53
Building societies, 70, 210; industry, 78
bungalows, 142–5; demand, 146; design, 147–8; cost, 154

Cairncross, A. K., 128
Canadian National Employment Service, 73
case work, 177–8
Census of Great Britain 1951, age distribution, 14, 16, 218; hospital inmates, 182; industrial status, 15, 32; living alone, 171; married women employed, 37; occupational distribution, 23, 25–7; part-time employment, 39; post-pension age employment, 25; ratio of older workers, 25; residential care, 134; shared dwellings, 136
Chief Inspector of Factories, 49
Children's Officer, 160
chiropody, 170, 176, 190
chronic hospitals, 166, 170, 184, 191; sickness, 65, 67, 165, 168, 180–1, 183
clubs, 172–5, 177, 228–9

INDEX

Coalition Government, 98
Columbia, District of, 115
convalescence, 165–6
contributory pensions (1925), 76
Co-operative societies, 70
Cosin, L. Z., 183
cost of living indices, 11–12, 100–1

Darby and Joan clubs, 174
Day Centres, 173
Day Hospitals, 173, 184–5
dependency, 3–6, 11–13, 17–18, 40
de-retirement, 63
Determination of Needs Act, 95
Development Corporations, 154
Director, The, 25
Disabled Persons Quota, 29
Distributive trades, 30–1, 38–9
domestic help, 152, 167, 170, 225–6, 230
domiciliary nursing, 163, 168–70, 189; welfare services, 166–70, 185
Dunne, A. C., 84

Eccles, Sir David, 13
Economica, 12
Economic Survey, 1947, 22
Economist, The, 105, 118
education, 13, 42
Elphinstone, M. D. W., 87
Employers' Associations, 21
employees, age analysis, 10
employment of older workers, former occupations, 22, 32–4, 37–9, 199; heavy industry, 30, 45, 51–2; light work, 23, 29, 45, 47, 49, 50–2, 54, 202; mobility, 72, 208–9; numbers, 10, 23–4, 27; occupational distribution, 25–7, 38; part-time, 39, 77, 80–1, 128–29; ratio to younger workers, 9–10, 24–6; substitution for juveniles, 41–4, 48, 202–3

Family Allowances, 12–13; care, 16, 140, 152, 163–4, 168–70, 178–9, 185; structure, 140–1, 150–1, 162, 191
Finsbury Employment Scheme, 40

flats, 142, 144–5, 148–9, 153–4
Fleming, C., 52
frail ambulants, 156, 160, 163, 183, 186
Ffrangcon Roberts, 191
Friendly Societies, 70, 93, 210
Friends Relief Services, 156
full employment, 7, 9–10, 21, 34, 41, 44, 46–7

General practitioners, 188–9
Geriatric clinics, 189; medicine, 180, 182–3; units, 180, 183
Gerontological Conference, U.S.A., 185; Congress, London, 189
Ghiselli, E. E., 53
Government Actuary, 20, 98; Report for Phillips Committee, 1–2, 5, 15, 19; 1st Quinquennial Review, National Insurance Funds, 4, 37
Greenwood, J., 183
Griffiths, James, 100
Group Life Pension Schemes, 105
Guillebaud Committee, 182, 186, 188, 191

Hagenbuch, W., 123
Hansard, P., 11–12, 23, 91, 100, 103
health, 152, 226–7, 230; older workers, 65, 77–8, 83, 206–7; Minister of, 190; Ministry of, 156–7; Parliamentary Secretary, 184
heavy occupations, 23, 30, 45, 51–2, 54
Heughan, H., 30
Hobson, W., 79
Hohman, H. F., 100
holidays, 168, 173, 177, 229–30
home-helps, 167, 169–70, 230
home nursing, 163, 168–70, 185
Homes, cost, 158, 170; half-way, 165, 186–7; local authority (Welfare), 156, 158–9; 160–1, Rest, 165; voluntary, 157–9, 161, 165
Hospital almoners, 185
Hospital discharges, 185
Hospital waiting lists, 184

INDEX

Hospitals, admissions, 181–2, 184–185

Hostels, 149, 153

households, 134, 136, 150, 153, 218

house-work, 152, 162–3, 167, 225–6

Housing Act, 1936, 143, 157; 1949, 147, 149

Housing Associations, 142, 148, 154, 157, 170

housing, conversions, 143–4; cost, 140, 143, 154; designated for old people, 141–5, 147–8, 153–4; estates, 138; sanitary facilities, 136–7, 147; shared dwellings, 136–7, 147, 150; siting, 138, 140–141; subsidies, 147, 149, 154–5

Housing Manual, 149

Housing Rent and Repairs Act, 154

Howell, T., 182

Income Tax Act, 1952, 106

incontinence, 167

Industrial Injury benefit, 49

Industrial Welfare Society, 52, 71, 110

infirmaries, 180–1

infirmity, 15, 156, 164, 185–7, 191, 226–7, 230

Inland Revenue Authorities, 110, 129

Institute of Actuaries, 87

International Association of Gerontology, 46, 73

job-analysis, 45

Journal of Occupational Psychology, 48

Journal of Public Health, 183

juveniles, 41–4, 48, 202

King Edward Hospital Fund, 165

King George VI Jubilee Trust, 178

Kossoris, M. D., 50

Labour exchanges, 70, 73–4

Labour, Ministry of, 73, 193; age-analysis of employees, 10; Budget Inquiry, 137; manpower statistics, 6–7, 10–11, 194; occupational pensions inquiry, 70–1; Wages Council, 36

Labour Government, 92

Labour Party, 93–4, 98

Lancet, The, 185

laundry, 150, 163, 167

Lavers, 87

Le Gros Clark, F., 45, 78, 84

leisure, 172–3, 228

Leser, C. E. V., 4

Lewis (Shenfield), B. E., 23, 34

Liberal Party, 92

Life Office Associations, 71

Liverpool Survey, 171, 172, 175; housing, 142

living alone, 15, 135, 137, 140, 147, 151, 181, 219

Lloyds Bank Review, 3, 111, 123

Local Government superannuation, 69

London, 136, 159, 171

London and Cambridge Economic Service, 118

loneliness, 162, 171–3, 175, 227

longevity, 2, 15, 19–20

long-stay annexes, 165, 183

Lord Mayor's Fund, 156

Louisiana, 115

Lowe, C., 166, 181

McKay, W., 93

McKeown, T., 166, 181

maisonettes, 142, 153

Manchester Guardian, 23, 108, 184

manpower, 6–11, 17, 22, 25, 35, 41, 47

marital status, 7–8, 16, 218; employment, 15, 36–7, 39, 67; hospital care, 16–17, 182, 191; housing, 17, 146–7, 151, 153, 224; pension costs, 17, 36–7, 126; living alone, 219

married women, 36–7, 39–40, 48, 202

Marples, E., 11

masculinity ratio, 14–16

Maudling, R. H., 12

meals, 150, 225; on wheels, 225

means test, 89–90, 92, 95–7, 104

medical care, general practice, 164, 170, 188–9, 191; geriatric units,

INDEX

Annual Reports, 23–4, 99; Retirement Inquiry, 9, 63–7, 78–9

Personnel Psychology, 53

Phillips Report, 1–2; age distribution of pensioners, 15; elderly living alone, 171; finance, 120, 124; occupational pensions, 130; pension contributions and savings, 108; poverty among the elderly, 87; size of working population, 6–9, 11; Appendix II, 1, 5, 19; Appendix III, 11

piece-rates, 53

Pingstone, G. W., 71

Planning (P.E.P.), 17, 89, 94, 111

Political Quarterly, The, 90

Poor Law, 91, 93, 100, 161, 181

population, age-structure, 1, 3–6, 14–15, 22; birth rates, 1, 3; death rates, 1–2, 19–20; future trends, 2, 6, 19–20; Royal Commission (1947), 22; see also, dependency, masculinity ratio, and marital status

Population Studies, 4

poverty, 87, 89, 94, 97

promotion, 58, 68

Public Assistance, 91, 94, 96, 133–4, 161, 180, 218

Public Work Loans Board, 170

Quinquennial Review, National Insurance, 4, 37, 120

Reed, D. B., 142

Regional hospital boards, 159, 160, 166

Registrar-General, 150–1

rehabilitation, 182–3

Rent Acts, 121, 154; restriction, 121

Rest Homes, 165

retirement, age, 56, 79; compulsory, 9, 66–7, 70–1, 84, 107; deferred, 8–9, 15, 23–4, 35, 52, 68, 124–5; earnings during, 21, 75–6, 81, 105; health effects, 59, 83; increments for postponement, 21, 57, 75–6; rates by occupations, 26–7,

38, 78; rates by status, 31–2; reasons for, 57–8, 60–9

Richardson, I. M., 28, 51, 62

Roberts, A., 46–7

Rowntree, B. S., 18, 87, 94, 134, 136, 141, 217

Royal College of Physicians, 148

St. Helier hospital, 186

Schoolmaster, The, 85

Scott, W. G., 73

Seldon, A., 34

Sheldon, J. H., 16, 59, 134, 140, 151–2, 163, 222

Shenfield, B. E., see Lewis

Social security and unemployment, 89

Social insurance principles, 120–4

Social Service Review, The, 100

Social Survey, The, 45, 60

Social Work Year Book, 115

Sociological Review, The, 140

South Staffordshire, 194

statistical abstract for U.K., 93

subsistence pensions, see pensions

Summerfield Hospital, 184

taxation, treatment of pensions, 106–7, 109, 120, 130; committee on, 106, 130–2

Taylor, W., 19

Teachers' Pension Account, 85; report, 85

Thomas, G., 45, 60, 63, 72, 79, 209, 211

Thomson, A. P., 166, 180–1

Times, The, 12

Titmuss, R., 17, 90, 182

Townsend, P., 85, 108, 140, 162

Trade Unions, 21, 46–7, 91, 94, 206; Congress, 22, 95, 131

training, 29, 53–4, 80, 201

transport, 33–5

tripartite administration (health and welfare services), 159–60, 186–7

Umpire, insurance claims, 99

under-crowding, 137–8

unemployment, 7, 10, 46, 70–4, 80

INDEX

Unionist Party, 92
United States, 113

voluntary Societies, 157, 161, 167, 170, 173, 177; Homes, 157–9, 161, 165; Social services, 176–7, 228; visiting, 175–6, 228

Walsh, R. C., 189
Warren, M., 182

Welfare Authorities (local), 160, 186–7; Homes, 133, 156–9, 161, 187
Welford, A. T., 48, 52, 53
West Midlands, 143
Wilson, A., 93
Wolverhampton, 140, 163, 217, 227
woman power, 36–7, 40, 166
Woman's Voluntary Services, 167

York, 94

236

Founded by KARL MANNHEIM
Late Professor of Education in the University of London

Edited by W. J. H. SPROTT
Professor of Philosophy in the University of Nottingham

The International Library

of

Sociology and Social

Reconstruction

ROUTLEDGE & KEGAN PAUL

BROADWAY HOUSE, CARTER LANE, LONDON, E.C.4

SOCIOLOGY OF EDUCATION

Mission of the University
JOSÉ ORTEGA Y GASSET. Translated and introduced by Howard
Lee Nostrand   *Second Impression. 12s. 6d.*

Total Education
A Plea for Synthesis
M. L. JACKS, *Director of the Institute of Education, Oxford*
                                          Fourth Impression. 16s.

The Social Psychology of Education
An Introduction and Guide to its Study
C. M. FLEMING, *Reader in Education, Institute of Education, London*
                                          Eighth Impression. 10s.

Education and Society in Modern Germany
R. H. SAMUEL, *Professor of Germanic Languages, Melbourne,* and
R. HINTON THOMAS, *Lecturer in German, Birmingham*   16s.

The Museum
Its History and Its Tasks in Education
ALMA S. WITTLIN   *Illustrated. 28s.*

The Educational Thought and Influence of Matthew Arnold
W. F. CONNELL, *Senior Lecturer in Education, Sydney.* With an Introduction by Sir Fred Clarke   23s.

Comparative Education
A Study of Educational Factors and Traditions
NICHOLAS HANS, *Reader in Education, Institute of Education, London*
                                          Fourth Impression. 23s.

New Trends in Education in the 18th Century
NICHOLAS HANS   21s.

From School to University
A Study, with special reference to University Entrance
R. R. DALE, *Lecturer in Education, University College, Swansea*   21s.

Education and Society

An Introduction to the Sociology of Education

A. K. C. OTTAWAY, *Lecturer in Education, Leeds*. With an Introduction by W. O. Lester Smith   *Second Impression.* 18s.

German Youth : Bond or Free

HOWARD BECKER, *Professor of Sociology, University of Wisconsin*
18s.

Parity and Prestige in English Secondary Education

OLIVE BANKS, *Lecturer in Sociology, Liverpool*   25s.

Helvetius

His Life and Place in the History of Educational Thought

IAN CUMMING, *Senior Lecturer in Education, Auckland University College*
25s.

Adolescence

Its Social Psychology: With an Introduction to recent findings from the fields of Anthropology, Physiology, Medicine, Psychometrics and Sociometry

C. M. FLEMING, *Reader in Education, Institute of Education, London*
Fourth Impression. 18s.

Studies in the Social Psychology of Adolescence

J. E. RICHARDSON, J. F. FORRESTER, J. K. SHUKLA and P. J. HIGGINBOTHAM

Edited by C. M. FLEMING   23s.

From Generation to Generation

Age Groups and Social Structure

S. N. EISENSTADT, *Head of the Department of Sociology, Hebrew University, Jerusalem*   42s.

SOCIOLOGY OF RELIGION

Sociology of Religion

JOACHIM WACH, *Professor of the History of Religions, Chicago*   30s.

The Economic Order and Religion

FRANK KNIGHT, *Professor of Social Science, Chicago,* and
THORNTON W. MERRIAM   18s.

SOCIOLOGY OF ART AND LITERATURE

Chekhov and His Russia: A Sociological Study
W. H. BRUFORD, *Schröder Professor of German, Cambridge*   18s.

The Sociology of Literary Taste
LEVIN L. SCHÜCKING   *Third Impression. 9s. 6d.*

Men of Letters and the English Public in the 18th Century, 1660-1744, Dryden, Addison, Pope
ALEXANDRE BELJAME, Edited with an Introduction and Notes by Bonamy Dobrée. Translated by E. O. Lorimer   28s.

SOCIOLOGICAL APPROACH TO THE STUDY OF HISTORY

The Aftermath of the Napoleonic Wars
The Concert of Europe—An Experiment

H. G. SCHENK, *Lecturer in Political Economics, Fellow of Exeter College, Oxford*   *Illustrated. 18s.*

Military Organization and Society
STANISLAW ANDRZEJEWSKI, *Simon Fellow, Manchester.* Foreword by A. Radcliffe-Brown   21s.

Population Theories and the Economic Interpretation
SYDNEY COONTZ, *Assistant Professor in Forest Economics, State University of New York, Syracuse*   *In preparation.*

SOCIOLOGY OF LAW

Sociology of Law
GEORGES GURVITCH, *Professor of Sociology, Sorbonne.* With an Introduction by Roscoe Pound   *Second Impression. 21s.*

The Institutions of Private Law and their Social Functions
KARL RENNER. Edited with an Introduction and Notes by O. Kahn-Freund   28s.

Legal Aid

ROBERT EGERTON. With an Introduction by A. L. Goodhart
Second Impression. 12s. 6d.

Soviet Legal Theory: Its Social Background and Development

RUDOLF SCHLESINGER, *Lecturer in Soviet Social and Economic Institutions, Glasgow* *Second Edition. 28s.*

CRIMINOLOGY

Juvenile Delinquency in an English Middletown

HERMANN MANNHEIM, *Reader in Criminology, London School of Economics* *14s.*

Criminal Justice and Social Reconstruction

HERMANN MANNHEIM *Second Impression. 20s.*

Group Problems in Crime and Punishment

HERMANN MANNHEIM *28s.*

The Psycho-Analytical Approach to Juvenile Delinquency: Theory, Case Studies, Treatment

KATE FRIEDLANDER, *Late Hon. Psychiatrist, Institute for the Scientific Treatment of Delinquency* *Fourth Impression. 23s.*

The English Prison and Borstal Systems

LIONEL FOX, K.C.B., M.C., *Chairman of the Prison Commission for England and Wales* *32s.*

Crime and the Services

JOHN SPENCER, *Director of the Bristol Social Project, Bristol University* *28s.*

Delinquent Boys: The Culture of the Gang

ALBERT K. COHEN, *Assistant Professor of Sociology, Indiana* *21s.*

THE SOCIAL SERVICES

Social Service and Mental Health

An Essay on Psychiatric Social Workers
M. ASHDOWN and S. C. BROWN *18s.*

The Social Services of Modern England

M. PENELOPE HALL, *Lecturer in Social Science, Liverpool* *Third Edition (Revised). 28s.*

Lunacy, Law and Conscience, 1744-1845
The Social History of the Care of the Insane
KATHLEEN JONES   21*s.*

British Social Work in the 19th Century
A. F. YOUNG and E. T. ASHTON, *Department of Social Studies,*
Southampton University   25*s.*

Social Policies for Old Age
B. E. SHENFIELD, *Lecturer in Social Studies, University of Birmingham*
In preparation

SOCIOLOGY AND POLITICS

Social-Economic Movements
An Historical and Comparative Survey of Socialism, Communism, Co-
operation, Utopianism; and Other Systems of Reform and Reconstruc-
tion
H. W. LAIDLER, *Executive Director, League for Industrial Democracy*
Second Impression. Illustrated. 37*s.* 6*d.*

The Analysis of Political Behaviour: An Empirical
Approach
HAROLD D. LASSWELL, *Professor of Law, Yale. Third Impression.* 23*s.*

Dictatorship and Political Police
The Technique of Control by Fear
E. K. BRAMSTEDT   20*s.*

Nationality in History and Politics
A Psychology and Sociology of National Sentiment and Nationalism
FRIEDRICH HERTZ   *Third Impression.* 30*s.*

The Logic of Liberty: Reflections and Rejoinders
MICHAEL POLANYI, F.R.S., *Professor of Social Studies, Manchester*
18*s.*

Power and Society
A Framework for Political Inquiry
HAROLD D. LASSWELL, *Professor of Law, Yale,* and
A. KAPLAN, *Professor of Liberal Studies, Indiana*   25*s.*

The Political Element in the Development of Economic Theory

GUNNAR MYRDAL, *Professor of Economics, Stockholm. Executive Secretary, United Nations Economic Commission for Europe*. Translated from the German by Paul Streeten   25s.

Higher Civil Servants in Britain

From 1870 to the Present Day
R. K. KELSALL, *Senior Research Officer, London School of Economics*   25s.

Democracy and Dictatorship: Their Psychology and Patterns of Life

Z. BARBU, *Lecturer in Social Psychology, Glasgow*   28s.

How People Vote: A Study of Electoral Behaviour in Greenwich

MARK BENNEY, A. P. GRAY, and R. H. PEAR   25s.

Economy and Society

A Study in the Integration of Economic and Social Theory
TALCOTT PARSONS, *Chairman of the Department of Social Relations, Harvard*, and NEIL J. SMELSER   35s.

The Functions of Social Conflict

LEWIS COSER   18s.

FOREIGN AFFAIRS, THEIR SOCIAL, POLITICAL & ECONOMIC FOUNDATIONS

Patterns of Peacemaking

DAVID THOMSON, *Research Fellow, Sidney Sussex College, Cambridge*, E. MEYER and ASA BRIGGS, *Fellow of Worcester College, Oxford*   25s.

French Canada in Transition

EVERETT C. HUGHES, *Professor of Sociology, Chicago*   16s.

State and Economics in the Middle East

A Society in Transition
A. BONNÉ, *Professor of Economics. Director, Economic Research Institute, Hebrew University, Jerusalem*   *Second Edition (Revised).*   40s.

The Economic Development of the Middle East
An Outline of Planned Reconstruction
A. BONNÉ   *Third Impression.* 16s.

Peasant Renaissance in Yugoslavia, 1900-1950
A Study of the Development of Yugoslav Peasant Society as Affected by Education
RUTH TROUTON   28s.

Transitional Economic Systems
The Polish-Czech Example
DOROTHY W. DOUGLAS   25s.

Political Thought in France from the Revolution to the Fourth Republic
J. P. MAYER   14s.

Central European Democracy and its Background
Economic and Political Group Organization
RUDOLF SCHLESINGER   30s.

ECONOMIC PLANNING

Private Corporations and their Control
A. B. LEVY   *Two Volumes.* 70s. *the set*

The Shops of Britain
A Study of Retail Distribution
HERMANN LEVY   *Second Impression.* 21s.

SOCIOLOGY OF THE FAMILY AND ALLIED TOPICS

The Family and Democratic Society
J. K. FOLSOM, *Professor of Economics, Vassar College*   35s.

Nation and Family
The Swedish Experiment in Democratic Family and Population Policy
ALVA MYRDAL, *Swedish Ambassador to India*

Second Impression. 28s.

The Deprived and the Privileged
Personality Development in English Society
B. M. SPINLEY, *Educational Psychologist, Sheffield Child Guidance Clinic* 20s.

Prosperity and Parenthood
J. A. BANKS, *Assistant Lecturer in Sociology, Liverpool*   21s.

Family, Socialization and Interaction Process
TALCOTT PARSONS and ROBERT F. BALES, *Lecturer in Sociology, Harvard University*   30s.

The Home and Social Status
DENNIS CHAPMAN, *Senior Lecturer in Social Science, Liverpool University*
119 tables, diagrams and plates, 35s.

Women's Two Roles
Home and Work :
ALVA MYRDAL, and VIOLA KLEIN

      25s.

TOWN AND COUNTRY PLANNING. HUMAN ECOLOGY

The Social Background of a Plan: A Study of Middlesbrough
Edited by RUTH GLASS. With Maps and Plans   42s.

City, Region and Regionalism
A Geographical Contribution to Human Ecology
ROBERT E. DICKINSON. With Maps and Plans
Second Impression. 25s.

The West European City: A Study in Urban Geography
ROBERT E. DICKINSON. With Maps and Plans   42s.

Revolution of Environment
E. A. GUTKIND   *Illustrated.* 32s.

The Journey to Work
Its Significance for Industrial and Community Life
K. LIEPMANN, *Research Fellow in Economics, Bristol.* With a Foreword
by Sir Alexander Carr-Saunders   *Second Impression* 16s.

Stevenage: A Sociological Study of a New Town
HAROLD ORLANS   30*s*.

The Genesis of Modern British Town Planning
A Study in Economic and Social History of the Nineteenth and Twentieth Centuries
W. ASHWORTH, *Lecturer in Economic History, London School of Economics*
21*s*.

SOCIOLOGICAL STUDIES OF MODERN COMMUNITIES

Negroes in Britain
A Study of Racial Relations in English Society
K. L. LITTLE, *Reader in Anthropology, Edinburgh*   25*s*.

Co-operative Living in Palestine
HENRIK F. INFIELD. With a Foreword by General
Sir Arthur Wauchope   *Illustrated*. 12*s*. 6*d*.

Co-operative Communities at Work
HENRIK F. INFIELD   18*s*.

Colour Prejudice in Britain
A Study of West Indian Workers in Liverpool, 1941-1951
ANTHONY H. RICHMOND, *Lecturer in Social Theory, Edinburgh*   18*s*.

Social Mobility in Britain
Edited by DAVID V. GLASS, *Professor of Sociology, London School of Economics*
36*s*.

The Absorption of Immigrants
S. N. EISENSTADT   25*s*.

Studies in Class Structure
G. D. H. COLE, *Chichele Professor of Social and Political Theory, Oxford*
21*s*.

The Study of Groups
JOSEPHINE KLEIN, *Lecturer in Social Studies, Birmingham*   21*s*.

SOCIOLOGY OF INDUSTRY

ANTHROPOLOGY & RURAL SOCIOLOGY

SOCIOLOGY AND PSYCHOLOGY OF THE PRESENT CRISIS

Diagnosis of Our Time
Wartime Essays of a Sociologist
KARL MANNHEIM   18*s.*

Farewell to European History or the Conquest of Nihilism
ALFRED WEBER   18*s.*

The Fear of Freedom
ERICH FROMM   21*s.*

The Sane Society
ERICH FROMM   25*s.*

Freedom, Power, and Democratic Planning
KARL MANNHEIM. Edited by Hans Gerth and E. K. Bramstedt 28*s.*

Essays on Sociology and Social Psychology
KARL MANNHEIM. Edited by Paul Kecskemeti   28*s.*

Essays on the Sociology of Culture
KARL MANNHEIM. Edited by Ernest Manheim and Paul
Kecskemeti   28*s.*

SOCIAL PSYCHOLOGY AND PSYCHO-ANALYSIS

Psychology and the Social Pattern
JULIAN BLACKBURN, *Associate Professor of Psychology, McGill University, Canada*   *Fifth Impression.* 14*s.*

The Framework of Human Behaviour
JULIAN BLACKBURN   *Second Impression.* 15*s.*

A Handbook of Social Psychology
KIMBALL YOUNG, *Professor of Sociology, North-western University*
                                          Fifth Impression. 30*s.*

Solitude and Privacy
A Study of Social Isolation, Its Causes and Therapy
PAUL HALMOS, *Lecturer in Social Psychology, Social Studies Dept., South West Essex Technical College*   21*s.*

The Human Group

GEORGE C. HOMANS, *Associate Professor of Sociology, Harvard*   28s.

Sigmund Freud: An Introduction

A Presentation of his Theories and a Discussion of the Relationship between Psycho-analysis and Sociology

WALTER HOLLITSCHER, *Professor of Philosophy and Sociology, Humboldt University, Berlin*   *Second Impression.* 12s.

The Social Problems of an Industrial Civilization

ELTON MAYO, *Late Professor of Industrial Research, Harvard Business School*   *Second Impression.* 15s.

Oppression

A Study in Social and Criminal Psychology

TADEUSZ GRYGIER. Foreword by Hermann Mannheim   28s.

Mental Health and Mental Disorder

A Sociological Approach

Edited by ARNOLD M. ROSE, *University of Minnesota*   40s.

APPROACHES TO THE PROBLEM OF PERSONALITY

The Cultural Background of Personality

RALPH LINTON, *Professor of Anthropology, Yale*

Third Impression. 12s. 6d.

The Feminine Character: History of an Ideology

VIOLA KLEIN. With an Introduction by Karl Mannheim   16s.

A History of Autobiography in Antiquity

GEORG MISCH, *Professor of Philosophy, Göttingen,* Translated by E. W. Dickes.   *Two volumes.* 45s. *the set*

Personality and Problems of Adjustment

KIMBALL YOUNG   *Second Edition (Revised).* 35s.

Towards a Measure of Man

The Frontiers of Normal Adjustment

PAUL HALMOS   *In preparation*

PHILOSOPHICAL AND SOCIAL FOUNDATIONS OF THOUGHT

Homo Ludens: A Study of the Play Element in Culture
J. HUIZINGA   18s.

The Ideal Foundations of Economic Thought
Three Essays on the Philosophy of Economics
WERNER STARK, *Reader in Economics, Manchester*
                                                    Third Impression.   16s.

The History of Economics in its Relation to Social Development
WERNER STARK   Third Impression.   12s.

America: Ideal and Reality
The United States of 1776 in Contemporary European Philosophy
WERNER STARK   12s.

The Decline of Liberalism as an Ideology
With Particular Reference to German Politico-Legal Thought
J. H. HALLOWELL   14s.

Society and Nature: A Sociological Inquiry
HANS KELSEN, *Department of Political Science, California*   25s.

Marx: His Time and Ours
R. SCHLESINGER   Second Impression.   32s.

The Philosophy of Wilhelm Dilthey
H. A. HODGES, *Professor of Philosophy, Reading*   30s.

Essays on the Sociology of Knowledge
KARL MANNHEIM   28s.

GENERAL SOCIOLOGY

A Handbook of Sociology
W. F. OGBURN, *Professor of Sociology, Chicago,* and
M. F. NIMKOFF, *Professor of Sociology, Bucknell*
                                              Third Edition (Revised).   30s.

Social Organization
ROBERT H. LOWIE, *late Professor of Anthropology, Chicago*   35s.

FOREIGN CLASSICS OF SOCIOLOGY

Wilhelm Dilthey: An Introduction

A comprehensive account of his sociological and philosophical work, with translations of selected passages.

H. A. HODGES   *Second Impression.* 14s.

From Max Weber: Essays in Sociology

Translated, Edited and with an Introduction by H. H. GERTH and C. W. MILLS   *Second Impression.* 28s.

Suicide: A Study in Sociology

EMILE DURKHEIM. Translated by J. A. Spaulding and George Simpson   28s.

Community and Association

FERDINAND TONNIES. Edited and supplemented by Charles P. Loomis   21s.

DOCUMENTARY

Changing Attitudes in Soviet Russia

Documents and Readings. Edited with an Introduction by
RUDOLF SCHLESINGER

Volume 1: *The Family in the U.S.S.R.*   30s.

Volume 2: *The Nationalities Problem and Soviet Administration*   30s.

Psychology in the Soviet Union

BRIAN SIMON, *Lecturer in Education, University College, Leicester*
In preparation

Soviet Youth: Some Achievements and Problems

Excerpts from the Soviet Press
Edited and translated by DOROTHEA L. MEEK   *In preparation*

All prices are net

1956   Clarke, Doble & Brendon, Ltd., Oakfield Press, Plymouth